Adapt

Also by Tim Harford

The Undercover Economist

The Logic of Life

Dear Undercover Economist

Adapt

Why Success Always Starts with Failure

Tim Harford

BOND
STREET
BOOKS
DOUBLEDAY
CANADA

The Bond Street Books colophon is a registered trademark of Random House of Canada

Library and Archives Canada Cataloguing in Publication

Harford, Tim, 1973-
        Adapt : saving the world one failure at a time / Tim Harford.

Issued also in electronic format.
ISBN 978-0-385-67024-1

        1. Business. 2. Economics. 3. Civilization, Modern--21st century. 4. Social problems. I. Title.

HF1008.H37 2011   650   C2010-907585-4

Printed and bound in the USA

Published in Canada by Bond Street Books, an imprint of Doubleday Canada, a division of Random House of Canada Limited

Visit Random House of Canada Limited's website: www.randomhouse.ca

10 9 8 7 6 5 4 3 2 1

To Jess, Sophy and Emily, with love

Contents

Adapt

One

Adapting

1 'You could easily spend your life making a toaster'

The electric toaster seems a humble thing. It was invented in 1893, roughly halfway between the appearance of the light bulb and that of the aeroplane. This century-old technology is now a household staple. Reliable, efficient toasters are available for less than an hour's wage.

Nevertheless, Thomas Thwaites, a postgraduate design student at the Royal College of Art in London, discovered just what an astonishing achievement the toaster is when he embarked on what he called the 'Toaster Project'. Quite simply, Thwaites wanted to build a toaster from scratch. He started by taking apart a cheap toaster, to discover that it had over four hundred components and sub-components. Even the most primitive model called for:

Copper, to make the pins of the electric plug, the cord, and internal wires. Iron to make the steel grilling apparatus, and the spring to pop up the toast. Nickel to make the heating element. Mica (a mineral a bit like slate) around which the heating element is wound, and of course plastic for the plug and cord insulation, and for the all important sleek looking casing.

The scale of the task soon became clear. To get iron ore, Thwaites had to travel to an old mine in Wales that now serves as a museum. He tried to smelt the iron using fifteenth-century technology, and failed dismally. He fared no better when he replaced bellows with hairdryers and a leaf-blower. His next attempt was even more of a cheat: he used a recently patented smelting method and two microwave ovens, one of which perished in the attempt, to produce a coin-sized lump of iron.

Plastic was no easier. Thwaites tried but failed to persuade BP to fly him out to an offshore rig to collect some crude oil. His attempts to make plastic from potato starch were foiled by mould and hungry snails. Finally, he settled for scavenging some plastic from a local dump, melting it down and moulding it into a toaster's casing. Other short cuts followed. Thwaites used electrolysis to obtain copper from the polluted water of an old mine in Anglesey, and simply melted down some commemorative coins to produce nickel, which he drew into wire using a specialised machine from the RCA's jewellery department.

Such compromises were inevitable. 'I realised that if you started absolutely from scratch, you could easily spend your life making a toaster,' he admitted. Despite his Herculean efforts to duplicate the technology, Thomas Thwaites's toaster looks more like a toaster-shaped birthday cake than a real toaster, its coating dripping and oozing like an icing job gone wrong. 'It warms bread when I plug it into a battery,' he told me, brightly. 'But I'm not sure what will happen if I plug it into the mains.' Eventually, he summoned up the courage to do so. Two seconds later, the toaster was toast.

2 Problem solving in a complicated world

The modern world is mind-bogglingly complicated. Far simpler objects than a toaster involve global supply chains and the coordinated efforts of many individuals, scattered across the world. Many do not even know the final destination of their efforts. As a lumberjack fells a giant of the Canadian forest, he doesn't know whether the tree he topples will make bed frames or pencils. At the vast Chuquicamata mine in Chile, a yellow truck the size of a house growls up an incline blasted into the landscape; the driver does not trouble himself to ask whether the copper ore he carries is destined for the wiring of a toaster or the casing of a bullet.

The range of products, too, is astounding. There are a hundred thousand or so distinct items in an ordinary Wal-Mart. Eric Beinhocker, a complexity researcher at the McKinsey Global Institute, reckons that if you were to add up all the different sizes and shapes of shoes, shirts and socks, the different brands and flavours and sizes of jams and sauces, the millions of different books, DVDs and music downloads on offer, you would find that a major economy such as New York or London offers over ten billion distinct types of product. Many of these products were undreamt of when the toaster was first invented, and millions of new ones appear every month. The complexity of the society we have created for ourselves envelops us so completely that, instead of being dizzied, we take it for granted.

I used to view this sophistication as cause to celebrate. Now I am less sure. Certainly, this complex economy produces vast material wealth. Not everyone gets a share, but far more people today enjoy a high material standard of living than at any time in history; and, notwithstanding the occasional recession, the wealth continues to grow more quickly than it ever used to. The process that produces this wealth is near miraculous, and the job is far harder than we tend to acknowledge. Alternative systems, from feudalism to central planning, have attempted the same task and been consigned to the history books.

Yet the Toaster Project should give us pause for thought. Because it is a symbol of the sophistication of our world, the toaster is also a symbol of the obstacles that lie in wait for those who want to change it. From climate change to terrorism, fixing the banks to ending global poverty, there is no shortage of big policy problems out there. They are always up for debate, yet we never seem to move any closer to a solution. Humbler problems in business and everyday life also tend to conceal the same unexpected complexity as the Toaster Project.

This is partly a book about those problems. But more fundamentally, it's a book that aims to understand how any problem – big or small – really gets solved in a world where even a toaster is beyond one man's comprehension.

The toasting problem isn't difficult: don't burn the toast; don't electrocute the user; don't start a fire. The bread itself is hardly an active protagonist. It doesn't deliberately try to outwit you, as a team of investment bankers might; it doesn't try to murder you, terrorise your country, and discredit everything you stand for, as a terrorist cell or a group of insurgents in Iraq would. The toaster is merely an improved way to solve an old problem – the Romans loved toast – unlike the World Wide Web or the personal computer, which provide solutions to problems we never realised we had. The toasting problem is laughably simple compared to the problem of transforming a poor country such as Bangladesh into the kind of economy where toasters are manufactured with ease and every household can afford one, along with the bread to put into it. It is dwarfed by the problem of climate change – the response to which will require much more than modifying a billion toasters.

Such problems are the stuff of this book: how to fight insurgents who, of course, fight back; how to nurture ideas that matter when so many of those ideas are hard even to imagine; how to restructure an economy to respond to climate change, or to make poor countries rich; how to prevent rogue investment bankers from destroying the banking system again. These are complex, fast-moving problems in a complex, fast-moving world. I will argue that they have far more in common with each other than we realise. Curiously, they also have something in common with the more humble problems we face in our own lives.

Whenever such problems are solved, it is little short of a miracle. This book is about how such miracles happen, why they matter so much, and whether we can make them happen more often.

3 The experts are humbled

> We're proud of the change we've brought to Washington in these first hundred days, but we've got a lot of work left to do, as all of you know. So I'd like to talk a little bit about what my administration plans to achieve in the next hundred days. During the second hundred days, we will design, build and open a library dedicated to my first hundred days ... I believe that my next hundred days will be so successful I will be able to complete them in 72 days. And on the 73rd day, I will rest.

This was President Obama addressing the White House Correspondents' Dinner, traditionally a venue for a joke or two, a few months after a tidal wave of hope and high expectations had swept him into power in November 2008. It seems a long time ago now, but Obama's joke cut close to the bone even then: people were expecting too much of one man.

We badly need to believe in the potency of leaders. Our instinctive response, when faced with a complicated challenge, is to look for a leader who will solve it. It wasn't just Obama: every president is elected after promising to change the way politics works; and almost every president then slumps in the polls as reality starts to bite. This isn't because we keep electing the wrong leaders. It is because we have an inflated sense of what leadership can achieve in the modern world.

Perhaps we have this instinct because we evolved to operate in small hunter–gatherer groups, solving small hunter–gatherer problems. The societies in which our modern brains developed weren't modern: they contained a few hundred separate products, rather than ten billion. The challenges such societies faced, however formidable, were simple enough to have been solved by an intelligent, wise, brave leader. They would have been vastly simpler than the challenges facing a newly elected US president.

Whatever the reason, the temptation to look to a leader to fix our problems runs deep. Of course, a leader doesn't have to solve every problem by himself. Good leaders surround themselves with expert advisers, seeking out the smartest specialists with the deepest insights into the problems of the day. But even deep expertise is not enough to solve today's complex problems.

Perhaps the best illustration of this comes from an extraordinary two-decade investigation into the limits of expertise, begun in 1984 by a young psychologist called Philip Tetlock. He was the most junior member of a committee of the National Academy of Sciences charged with working out what the Soviet response might be to the Reagan administration's hawkish stance in the Cold War. Would Reagan call the bluff of a bully or was he about to provoke a deadly reaction? Tetlock canvassed every expert he could find. He was struck by the fact that, again and again, the most influential thinkers on the Cold War flatly contradicted one another. We are so used to talking heads disagreeing that perhaps this doesn't seem surprising. But when we realise that the leading experts cannot agree on the most basic level about the key problem of the age, we begin to understand that this kind of expertise is far less useful than we might hope.

Tetlock didn't leave it at that. He worried away at this question of expert judgement for twenty years. He rounded up nearly three hundred experts – by which he meant people whose job it was to comment or advise on political and economic trends. They were a formidable bunch: political scientists, economists, lawyers and diplomats. There were spooks and think-tankers, journalists and academics. Over half of them had PhDs; almost all had postgraduate degrees. And Tetlock's method for evaluating the quality of their expert judgement was to pin the experts down: he asked them to make specific, quantifiable forecasts – answering 27,450 of his questions between them – and then waited to see whether their forecasts came true. They rarely did. The experts failed, and their failure to forecast the future is a symptom of their failure to understand fully the complexities of the present.

It wasn't that expertise was entirely useless. Tetlock compared his experts' responses to those of a control group of undergraduates, and the experts did better. But by any objective standard, they didn't do well. And the return on expertise was distinctly limited. Once experts have acquired a broad knowledge of the political world, deeper expertise in a specific field doesn't seem to help much. Predictions about Russia from experts on Russia were no more accurate than predictions about Russia from experts on Canada.

Most accounts of Tetlock's research savour the humbling of the professional pundits. And why not? One of Tetlock's more delicious discoveries was that the more famous experts – those who spent a lot of time as talking heads on television – were especially incompetent. Louis Menand, writing in the *New Yorker*, enjoyed the notion of bumbling seers, and concluded, 'the best lesson of Tetlock's book may be the one that he seems most reluctant to draw: Think for yourself'.

Yet there is a reason why Tetlock himself hesitates to draw that conclusion: his results clearly show that experts do outperform non-experts. These intelligent, educated and experienced professionals have insights to contribute – it's just that those insights go only so far. The problem is not the experts; it is the world they inhabit – the world we all inhabit – which is simply too complicated for anyone to analyse with much success.

So, if expertise is of such limited help in the face of our complex, ever-changing human society, what can we do to solve the problems we face? Perhaps we should look for clues in the success story we've already encountered: the amazing material wealth of modern developed countries.

4 The long, tangled history of failure

In 1982, just a couple of years before Philip Tetlock began his painstaking examination of expertise, two management consultants, Tom Peters and Robert Waterman, concluded their own detailed study of excellence in business. *In Search of Excellence* was published to great acclaim and launched Peters's career as one of the world's most recognisable management gurus. The two authors, working with their colleagues at McKinsey, used a mixture of data and subjective judgement to settle on a list of forty-three 'excellent' companies, which they then studied intensively in a bid to unlock their secrets.

Just two years later, *Business Week* ran a cover story entitled 'Oops! Who's Excellent Now?' Out of the forty-three companies, fourteen, almost a third, were in serious financial trouble. Excellence – if that was what Peters and Waterman really found when they studied the likes of Atari and Wang Laboratories – appears to be a fleeting quality.

It seems strange that so many apparently excellent companies could find themselves in deep trouble so quickly. Perhaps there was something uniquely silly about Peters and Waterman's project. Or perhaps there was something uniquely turbulent about the early 1980s – *In Search of Excellence* was published during a severe recession, after all.

But perhaps not. The 'who's excellent now?' experience is reinforced by a careful study from the economic historian Leslie

Hannah, who in the late 1990s decided to trace the fortunes of every one of the largest companies in the world in 1912. These were corporate giants that had survived a merger shakedown over the preceding few years and typically employed at least ten thousand workers.

At the top of the list was US Steel, a gigantic corporation even by today's standards, employing 221,000 workers. This was a company with everything going for it: it was the market leader in the largest and most dynamic economy in the world; and it was in an industry that has been of tremendous importance ever since. Yet US Steel had disappeared from the world's top hundred companies by 1995; at the time of writing, it was not even in the top five hundred.

Next on the list was Jersey Standard, which these days continues to prosper under the name Exxon. General Electric and Shell were also in the top ten both in 1912 and in 1995. But none of the other top-ten titans was in the top ten by 1995. More remarkably, none of them was even in the top hundred. Names such as Pullman and Singer recall a bygone age. Others, such as J&P Coats, Anaconda and International Harvester, are barely recognisable. It is hard to imagine just how large and powerful these companies once were – the closest parallels would be the likes of Microsoft and Wal-Mart today – and how permanent their success must have seemed. And while it could be said that Pullman and Singer suffered from being market leaders in declining industries, their fate was not inevitable. Singer made sewing machines, but Toyota's origins as a manufacturer of looms were no more promising. Other former titans, such as Westinghouse Electric, Cudahy Packing and American Brands, were in the same dynamic industries as the rare success stories General Electric and Procter & Gamble. Yet they failed.

Just as Philip Tetlock's experts have proved less capable than we tend to think, in the face of a complex world, these great companies are more transient than we realise. Ten of Hannah's top hundred had vanished within a decade; over half disappeared over the next 83 years. The lesson seems to be that failure is fundamental to the way the market creates sophisticated and wealthy economies. But perhaps what Peters, Waterman and Hannah found merely reflects the fact that if you start at the top, the only way is down. What happens when we look at survival rates in young, dynamic industries?

The answer is that failure rates are even higher. Consider the early printing industry. The printing press was invented by Johannes Gutenberg, a man who changed the world utterly, and produced the celebrated Gutenberg Bible in 1455. But the Gutenberg Bible was a ruinous project that put him out of business. The centre of the printing industry quickly moved to Venice, where twelve companies were established by 1469. Nine of them were gone in just three years, as the industry fumbled for a profitable business model. (It eventually found one: printing pre-packaged relief from divine punishment in the form of religious indulgences.)

At the dawn of the automobile industry, two thousand firms were operating in the United States. Around 1 per cent of them survived. The dot-com bubble spawned and killed countless new businesses. Today, 10 per cent of American companies disappear every year. What is striking about the market system is not how few failures there are, but how ubiquitous failure is even in the most vibrant growth industries.

Why, then, are there so many failures in a system that seems to be so economically successful overall? It is partly the difficulty of the task. Philip Tetlock showed how hard it was for expert political and economic analysts to generate decent forecasts, and there is no reason to believe that it is any easier for marketers or product developers or strategists to predict the future. In 1912, Singer's managers probably did not forecast the rise of the off-the-peg clothing industry. To make things even more difficult, corporations must compete with each other. To survive and be profitable it is not enough to be good; you must be one of the best. Asking why so many companies go out of business is the same as asking why so few athletes reach Olympic finals. In a market economy, there is usually room for only a few winners in each sector. Not everyone can be one of them.

The difference between market-based economies and centrally planned disasters, such as Mao Zedong's Great Leap Forward, is not that markets avoid failure. It's that large-scale failures do not seem to have the same dire consequences for the market as they do for planned economies. (The most obvious exception to this claim is also the most interesting: the financial crisis that began in 2007. We'll find out why it was such a catastrophic anomaly in chapter six.) Failure in market economies, while endemic, seems to go hand in hand with rapid progress.

The modern computer industry is a striking example: the most dynamic sector of the economy has also been the one in which failure is everywhere you look. The industry started with failure: when transistors replaced vacuum tubes as the basic elements of the computer, vacuum-tube manufacturers failed to make the switch. The likes of Hughes, Transitron and Philco took over, before stumbling in turn as integrated circuits replaced transistors, and the baton passed to Intel and Hitachi.

Meanwhile, Xerox, struggling to survive the expiry of its patents on photocopying, established the Palo Alto Research Center (or Parc), which developed the fax machine, the graphical interface that defines all modern computers, the laser printer, the Ethernet, and the first personal computer, the Alto. Yet Xerox did not become a powerhouse in personal computing. Many of the Alto's successors – including the ZX Spectrum, the BBC Micro and Japan's MSX standard – were dead-ends in the history of computing. It fell to IBM to produce the direct ancestor of today's personal computer – only to then unwittingly hand over control of the most valuable part of the package, the operating system, to Microsoft. IBM eventually bowed out of the personal computer business in 2005, selling its interests to a Chinese company. Apple also lost out to Microsoft in the 1980s, despite perfecting the user-friendly computer (although it was later to bounce back selling music, iPods and phones). Microsoft itself was caught unawares by the internet, lost the search-engine war with Google, and may soon lose its dominant position in software altogether. Who knows? Only the most arrogant forecaster would be able to convince himself that he could predict the next twist or turn in this market. The most successful industry of the last forty years has been built on failure after failure after failure.

The humble toaster which so baffled Thomas Thwaites is itself a product of trial and error. The Eclipse of 1893 was not a success: its iron heating element was prone to rust and tended to melt and start fires. The company that marketed it no longer exists. The first successful toaster did not emerge until 1910. It boasted a superior nickel-chrome alloy for the heating element but was still flawed. Most notably, that heating element was exposed, making it a potential source of household fires, burns and electrocutions. It took several decades for the practical and familiar pop-up toaster design to emerge, by which time many manufacturers had quit the business or gone bankrupt.

The market has solved the problem of generating material wealth, but its secret has little to do with the profit motive or the superior savvy of the boardroom over the cabinet office. Few company bosses would care to admit it, but the market fumbles its way to success, as successful ideas take off and less successful ones die out. When we see the survivors of this process – such as Exxon, General Electric and Procter & Gamble – we shouldn't merely see success. We should also see the long, tangled history of failure, of all of the companies and all of the ideas that didn't make it.

5 A shifting landscape

Biologists have a word for the way in which solutions emerge from failure: evolution. Often summarised as survival of the fittest, evolution is a process driven by the failure of the less fit.

Disconcertingly, given our instinctive belief that complex problems require expertly designed solutions, it is also completely unplanned. Astounding complexity emerges in response to a simple process: try out a few variants on what you already have, weed out the failures, copy the successes – and repeat for ever. Variation, and selection, again and again.

We are used to thinking about evolution as something that happens in the natural world – a biological phenomenon. But it doesn't have to be. Anyone can watch evolution taking place in a digital world, thanks to a graphics expert named Karl Sims. If you've ever seen *Titanic*, or the *Lord of the Rings* trilogy, or the *Spider-Man* films, then you've enjoyed the work of Karl Sims, who founded the special-effects company GenArts. But in the early 1990s, before Sims turned his attention to the visual-effects business, he produced moving images that are far cruder and yet, in some ways, more remarkable.

Sims wanted to watch evolution in progress. More than that, he wanted to create a virtual environment in which he could set its direction. Sims programmed simulations of settings such as a tank of water, and into them he dropped crude virtual creatures consisting of simple control systems, some sensors and random assortments of articulated blocks. Most of these jumbled creatures sank to the bottom and thrashed about without any great success. A few, however, were able to swim a little. Sims then applied the evolutionary process, instructing his computer to discard the floundering creatures and to create mutations based on the more successful swimmers: variation and selection. Most of the mutations were failures, of course. But the failures were continuously discarded, the occasional successes were allowed to flourish. From the most mindless and random of processes, remarkable results emerged: virtual creatures that resembled tadpoles, eels and rays, along with a number of apparently successful entities that looked like nothing on earth.

On another evolutionary run, Sims rewarded creatures for

successfully taking possession of a green cube, in competition with each other. The trial-and-error process of evolution produced a wide range of workable solutions, some obvious, others less so, from ignoring the cube and lunging at the opponent, to making a quick grab for the cube and then dashing off, to simply toppling forward and covering the cube with a heavy slab of a body. Sims was not the designer, nor even the subjective judge of success after the fact: he simply set up an evolutionary environment and recorded what happened. The process he created was entirely blind and stupid: there was no foresight, planning or conscious design in any of the mutations. Yet the blind evolutionary process produced marvellous things.

Why is trial and error such an effective tool for solving problems? The evolutionary algorithm – of variation and selection, repeated – searches for solutions in a world where the problems keep changing, trying all sorts of variants and doing more of what works. One way to think about this quest for solutions is to imagine a vast, flat landscape, divided into a grid of billions of squares. On each square is a document: a recipe describing a particular strategy. Evolutionary theorists call this a 'fitness landscape'. If the fitness landscape is biological, each strategy is a different genetic recipe: some squares describe fish; some describe birds; some describe human beings; while the majority describe a genetic mush that represents nothing that could ever survive in reality. But the fitness landscape might equally represent recipes for dinner: some produce curries; others produce salads; many produce dishes that are nauseating or even poisonous. Or the fitness landscape might contain business strategies: different ways to run an airline or a fast-food chain.

For any problem, it's possible to imagine a huge range of potential solutions, each one carefully written down and scattered on this vast landscape. Imagine, too, that each recipe is very similar to its neighbours: two adjacent dinner recipes might be identical save for one demanding a little more salt and the other a slightly longer cooking time. Two neighbouring business strategies might advocate doing everything the same, except that one prescribes slightly higher prices and a bit more marketing.

We've been imagining a flat plane stretching in every direction, but now let's change the picture and say that on our fitness landscape: the better the solution, the higher the altitude of the square that contains it. Now the fitness landscape is a jumble of cliffs and chasms, plateaus and jagged summits. Valleys represent bad solutions; mountain tops are good. In an ecosystem, the latter are creatures more likely to survive and reproduce; in the market place, they are the profitable business ideas; and at the dinner party, they are the tastiest dishes. In our dinner-party landscape, a deep, dark pit might contain a recipe for spaghetti with fish fingers and a jar of curry sauce. From there, the only way is up. Trek in one direction and you might eventually ascend to the soaring peak of Bolognese ragù. Head off in the opposite direction and you might eventually climb to the summit of a Bangladeshi fish curry.

Problem-solving on a contoured fitness landscape means trying to find the high peaks. In dinner-party space, that's not so hard. But in a biological ecosystem, or an economy, the peaks keep moving – sometimes slowly, sometimes quickly. Pullman and Singer went out of business because the peaks they were standing on suddenly disappeared. The peak that McDonald's currently occupies has been around for a while, moving slowly as new technologies become available and new tastes develop. The Google peak is very young, and it exists only because of earlier developments, such as the computer and the World Wide Web, just as squirrels exist only because there are trees for them to inhabit. And the Google peak is moving fast, more like a rolling wave than a mountain. At the moment, Google is surfing along, adapting its strategy to stay on or near the crest of the wave. Like surfing itself, this is harder than it looks.

As one peak subsides, others may not be clearly visible. The biological process of evolution through natural selection is entirely blind; finding a corporate strategy may or may not be a more deliberate and far-sighted process, as we shall shortly see. But Tetlock's research on expertise suggests that, even if other peaks in corporate strategy are sometimes visible, executives see them only fleetingly, through heavy cloud.

We can imagine many ways to search for peaks in this changeable and mysterious landscape. Biological evolution usually moves in small steps, but occasionally takes wild leaps – a single mutation might give a creature an extra pair of legs or totally different skin pigmentation. This combination, along with the culling of failed experiments, works well. Some strategies will cling to a familiar summit as it shifts around; others, by darting off, may find a new peak rising up. The process of evolution strikes a balance between discovering the new and exploiting the familiar very well. In fact, Stuart Kauffmann and John Holland, both complexity theorists affiliated with the multidisciplinary Santa Fe Institute, have shown that the evolutionary approach is not just another way of solving complex problems. Given the likely shape of these ever-shifting landscapes, the evolutionary mix of small steps and occasional wild gambles is the best possible way to search for solutions.

Evolution is effective because, rather than engaging in an exhaustive, time-consuming search for the highest peak – a peak that may not even be there tomorrow – it produces ongoing, 'works for now' solutions to a complex and ever-changing set of problems. In biological evolution, solutions include photosynthesis, pairs of eyes and mothers' milk. In economic evolution, solutions include double-entry book-keeping, supply-chain management and 'buy one, get one free'. Some of what works seems to be perennial. The rest, such as being a *Tyrannosaurus rex* or the world's most efficient manufacturer of VHS video cassettes, is rooted in a particular place and time.

We know that the evolutionary process is driven by variation and selection. In biology, variation emerges from mutations and from sexual reproduction, which mixes the genes from two

parents. Selection happens through heredity: successful creatures reproduce before they die and have offspring that share
some or all of their genes. In a market economy, variation and
selection are also at work. New ideas are created by scientists
and engineers, meticulous middle managers in large corporations or daring entrepreneurs. Failures are culled because bad
ideas do not survive long in the market place: to succeed, you
have to make a product that customers wish to buy at a price that
covers costs and beats obvious competitors. Many ideas fail these
tests, and if they are not shut down by management they will
eventually be shut down by a bankruptcy court. Good ideas
spread because they are copied by competitors, because staff
leave to set up their own businesses, or because the company
with the good ideas grows. With these elements of variation and
selection in place, the stage is set for an evolutionary process; or,
to put it more crudely, solving problems through trial and error.

6 We are blinder than we think

This is all rather counter-intuitive, not to say uncomfortable.
Many people assume that top corporate executives must be good
for something: the shareholders who pay them handsome
salaries certainly do; as do the millions of people who buy books
purporting to convey the wisdom of successful business chiefs.
Tetlock's experts were almost helpless in the face of the complex
situations he asked them to analyse. Are chief executives just as
impotent, fumbling around for workable strategies in an impen-
etrable fog?

That would be what the evolutionary analogy implies. In
biological evolution, the evolutionary process has no foresight.
It is the result of pure trial and error over hundreds of millions
of years. Could that also be true in an economy, despite the
best efforts of managers, corporate strategists and management
consultants?

A compelling clue comes from the economist Paul Ormerod. Ormerod had been reviewing what the fossil record tells us about extinctions over the last 550 million years – including mass extinctions that make the death of the dinosaurs look almost trivial. That record revealed a clear relationship between the scale of an extinction event and how often such events occur: if the extinction event is twice as severe, it is four times as rare; if it is three times as severe, it is nine times as rare. Eras in which very few extinctions take place are the most common of all. The pattern is very clear, and biologists now have mathematical models that show how a blind evolutionary process, when combined with an ever-changing contest for resources and the occasional asteroid strike, produces this distinctive signature.

Ormerod is a blunt, widely-read iconoclast from Lancashire in northern England, with a taste for disarming fellow economists with their own favourite weapon – mathematics. He decided to take a look at the data for corporate extinctions as well. He studied Leslie Hannah's statistics on the death of corporate titans and compared them with half a billion years of data from the fossil record. The timescales were different, but the relationship between the size of an extinction event and its frequency proved to be exactly the same. (By far the worst year for the corporate titans was 1968, when six of them 'died'.) Next, Ormerod turned to a much bigger database of smaller corporate extinctions in the United States, state by state, sector by sector, with thousands of data points describing literally millions of small companies. He discovered the same thing. He cast the net even wider, looking at corporate extinctions across eight other rich countries. He found the same thing again.

Biological extinctions and corporate extinctions share that special signature. This does not prove that the economy is an evolutionary environment and that corporate strategies evolve through trial and error rather than successful planning, but it does offer a big hint. And Ormerod went further, again building on work by biologists. He took a stripped-down mathematical model of biological extinction that produced the tell-tale extinction signature and adapted it to represent corporate life and death. But he added a twist: he changed the rules of his model so that some companies were allowed to be successful planners. These planners were able to adjust their strategies to maximise the advantage they gained from interacting with other companies in the economy; some could do this perfectly, while others had just a tiny edge over a company whose strategy was determined entirely at random.

Ormerod discovered something disturbing: it was possible to build a model that mimicked the real extinction signature of firms, and it was possible to build a model that represented firms as modestly successful planners; but it was not possible to build a model that did both. The patterns of corporate life and death are totally different from reality in the 'planning is possible' model, but uncannily close to reality in the 'planning is impossible' model. If companies really could plan successfully – as most of us naturally assume that they can, despite what Tetlock tells us about the limitations of expert judgement – then the extinction signature of companies would look totally different to that of species. In reality, the signatures could hardly be more similar.

We should not leap to conclusions based on an abstract mathematical model, but Ormerod's discovery strongly implies that effective planning is rare in the modern economy. I wouldn't go so far as to suggest that Apple might as well replace Steve Jobs with a dart-throwing chimpanzee – even though it would certainly liven up Apple product launches. But the evidence suggests that in a competitive environment, many corporate decisions are not successful, and corporations constantly have to cull bad ideas and search for something better.

The same conclusion is suggested by Tetlock's studies of expert judgement and by the history of 'excellent' companies that so often lose their way: we are blinder than we think. In a complex, changeable world, the process of trial and error is essential. That is true whether we harness it consciously or simply allow ourselves to be tossed around by the results.

While trial and error is fundamental to the way that markets work, it makes for a challenging approach to life. Who wants to grope her way to a successful solution, with her repeated failures in full view of the world? Who wants to vote for a politician who takes that approach, or promote a middle manager whose strategy seems to be to throw around random ideas and see what works? Remember that President George W. Bush vowed to 'stay the course' while his opponent, John Kerry, lost the Presidential election in part because he had a reputation for changing his mind. Kerry's fans agreed that 'flip-flopper' was an insult, although they felt it was ill-deserved. But if we took trial and error seriously, 'flip-flopper' would be a badge of flexibility, worn with pride. A similar attitude prevails in British politics. Margaret Thatcher famously declared, 'You turn if you want to. The lady's not for turning.' Tony Blair was proud of the fact that he didn't have a reverse gear. Nobody would buy a car that didn't turn or go backwards, so it is unclear why we think of these as desirable qualities in Prime Ministers. But British voters rewarded Thatcher and Blair for their self-professed lack of adaptability with three general election victories apiece.

But whether we like it or not, trial and error is a tremendously powerful process for solving problems in a complex world, while expert leadership is not. Markets harness this process of trial and error, but that does not mean that we should leave everything to the market. It does mean – in the face of seemingly intractable problems, such as civil war, climate change and financial instability – that we must find a way to use the secret of trial and error beyond the familiar context of the market.

We will have to make an uncomfortable number of mistakes, and learn from them, rather than cover them up or deny they happened, even to ourselves. This is not the way we are used to getting things done.

7 A failure to adapt

A railroad foreman named Phineas Gage has the unfortunate distinction of being the world's most famous victim of a brain injury. In 1848, he was preparing an explosive charge when it detonated unexpectedly, driving his tamping iron – a rod over a yard long and an inch thick – through his cheek, behind his left eye, through his left front brain and out of the top of his head. The rod landed eighty feet away. Astonishingly, Gage survived, but his character was changed radically: previously sober and reliable, he became feckless, stubborn, unable to settle on any plan and prone to yelling obscenities. Along with a chunk of his brain, a particular part of his mind had gone. His friends said he was 'no longer Gage'.

The Soviet Union is to economics what Phineas Gage is to neuroscience. Neuroscientists study patients with damage to specific regions of the brain because their plight illuminates how the brain is ordinarily supposed to work. In much the same way, economists study dysfunctional economies when attempting to figure out the secrets of healthy ones. It is of course not a new insight that the Soviet system failed, but the unexpected details of why it failed are often glossed over – and they hold an important lesson for our mission to understand how to harness trial and error to solve problems.

The story starts in Russia's coal-rich Don Basin, north of the Black Sea, in 1901, before the Soviet Union even existed. A twenty-six-year-old engineer named Peter Palchinsky was sent by the Tsar's government to study the area's coal mines. Palchinsky gathered reams of data, paying attention to every local detail, and in particular building up a dossier on working conditions. The miners, he discovered, were housed forty or even sixty to a room, stacked in shared wooden bunks like cheap goods in a warehouse. In order to sleep, they had to crawl into position from the foot of the bed because there was no headroom to clamber over their fellows. Toilets and other facilities were rudimentary.

When Palchinsky sent back his findings, his superiors realised that his research was political dynamite: Palchinsky was sent to Siberia to perform less sensitive assignments. Palchinsky and his stubborn streak were inextricably linked. A few years earlier, winning a place at Russia's top engineering school, he had taken pride that he had based his application on the strength of his exam results, rather than relying on the right connections. In short, Palchinsky was bright, energetic, confident – and almost absurdly honest.

Palchinsky's early brush with the authorities worked to his advantage. He slipped across the Russian border to work in Western Europe. Palchinsky soaked up knowledge in Paris, Amsterdam, London and Hamburg, making copious notes on the new industries those cities were developing, and paying just as much attention to new ideas in management as in engineering. He wanted to absorb the latest thinking on organising a workforce as well as cutting-edge science and technology. Hungry to understand as much as he could, he became a successful industrial consultant, and was as eager to spread expertise as to gain it.

Incredibly, Palchinsky began writing articles suggesting suitable reforms for the Russian economy, advising the very Tsarist government that had exiled him to Siberia. But that was Palchinsky through and through: he just couldn't stop telling it the way he saw it. He wrote letters to his wife Nina freely admitting that he had had an affair while travelling in Europe. (She received the news stoically.) When he returned to Russia after receiving a pardon in 1913, he became an influential adviser to the Tsar's government, and – after narrowly escaping being bayoneted during the revolution – later he advised the Soviet government, too. But his stubborn honesty continued: he refused to join any scientific or engineering organisation that was controlled by the Communist Party, on the grounds that engineering advice should not be distorted by politics. He frequently criticised foolhardy engineering. He even drafted a letter to the Soviet leadership, offering the helpful observation that technology and science were more important than communism; friends begged him not to send it, and he relented.

Yet while Palchinsky's political antennae were missing, his technical judgement and humanitarian instincts were sharp. He warned against prestige projects: why drill oil wells just for the spectacular 'gush' when cheap coal and gas were widely available? He defended small projects that, according to his own painstaking research, were often more efficient than gigantic ones. He defended workers' rights throughout.

It is easy to forget just how successful the Soviet economy was ... for a time. We tend to assume that the planned economy fell apart because it lacked the galvanising force of the profit motive and the creativity of private-sector entrepreneurs. But this does not really make sense: there were many creative people in the Soviet Union, including Palchinsky. It is not immediately obvious why they would lose their creativity merely because they worked for state-owned enterprises. Nor did the Soviet Union lack motivational techniques: in fact, it possessed as great a range of incentives, positive and horrifyingly negative, as any civilisation in history, and deployed them ruthlessly. And the results were initially impressive. So much so that, by the 1950s, many Western experts had concluded that communism – while anti-democratic and cruel – was more effective than capitalism as a way to run an economy.

The Soviet failure revealed itself much more gradually: it was a pathological inability to experiment. The building blocks of an evolutionary process, remember, are repeated variation and selection. The Soviets failed at both: they found it impossible to tolerate a real variety of approaches to any problem; and they found it hard to decide what was working and what was not. The more the Soviet economy developed, the less of a reference point the planners had. The whole system was unable to adapt.

Peter Palchinsky, with his international experience and his painstaking analysis of local conditions, was just the kind of man who could have changed that. He was assigned to advise on two of the most important projects in Stalin's first five-year plan: the Lenin Dam and Magnitogorsk. The Lenin Dam, on the Dnieper River in modern Ukraine, was the world's largest when it was commissioned in the late 1920s. Palchinsky was unmoved by its scale. Stalin's brainchild it might be, but he warned that the river was too slow and, on a flood plain, the reservoir would be huge and would swamp many thousands of homes and much prime farming land. Nobody knew how much, he pointed out, because no hydrological surveys had been carried out; but the reservoir eventually proved to be so large that simply growing hay on the land it had covered and burning it in a power plant would have generated as much energy as the dam did. There was a dry season, Palchinsky admonished, so coal-fired power stations would have to be built and run for three months a year in any case. He advocated a step-by-step approach as the local economy expanded, combining small coal-fired plants with more modest dams. He pointed out that smaller dams would likely be more effective. In every detail, his concerns were later proved correct. But Stalin was not interested: he simply wanted the world's largest hydroelectric project and gave the order to proceed anyway. The project suffered huge cost overruns and was an economic and engineering disaster, even setting aside the ecological costs, the forced relocation of ten thousand farmers and the appalling labour conditions.

The steel mills of Magnitogorsk, the 'City of Magnet Mountain', were if anything more ambitious. The city was to be built in the remote heart of Russia, far to the east of Moscow, but near apparently plentiful iron-ore deposits. It was designed to exceed the entire steel output of the United Kingdom. Again, Palchinsky counselled caution – he wanted more analysis and a step-by-step approach. His old studies of workers' conditions in the coal mines of the Don Basin led him to worry about the fate of Magnitogorsk's workers. But he also pointed out the key technical objections to the project, which seemed to be cast from the same mould as the Lenin Dam: it was begun without a detailed study of the area's geology and without any interest in the availability of the coal needed to fire the mills.

Palchinsky's warnings were ignored, and again they were horribly accurate. One witness described conditions on the cattle wagons transporting workers to the site: 'For a day and a half, the door was not even opened ... mothers had children die in their arms ... From only the wagon in which we travelled, four little corpses were removed. More were carried out from other wagons.' Over three thousand people died in the first winter of construction work. Promised a garden city, Magnitogorsk's forced labourers were housed downwind of the blast furnaces. The iron ore ran out in the early 1970s, and then both coal and iron had to be shipped to what were the world's largest steel mills over vast distances. When the US historian Stephen Kotkin spent time living in the city in 1987, he discovered endemic alcoholism, shortages of almost everything, crumbling infrastructure, 'almost unfathomable pollution and a health catastrophe impossible to exaggerate'.

What Palchinsky realised was that most real-world problems are more complex than we think. They have a human dimension, a local dimension, and are likely to change as circumstances change. His method for dealing with this could be summarised as three 'Palchinsky principles': first, seek out new ideas and try new things; second, when trying something new, do it on a scale where failure is survivable; third, seek out feedback and learn from your mistakes as you go along. The first principle could simply be expressed as 'variation'; the third as 'selection'. The importance of the middle principle – survivability – is something which will become clear in chapter six, which explores the collapse of the banking system.

The monstrous moral flaws of the Soviet system are now obvious. The economic flaw was more subtle: its inability to produce variation and selection, and therefore its inability to adapt. Central planners decided what would be built, lulled into a sense of omniscience by having a map or a table of statistics in front of them. Such plans inevitably missed the messy complexities of the situation on the ground, and also produced far too little variation. Almost every apartment in 1960s Moscow had the same iridescent orange lampshade. In Magnitogorsk, there were two types of apartment, named 'A' and 'B'. They were the city's sole concession to variety.

Above all, feedback is essential for determining which experiments have succeeded and which have failed. And in the Soviet Union, feedback was ruthlessly suppressed.

One icy Leningrad night in April 1928, there was a knock on the door of Peter Palchinsky's apartment. He was arrested by the secret police and was never seen by his wife again. Over a year later, it was announced that he had been executed. There had been no trial, but a secret police dossier on Palchinsky, unearthed and smuggled out of Moscow many decades later by the historian Loren Graham, documented his 'crimes'. He was accused of 'publishing detailed statistics' and sabotaging Soviet industry by trying to set 'minimal goals'. In other words, Peter Palchinsky was murdered for trying to figure out what would work, and for refusing to shut up when he saw a problem.

Palchinsky was not alone. Three thousand of the USSR's ten thousand engineers were arrested in the late 1920s and early 1930s, mostly bound for near-certain death in Siberia. (Palchinsky's wife, Nina, also met that fate.) Anyone who tried to object to looming technological disasters and to suggest alternatives was denounced as a 'wrecker'. Palchinsky's secret execution was unusual – perhaps because, stubborn to the end, he refused to recant. His persecution was not.

The Soviet Bloc began to fall apart in the late 1980s, punctuated with famous events such as the victory of the newly legalised Solidarity movement in the Polish elections of June 1989, and the fall of the Berlin Wall in November of that year.

In the heart of the Soviet Union itself, a momentous but less famous revolt was also taking place: the first major strike in Soviet history. In July 1989, a quarter of a million coal miners walked away from their jobs. Part of the protest was about grotesquely dangerous conditions: the death rate for Soviet miners was fifteen to twenty times higher than it was for their American equivalents, with the local pits claiming the lives of over fifty men every month. But the strike was also provoked by simple deprivation: the miners often had no meat or fruit to eat, and few had access to soap or hot water. After risking their lives each day in the suffocating depths, they couldn't even wash themselves or rest in a comfortable bed. President Mikhail Gorbachev was forced to appear on national television, acknowledging the justice of the miners' cause and offering substantial concessions. It was a notable moment in the downfall of the Soviet system.

The miners who had walked out and humiliated Gorbachev worked, of all places, in the Don Basin. Sixty years after Peter Palchinsky's execution, and eighty-eight years after he had initially pointed to the problem of working conditions in the Don coal mines, the Soviet system had still failed to adapt.

8 Beyond Coca-Cola problems

The Soviet Union, like poor Phineas Gage, is a grotesquely extreme example. Only the worst dictatorships have exhibited the same pathological immunity to feedback. Yet, in a gentler way, most organisations and most forms of politics have the same difficulty in carrying out the simple process of variation and selection.

Variation is difficult because of two natural tendencies in organisations. One is grandiosity: politicians and corporate bosses both like large projects – anything from the reorganisation of a country's entire healthcare system to a gigantic merger –

because they win attention and show that the leader is a person who gets things done. Such flagship projects violate the first Palchinsky Principle, because errors are common and big projects leave little room to adapt. The other tendency emerges because we rarely like the idea of standards that are inconsistent and uneven from place to place. It seems neater and fairer to provide a consistent standard for everything, whether it's education, the road network or the coffee at Starbucks. Such uniformly high standards sound tempting: as Andy Warhol once commented, 'You can be watching TV and see Coca-Cola, and you know that the President drinks Coke, Liz Taylor drinks Coke, and just think, you can drink Coke, too. A Coke is a Coke and no amount of money can get you a better Coke than the one the bum on the corner is drinking. All the Cokes are the same and all the Cokes are good.'

But Warhol found Coke intriguing because it was an exception; and it still is. Producing a sweet, fizzy drink is a static, solved problem. No further experimentation is necessary, and it is perfectly possible to set uniformly high standards in the production of Coca-Cola. (The *delivery* of Coke to remote parts of the world is another matter, and is a minor miracle of local adaptation.) Ensuring uniformly high standards in more complex situations is much harder: it's the chief achievement of Starbucks and McDonald's, and even then the standardisation comes at a price in charm, flexibility and quality.

Running a hospital or a school is another matter altogether. We love the idea that every single one should deliver the same high quality. In the UK, we even have our own catchphrase, the 'postcode lottery', to describe the scandal that standards vary from place to place. It is something of a national obsession. We want all of our public services to be like Coca-Cola: all identical, all good. And they can't be.

If we are to take the 'variation' part of 'variation and selection' seriously, uniformly high standards are not only impossible but undesirable. When a problem is unsolved or continually changing, the best way to tackle it is to experiment with many different approaches. If nobody tries anything different, we will struggle to figure out new and better ways to do anything. But if we are to accept variation, we must also accept that some of these new approaches will not work well. That is not a tempting proposition for a politician or chief executive to try to sell.

It seems to be equally hard for traditional organisations to deliver the selection component of variation and selection. The difficulty is in selecting what is really working on the ground. Peter Palchinsky was all for taking things step by step, but politicians resist pilot schemes with objective measures of success. This is partly because politicians are in a hurry: they expect to hold on to a role for two to four years, not long enough for most experiments to deliver meaningful results.* Even more politically inconvenient is the fact that half of the pilot schemes will fail – many things do in a complex world – so the pilot will simply produce stark evidence of that failure. This is our fault as much as the fault of our politicians. We should tolerate, even celebrate, any politicians who test their ideas robustly enough to prove that some of them don't work. But, of course, we do not.

It's a sad truth that one of the most successful pilot schemes of recent years was implemented not by politicians but by a celebrity chef and a television crew. Jamie Oliver, chirpy Essex boy turned darling of the British middle class, created a national phenomenon in 2005 when he tried to persuade schools to serve healthier meals. Almost accidentally, he created a reasonable approximation of a controlled experiment. He convinced schools in the London borough of Greenwich to change their menus, and then mobilised resources, provided equipment and

---

*Donald Green, Professor of Political Science at Yale, tells me that one question in the social sciences has been thoroughly tested with field experiments: how to get out the vote. So politicians can use rigorous evaluation methods when it suits them.

trained dinner ladies. Other London boroughs with similar demographics received none of these advantages. Indeed, because the resulting television programme wasn't broadcast until after the project was well under way, they probably knew little about it.

Two economists, Michele Belot and Jonathan James, picked up the data generated by the cheeky chef's campaign and analysed it, discovering that if primary-school kids eat less fat, sugar and salt, and more fruit and vegetables, they are ill less often and do somewhat better at English and science. These conclusions would be more robust if the trial had been rigorously controlled, but until Jamie Oliver came along, none of the country's politicians had shown much interest in the experiment. Tony Blair, then British Prime Minister, fell over himself to endorse the campaign. He had been in power for eight years at the time.

If formal experiments hold few joys for traditional leaders, informal feedback will often fail to reach them, too. Few advisers face Peter Palchinsky's fate, but even so his compulsion to blurt out the truth is rare. There is a limit to how much honest feedback most leaders really want to hear; and because we know this, most of us sugar-coat our opinions whenever we speak to a powerful person. In a deep hierarchy, that process is repeated many times, until the truth is utterly concealed inside a thick layer of sweet-talk. There is some evidence that the more ambitious a person is, the more he will choose to be a yes-man – and with good reason, because yes-men tend to be rewarded.

Even when leaders and managers genuinely want honest feedback, they may not receive it. At every stage in a plan, junior managers or petty bureaucrats must tell their superiors what resources they need and what they propose to do with them. There are a number of plausible lies they might choose to tell, including over-promising in the hope of winning influence as go-getters, or stressing the impossibility of the task and the vast resources needed to deliver success, in the hope of providing a pleasant surprise. Actually telling the unvarnished truth is unlikely to be the best strategy in a bureaucratic hierarchy. Even if someone does tell the truth, how is the senior decision-maker supposed to distinguish the honest opinion of a Peter Palchinsky from some cynical protestation calculated to win a budget increase?

Traditional organisations are badly equipped to benefit from a decentralised process of trial and error. Static, solved problems are ideal for such organisations; as are tasks where generalised expertise counts for much more than local knowledge. But such 'Coca-Cola problems' are increasingly rare in a rapidly changing world, which is why – as we shall see – many businesses are beginning to decentralise and strip authority away from managers. In the next chapter, we'll see how adaptive organisations need to decentralise and become comfortable with the chaos of different local approaches and the awkwardness of dissent from junior staff. We'll also see the heroic effort required to force a traditional hierarchy to change its mind.

But there is a more fundamental problem here than the right way to design an organisation, because it isn't just organisations that struggle to acknowledge and adapt to their mistakes. Most individuals suffer from the same problem. Accepting trial and error means accepting error. It means taking problems in our stride when a decision doesn't work out, whether through luck or misjudgement. And that is not something human brains seem to be able to do without a struggle.

9 Why learning from mistakes is hard

I spent the summer of 2005 studying poker. I interviewed some of the best players in the world, attended the World Series of Poker in Las Vegas, analysed 'pokerbots' – poker-playing computers – and chronicled the efforts of highly rational players, such as Chris 'Jesus' Ferguson, a game theorist with a PhD who is a world champion and a formidable one-on-one player.

While poker can be analysed rationally, with big egos and big money at stake it can also be a very emotional game. Poker players explained to me that there's a particular moment at which players are extremely vulnerable to an emotional surge. It's not when they've won a huge pot or when they've drawn a fantastic hand. It's when they've just lost a lot of money through bad luck (a 'bad beat') or bad strategy. The loss can nudge a player into going 'on tilt' – making overly aggressive bets in an effort to win back what he wrongly feels is still his money. The brain refuses to register that the money has gone. Acknowledging the loss and recalculating one's strategy would be the right thing to do, but that is too painful. Instead, the player makes crazy bets to rectify what he unconsciously believes is a temporary situation. It isn't the initial loss that does for him, but the stupid plays he makes in an effort to deny that the loss has happened. The great economic psychologists Daniel Kahneman and Amos Tversky summarised the behaviour in their classic analysis of the psychology of risk: 'a person who has not made peace with his losses is likely to accept gambles that would be unacceptable to him otherwise'.

Even those of us who aren't professional poker players know how it feels to chase a loss. A few years ago, my wife and I had booked a romantic weekend in Paris. But she was pregnant, and a couple of hours before we were due to catch the train she began feeling sick. She was throwing up into a plastic bag in the taxi on the way to the station. But when I met up with her, she was determined to go to Paris because our tickets weren't refundable. She didn't want to accept the loss and was about to compound it.

Being an economist is rarely an advantage in a romantic situation, but this was perhaps an exception. I tried to convince my wife to forget about the tickets. Imagine that the money we had spent on them had been lost for ever, I told her, but also imagine that we stood on the steps of Waterloo station with no plans for the weekend, when somebody came up to us and offered us free tickets to Paris. That was the correct way to think about the situation: the money was gone; and the question was whether we wanted to travel to Paris for no further cost. I asked my wife whether she would accept such an offer. Of course not. She was feeling far too sick to go to Paris. She forced a faint smile as she realised what I was telling her, and we went home. (As if to confirm that we had made the right decision, the nice people at Eurostar refunded our tickets anyway. And a few months later, my wife somewhat more pregnant, we got to Paris in the end.)

The behavioural economist Richard Thaler, with a team of co-authors, has found the perfect setting to analyse the way we respond to losses. He studied the TV game show *Deal or No Deal*, which is a great source of data because the basic game is repeated incessantly, with similar rules, for high stakes, in over fifty countries. *Deal or No Deal* offers contestants a choice of between twenty and twenty-six numbered boxes, each containing some prize money, ranging from pennies to hundreds of thousands of dollars, pounds or euros. (The original Dutch version has a jackpot of five million euros.) The player holds one box, not knowing how much money is inside. Her task is to choose the other boxes in any order she likes. These are then opened and discarded. Every time she opens a box containing a token amount, she celebrates, because that means her own mystery box doesn't contain that low prize. Every time she opens a box with a large prize, she winces, because that reduces the odds that her own box will be lucrative.

All of this is pure chance. The interesting decision is the one that gives the game show its title. From time to time, the 'Banker', a mysterious and anonymous figure, calls the studio to offer the contestant cash in exchange for the unknown sum inside her box. Will it be a deal, or no deal?

The psychology of the game is revealing. Let's take a look at Frank, a contestant in the Dutch version of *Deal or No Deal*.

After a few rounds, the expected value of his box – that is, the average of all the remaining amounts – was just over €100,000. The Banker offered him €5,000 – serious money, but less than 75 per cent of his box's expected value. He turned it down. Then he received a nasty shock. Frank opened a box containing €500,000, the last big prize remaining. His expected winnings plunged to just €2,508. The Banker's offer plunged, too – from €75,000 to €2,400. Relative to Frank's likely winnings, this was a more generous offer than the previous one – 96 per cent of the expected value of playing on – but Frank rejected it. The next round, Frank spurned a Banker's offer that was actually greater than the average value of the remaining boxes. And in the final round, Frank's two remaining possibilities were €10 or €10,000. The Banker offered him a more-than-generous €6,000. Frank turned it down. He left the studio with €10. After being stunned by the loss of a guaranteed €75,000 and a decent chance of a €500,000 prize, Frank started taking crazy gambles. Frank had gone on tilt.

Frank's behaviour is typical. Thaler and his colleagues looked at how people responded to the Banker's offers immediately after making an unlucky choice, a lucky choice, or a choice that was broadly neutral. They found that the neutral choosers tended to be quite keen to accept the Banker's deal. Lucky choosers were cocky: they were more likely to turn down the Banker and keep going. But it was unlucky choosers who stood out. They were extremely unlikely to accept an offer from the Banker.* Why? Because if they did, it would lock in their 'mistake'. If they kept playing, there was a chance of some sort of redemption. The pattern was all the more striking because the Banker tended to make more generous offers to losers – lower in absolute terms, of course, but closer to the average of the

---

*Typical contestants accepted the Banker's offer 31 per cent of the time. 'Winners' accepted the offer 25 per cent of the time. 'Losers' accepted only 14 per cent of the time, despite receiving objectively more generous offers.

remaining boxes. Objectively, players who had just made an unlucky choice should have been more willing to deal than anyone, because they were receiving more attractive odds from the Banker.

Perhaps this is a phenomenon restricted to game shows and the poker tables of the Rio in Las Vegas? No such luck. The economist Terrance Odean has found that we tend to hang on grimly, and wrongly, to shares that have plunged in the hope that things will turn around. We are far happier to sell shares that have been doing well. Unfortunately, selling winners and holding on to losers has in retrospect been poor investment strategy.

All four examples – poker, Paris, *Deal or No Deal* and share portfolios – show a dogged determination to avoid crystallising a loss or drawing a line under a decision we regret. That dogged determination might occasionally be helpful, but it is counterproductive in all these cases and in many others. Faced with a mistake or a loss, the right response is to acknowledge the setback and change direction. Yet our instinctive reaction is denial. That is why 'learn from your mistakes' is wise advice that is painfully hard to take.

10 A recipe for adapting

We face a difficult challenge: the more complex and elusive our problems are, the more effective trial and error becomes, relative to the alternatives. Yet it is an approach that runs counter to our instincts, and to the way in which traditional organisations work. The aim of this book is to provide an answer to that challenge.

The adaptive, experimental approach can work almost anywhere, so we'll look at a huge range of problems. We'll meet the rebellious colonels who risked their careers – and their lives – to change the shape of the war in Iraq; and the doctor whose desperate gamble in a wartime prison camp should serve as an example to the staff of the World Bank today. We'll discover what the disasters at Three Mile Island and Deepwater Horizon have to tell us about preventing another Lehman Brothers crisis. We'll learn from a watchmaker, a street urchin, a Wall Street rebel, two aircraft designers and a failing choreographer. We'll study the corporate strategies of companies from Google to a simple high-street cobbler. We'll search for solutions to problems from the banking crisis to climate change.

Along the way, we'll also be learning about the recipe for successfully adapting. The three essential steps are: to try new things, in the expectation that some will fail; to make failure survivable, because it will be common; and to make sure that you know when you've failed. Palchinsky would have recognised these steps, but they involve formidable obstacles. To produce new ideas we must overcome our tendency to fall in step with those around us, and overcome those with a vested interest in the status quo. Making failure survivable sometimes means taking small steps, but not always: many innovations emerge from highly speculative leaps, and surviving such leaps is not easy. Nor is it easy to survive a failure in the financial system. And distinguishing success from failure, oddly, can be the hardest task of all: arrogant leaders can ignore the distinction; our own denial can blur it; and the sheer complexity of the world can make the distinction hard to draw even for the most objective judge.

Along the way, I hope that we'll learn something about how to adapt and experiment in business and in our own lives. Faced with the costs and risks of trial and error, should you and I try to experiment and adapt more than we do? What price would we pay in our quest to succeed?

Two

Conflict or: How organisations learn

'It's so damn complex. If you ever think you have the solution to this, you're wrong and you're dangerous.'

– H.R. McMaster

'In the absence of guidance or orders, figure out what they should have been . . . '

– part of a sign on a command-post door in west Baghdad, commandeered by David Petraeus

1 'I watched them shoot my grandfather . . . '

On Saturday 19 November 2005, the weekend before Thanksgiving, a US marine ran into a family home about 150 miles outside Baghdad and began shooting children. By his own account, he 'saw that children were in the room kneeling down. I don't remember the exact number but only that it was a lot.' He concluded that the children were hostile. 'I am trained to shoot two shots to the chest and two to the head and I followed my training.'

The marine's friend, Corporal Miguel Terrazas, a twenty-year-old from El Paso, was dead. A concealed bomb had blown his upper body apart. Two other marines had been wounded, and then a white Opel had approached the scene with five young Iraqi men in it – a possible threat. The young soldiers were shocked and under tremendous pressure.

What happened after the bomb exploded was pieced together by marine investigators and by journalists who questioned the marines' account. The five Iraqi men were shot. One marine sergeant admitted that he had urinated on the head of one of the dead men, and claimed that they'd been shot while trying to surrender.

The marines then swept through the houses on the side of the road. Five-year-old Zainab Salem was killed. So was her sister Aisha, who was three. Five other members of the family were shot and killed. The only survivor was a thirteen-year-old girl who had been playing dead. A baby was killed in another house; a man in a wheelchair was shot nine times. Eman Waleed, who was nine, was sheltered with her eight-year-old brother by the bodies of adult relatives. 'I watched them shoot my grandfather, first in the chest and then in the head,' she told journalists. 'Then they killed my granny.' In total, twenty-four Iraqis died at the hands of the marines.

Almost as appalling as the killings in the town of Haditha was the fact that the sudden death of twenty-four civilians was accepted as routine. The battalion commander thought it was 'very sad, very unfortunate' but saw nothing worthy of investigating. His commander saw 'nothing out of the ordinary, including the number of civilian dead'. The division commander agreed.

Haditha did not immediately damage the reputation of the US Army in Iraq. Violent deaths were by then so common that they were no more noticed by most Iraqis than by marine officers. But Haditha was a symbol of the utter failure of the US strategy in Iraq. The US and their allies desperately needed the support of ordinary Iraqis, and they were failing to get it. Haditha was a symptom of the stress, frustration, fatigue and sheer isolation of the US occupying forces. The marines at

Haditha saw their friend killed and they didn't have a proper response. Their tactics were failing and they had been given no effective strategy. The result was an atrocity.

2005 had been a dreadful year. 2006 turned out to be worse. On 22 February, the Golden Dome Mosque in Samarra was destroyed by a bomb – an act very roughly comparable to Catholics obliterating Westminster Abbey in London. It marked the beginning of a street-level civil war between the Shia Muslim majority whose holy site had been attacked, and who dominated the Iraqi government, and the Sunni Muslim minority who had been dominant under Saddam Hussein but who were being excluded from the post-Saddam order in Iraq. Some see the Samarra bombing as the trigger for the crisis; others argue that it was simply a mark of escalating tensions between Shia and Sunni. Car bombs became commonplace, but much of the violence was even simpler than that: one summer day in 2006, over fifty bodies were found in Baghdad alone. Each was handcuffed, blindfolded and shot. Shia militia would seize a Sunni man from a mixed area, take him to the edge of a Sunni district, shoot him in the back of the head, dump his body and drive off. Sunni insurgents also tried to clear mixed areas by picking off Shia one by one – first the barbers, then the estate agents, then the ice-sellers. A butcher was shot in the face in front of his customers; his adult son ran in and was shot too. His brother dashed in from the shop next door and met the same fate. Vast numbers of people fled the country, or moved from mixed to segregated areas, where they felt safer from casual violence.

Then there was Al Qaeda in Iraq (AQI), a vicious group of insurgents led by a Jordanian, Abu Musab al-Zarqawi, and pledging allegiance to Osama bin Laden's network. AQI seized control of Iraqi towns one by one, humiliating tribal leaders – for instance, with a public beating – and if necessary assassinating them on the way to cowing the local population.

The US and allied response to the unfolding catastrophe was

inept. The official policy remained that local police and army units were ready to stand up and be counted, but the official policy simply wasn't working. Iraqi army units refused to move away from their local patches. The police in Baghdad were Shia-dominated and had no interest in stopping the violence. Under the guise of 'pacification', they would move into a Sunni area and confiscate weapons, and then withdraw, tipping off the local Shia militia that the Sunnis were now defenceless.

Iraq was falling apart, and allied casualties were rising alarmingly. It was clear to anyone on the ground that the country was sliding ever further from peace and good government. Failure looked almost inevitable. And the Haditha massacre, shooting young children and men in wheelchairs, was not only a dreadful crime, but typified the isolation of the occupying forces from the people whose interests they were said to be serving. Strategies for dealing with insurgents such as AQI did exist, yet in 2005 and 2006, US forces seemed scarcely aware even of their existence. The occupation of Iraq was failing beyond the worst nightmares of the Pentagon and the White House.

Yet by 2008, the situation in Iraq had turned around completely. AQI was in full retreat, and the number of attacks, American deaths and Iraqi deaths had fallen dramatically. The damage done by the ill-planned Iraq invasion cannot be undone, and the future of the country remains very uncertain. But it is undeniable that a fragile success was snatched from the jaws of utter failure. The lesson of how the US military did so is important, because it defies everything we want to believe about how any large organisation should deal with problems.

2 The ideal organisation

Take a look at any organisational chart in the world and you'll see in a simple PowerPoint-friendly format the idealised view of how organisations make decisions. At the top, you have the leader: the CEO, the four-star General, the President. The leader is crucial: if he makes good decisions, all will be well. If he makes bad decisions, the organisation will suffer and may fail altogether.

And how should the leader make good decisions? That's easy. First, he should take advantage of the fact that he's in a position to see the big picture. The more technology he devotes to this task, the better he can see how everything fits together, enabling him to coordinate what's happening on the ground, be it the check-out, the factory floor, or the front line. The leader should also be surrounded by a supportive team with a shared vision of where the organisation is going. And to ensure that the strategy is carried out effectively, reporting lines should be clear. Information should flow to the top and be analysed, and instructions should flow back down in response – otherwise nothing but muddle and chaos lie ahead.

But while this is how we instinctively think about how leadership works and how organisations should operate, it's a dangerously misleading view. The problem is that no leader can make the right decision every time. Napoleon, perhaps the finest general in history, invaded Russia with half a million men and lost over 90 per cent of them to death and desertion. John F. Kennedy forced Khrushchev to back down during the Cuban missile crisis. Yet he will also be remembered for the Bay of Pigs fiasco, when he somehow persuaded himself both that 1400 US-trained Cuban exiles might defeat 200,000 troops and topple Fidel Castro, and that nobody would suspect that the US was involved. Mao Zedong was the greatest of all insurgent commanders, but a catastrophic peacetime leader whose blundering arrogance killed tens of millions of his own people. Winston Churchill offered fierce warnings about the rise of Hitler, and inspirational wartime leadership for the United Kingdom. But as the politician in charge of the British Navy in the First World War, Churchill forced through the disastrous Gallipoli campaign which claimed tens of thousands of allied soldiers without any success. In war, politics and business, we face complex problems, and adversaries who have their own plans. It is simply impossible to be right every time. As a Prussian general once put it, 'No plan survives first contact with the enemy'. What matters is how quickly the leader is able to adapt.

If even the best leaders make mistakes, a good organisation will need to have some way to correct those mistakes. Let's recall the features that make our idealised hierarchy an attractive machine for carrying out correct decisions: the refinement of information to produce a 'big picture'; the power of a team all pulling in the same direction; and the clear responsibilities producing a proper flow of information up and down the chain of command. Every one of these assets can become a liability if the task of the organisation is to learn from mistakes. The big picture becomes a self-deluding propaganda poster, the unified team retreats into groupthink, and the chain of command becomes a hierarchy of wastebaskets, perfectly evolved to prevent feedback reaching the top. What works in reality is a far more unsightly, chaotic and rebellious organisation altogether.

3 Mr Rumsfeld's 'epiphany'

It is impossible to read a history of the Iraq war without concluding that the invasion was misconceived. What is more remarkable, though, is that it was executed with staggering incompetence for many years. How did the fiasco persist for so long?

A clue lies in a press conference given just after Thanksgiving in 2005 by the two most senior figures in the US defence establishment. Donald Rumsfeld, the defense secretary, stood side by side with the chairman of the Joint Chiefs of Staff, General Peter Pace. This was ten days after the Haditha massacre, but the subject of the briefing was the conduct of the war in general.

Several observers noticed something very odd about the press conference. Throughout it, Rumsfeld carefully avoided referring to 'insurgents'. This was at a time when all three insurgencies – Sunni, Shia and Al Qaeda in Iraq – were on the rise. The quirk was so noticeable that a journalist asked the defense secretary why he was skirting around the word. Rumsfeld explained that he had enjoyed an 'epiphany' over Thanksgiving weekend. He'd realised that 'this is a group of people who don't merit the word "insurgency"'.

General Pace couldn't quite keep to his boss's surreal script. At one point, he hesitated while describing the situation on the ground and sheepishly admitted, 'I have to use the word "insurgent" because I can't think of a better word right now.' '"Enemies of the legitimate Iraqi government", how's that?' Rumsfeld interjected. When General Pace made the 'insurgent' slip later in the press conference, he offered a mock-rueful apology to Rumsfeld, to chuckles all round. General Pace also told a reporter that, 'No armed force in the world goes to greater effort than your armed force to protect civilians.' The facts about Haditha had hardly begun their slow crawl up the chain of command.

Rumsfeld's Orwellian performance at a press conference would have been less remarkable had it been merely an isolated piece of bluster to the media, but it wasn't. It had an impact on the day-to-day conduct of the war. It was becoming apparent that some kind of counterinsurgency strategy was needed, but that was hard to discuss without using the word 'insurgent'. The fear of the 'i-word' had already trickled down through the military. One captain complained to the journalist George Packer about a general who visited his unit and announced, 'This is not an insurgency.' His unspoken response had been, 'Well, if you could tell us what it is, that'd be awesome.'

Rumsfeld's denial of reality also typified his refusal to take advice from men who understood the situation. One of the very first opportunities for feedback had come before the Iraq war even started. General Eric Shinseki had warned a Senate committee that several hundred thousand troops would be needed to deal with the aftermath of the invasion, two or three times the number Rumsfeld had allocated. General Shinseki was not only the Army's chief of staff, but a former commander of peacekeeping forces in Bosnia. His comments, which later proved accurate, had been swiftly dismissed by Donald Rumsfeld's deputy as 'wildly off the mark'. Pentagon-watchers reported that General Shinseki had then been marginalised until his scheduled retirement a few months later.

A second opportunity for feedback came when Lt General John Abizaid had spoken to Rumsfeld and his third-in-command, Douglas Feith, six days into the war. Abizaid was the number two field commander in Iraq (he would later assume command of all US forces in the Middle East) and he was a man worth listening to. Of all the Army's top brass, he was the authority on the Middle East. He had moved with his pregnant wife and toddler daughter to Iraq's neighbour Jordan in 1978, living in humble accommodation in the capital, Amman. The family had embraced the local culture and Abizaid studied the Koran, witnessed the Jordanian response to the Iranian revolution, and travelled the country, earning the name 'Abu Zaid' from nomads. And after the first Gulf War, Abizaid had improvised a remarkable campaign in which he nudged Saddam Hussein's army back from the Iraqi Kurds, preventing a massacre without a shot being fired. His commanding officer had called it 'one of the greatest examples of military skill that I have ever seen'.

Twelve years on, the opening 'shock and awe' phase of the Iraq war had seemed to be going well. Abizaid, however, had plenty he wanted to discuss. Yet Rumsfeld didn't detect an opportunity to learn something: he left the conference call after fifteen minutes with a cheery wave. So it had fallen to Feith to hear Abizaid's opinion of how things were going. Abizaid had tried to share his profound disquiet. He knew from his previous Iraqi experience that ethnic and religious divisions ran deep, and was worried that the Pentagon had no plan for stabilising the country after Saddam's inevitable fall. Abizaid had argued that the allies needed to win over tens of thousands of low- and mid-level employees of Saddam's doomed Baath regime, including administrators, police and teachers. But Feith simply hadn't been interested. He had interrupted Abizaid to declare, 'The policy of the United States government is de-Baathification' – the removal of all of Saddam's party members, no matter how minor they were, and thus the removal of almost anyone in Iraq who knew anything about the functioning of the state. Abizaid had tried again, arguing that even the word was treacherous, laden with entirely misleading parallels with postwar Germany and 'de-Nazification'.

Feith had responded with the tried-and-true debating tactics of a five-year-old. He simply repeated himself: 'The policy of the United States government is de-Baathification'. General Abizaid's concerns were subsequently justified in almost every detail.

It is only with hindsight that we know that Generals Shinseki and Abizaid were correct. Yet even when the war effort had fallen apart, Rumsfeld's team continued to put their fingers in their ears. There was the case of Andy Krepinevich, a defence analyst who in September 2005 had written a sharp article in *Foreign Affairs* describing and arguing for a proper counterinsurgency strategy. Rumsfeld asked his advisers to have a word with Krepinevich, but when he was summoned for a breakfast briefing, rather than being asked for his advice, he was told he didn't understand the situation on the ground. According to Krepinevich, one Rumsfeld aide even joked that they should abandon him on the deadly road to Baghdad airport. The aide in question denies making any threat, but the story hardly shows an eagerness to learn from outsiders.

It's easy, and true, to blame the failures of the Iraq war on bad decisions at the top. But there was more going on than a simple failure of strategy. Strategic errors are common in war. This wasn't just about going into Iraq with the wrong strategy. It was a failure – worse, a *refusal* – to adapt.

4 'A kind of family'

Drawing parallels between Vietnam and Iraq can be deceptive. Yet in one respect Vietnam and Iraq are eerie echoes of each other: in both cases, it was almost impossible for dissenting ideas, especially from the battlefield, to penetrate the war rooms at the Pentagon and the White House. The situation in Iraq changed only when dissenting ideas were given space to breathe; in Vietnam, they never were.

The authoritative study of decision-making as the US was sucked into Vietnam was published in 1997, and based on a PhD thesis which itself relied on newly declassified documents. Its author, H.R. McMaster, was so incensed by the failures of President Lyndon Johnson, his defense secretary Robert McNamara, and the generals on the Joint Chiefs of Staff, that he called his book *Dereliction of Duty*.

McMaster's book shows clearly how the ideal hierarchy can backfire. Remember the three elements of the idealised, decisive hierarchy: a 'big-picture' view produced by the refined analysis of all available information; a united team all pulling in the same direction; and a strict chain of command. Johnson and McNamara managed to tick all those boxes, yet produce catastrophic results. The 'big-picture' information that could be summarised and analysed centrally wasn't the information that turned out to matter. A loyal, unified team left no space for alternative perspectives. And the strict chain of command neatly suppressed bad news from further down the organisation before it reached Johnson. Donald Rumsfeld was later to repeat the same mistakes, and the turnaround in Iraq came only when the US military abandoned its chain of command, love of unanimity and its aspirations to make big-picture decisions.

Robert McNamara was famous for his love of quantitative analysis, which he perfected to such effect at the Ford Motor Company that he was appointed the first Ford president outside the Ford family – before, just a few weeks later, being poached by John F. Kennedy and made defense secretary. McNamara thought that with enough computers and enough Harvard MBAs, he could calculate the optimal strategy in war, far from the front lines. That project brought the US Army no joy in Vietnam, but its spirit continued to animate Donald Rumsfeld. Even more damaging, though, was McNamara's management style.

H.R. McMaster shows that Lyndon Johnson and Robert McNamara were made for each other. Johnson, an insecure man with the Presidency thrust upon him by John F. Kennedy's murder, was eager for reassurance and disliked debate. McNamara was the quintessential yes-man, soothing Johnson at every step and ruthlessly enforcing the President's request to hear a single voice. Shortly after becoming President, and with the 1964 Presidential election looming closer, Johnson hosted a lunchtime discussion each Tuesday with three senior advisers, including McNamara. No military specialists were present, not even the chairman of the Joint Chiefs of Staff. McNamara and Johnson both distrusted the military – indeed, shortly after taking office, Johnson had sacked three military aides because 'they get in my way'.

Johnson and his advisers saw Vietnam primarily as a political football that might stall or strengthen Johnson's Presidential campaign. His three aides, who viewed themselves as 'a kind of family', were careful always to harmonise their advice before meeting Johnson, which was just the way he liked it. McNamara himself looked for 'team players', declaring that it was impossible for a government to operate effectively if departmental heads 'express disagreement with decisions' of the President. This was the idealised organisation at its worst. Loyalty wasn't enough. Merely to 'express disagreement' was a threat.

A famous set of experiments by the psychologist Solomon Asch shows why the McNamara–Johnson doctrine of unanimous advice was so dangerous. The classic Asch experiment sat several young men around a table and showed them a pair of cards, one with a single line, and one with three lines of obviously different lengths, labelled A, B and C. The experimenter asked subjects to say which of the three lines was the same length as the single line on the other card. This was a trivially easy task, but there was a twist: all but one of the people sitting around the table were actors recruited by Asch. As they went round the table, each one called out the same answer – a wrong answer. By the time Asch turned to the real experimental subject, the poor man would be baffled. Frequently, he would fall in with the group, and later interviews revealed that this was often because he genuinely believed his eyes were deceiving him. As few as three actors were enough to create this effect.

Less famous but just as important is Asch's follow-up experiment, in which one of the actors gave a different answer from the rest. Immediately, the pressure to conform was released. Experimental subjects who gave the wrong answer when outnumbered ten to one happily dissented and gave the right answer when outnumbered nine to two. Remarkably, it didn't even matter if the fellow dissenter gave the right answer himself. As long as the answer was different from the group, that was sufficient to free Asch's poor subjects from their socially-imposed cognitive straitjacket.

In a surreal variant, the psychologists Vernon Allen and John Levine ran a similar visual test with an elaborate pantomime in which one of the experimental participants had extravagantly thick glasses, specially manufactured by a local optometrist to look like bottle-bottoms. This Mr Magoo character – another actor – then started raising concerns with the experimenter. 'Will the experiment require any distance vision? I have a lot of trouble seeing objects that are some distance away.' After a series of set-pieces designed to fool the real subject into believing that Mr Magoo could hardly see his hand in front of his face, the experiment began and of course Magoo kept getting things wrong.

Again, subjects found it very hard to disagree with a unanimous –
and wrong – group verdict. Again, a single dissenting voice was
enough to liberate the subjects. And, astonishingly, this liberation
took place even if the fellow dissenter was just poor old Magoo
yelling out completely the wrong answer.

An alternative perspective on the value of an alternative perspective comes from the complexity theorists Lu Hong and
Scott Page. Their decision-makers are simple automatons inside
a computer, undaunted by social pressure. Yet when Hong and
Page run simulations in which their silicon agents are programmed to search for solutions, they find that a group of the
very smartest agents isn't as successful as a more diverse group of
dumber agents. Even though 'different' often means 'wrong',
trying something different has a value all of its own – a lesson
Peter Palchinsky learned as he travelled the industrial hubs of
Europe. Both because of the conformity effect Asch discovered,
and because of the basic usefulness of hearing more ideas, better
decisions emerge from a diverse group.

The doctrine of avoiding split advice, then, couldn't have
been more misguided. The last thing Lyndon Johnson needed
was to be confronted with a unanimous view. He desperately
needed to hear disagreement. Only then would he feel free to
use his own judgement, and only then would he avoid the trap
of considering too narrow a range of options. Even an incompetent adviser with a different perspective – the foreign-policy
equivalent of Allen and Levine's fake Mr Magoo – would probably have improved Johnson's decision-making. But unanimity
was what Johnson wanted, and McNamara made sure that he
got it.

To add to the trouble, Johnson set up a clear, idealised chain
of command and insisted that nobody stepped outside it. Rather
than speaking directly to the Joint Chiefs of Staff (who, to
Johnson's discomfort, often disagreed with each other) he used
the JCS chairman, and McNamara, to filter out news. Johnson
probably didn't realise how much was being hidden from him.

H.R. McMaster's book gives a telling example: when the Joint Chiefs of Staff commissioned a war game called SIGMA I in 1964, it largely predicted what later happened: a dismal and inexorable escalation into full-blown war. McNamara dismissed SIGMA I because his number-crunching analysts were producing a different conclusion. Johnson never saw the results of SIGMA I. This incident was typical of the abysmal communication between Johnson and his military advisers.

It would be tempting to blame McNamara alone for that – were it not for the fact that the Chiefs of Staff had tried to speak to Johnson through alternative, unofficial routes and the President had made it quite clear he wanted the military to talk to him 'through the McNamara channel'. Johnson talked only to his political advisers, and his decisions gave him short-term political success and eventual military disaster. The idealised hierarchy backfired with a vengeance, the wrong decisions taken by a team all pulling in the wrong direction, and the chain of command serving as a perfect barrier to the upward flow of vital information. As H.R. McMaster concludes, between November 1963 and July 1964, Johnson 'made the critical decisions that took the United States into war almost without realizing it'.

Forty years later, Donald Rumsfeld's refusal to listen to dissenting advice was dooming the allied forces in Iraq. Yes, the strategy was bad, but what was truly unforgivable was that Rumsfeld was preventing it from getting better. H.R. McMaster's book had documented a systematic failure to learn at the top of the US military establishment. Nothing, it seems, had changed.

5 The Tal Afar experiment

The US turnaround in Iraq had, in fact, begun months before the Haditha massacre and Donald Rumsfeld's bizarre press conference – it was just that Donald Rumsfeld didn't know it.

The first glimmerings of success came in a place called Tal Afar, in the spring of 2005. Tal Afar is an ancient Iraqi city with a quarter of a million citizens, not far from the border of Syria. US forces had repeatedly driven insurgents out of Tal Afar, but each time the Americans withdrew, the insurgents returned. By the end of 2004, Tal Afar was a stronghold for Sunni extremists and a jewel in the crown of Musab al-Zarqawi, the Jordanian terrorist who ran 'Al Qaeda in Iraq'. Always a smugglers' town, Tal Afar had become the destination of choice for foreign insurgents arriving from Syria, where they could be equipped, trained, and despatched against Shias, the US forces, and collaborators.

At this time, much of the US Army in Iraq was stationed in Forward Operating Bases, FOBs. Some of the FOBs were enormous, four miles or more along each side, with scheduled bus services to get soldiers around the base. FOBs offered soldiers some of the comforts of home, including Baskin Robbins ice cream, cinemas, swimming pools, and even stores where they could buy consumer electronics. The neat concrete symmetry of a FOB would have delighted many a modernist architect, and it made a certain amount of sense tactically, because FOBs in the middle of the desert were almost impregnable against a ragtag bunch of terrorists. Soldiers could be supplied more easily (the support staff were given the not entirely affectionate title, 'Fobbits'), even if one captain was overheard commenting with black humour that their mission was 'to guard the ice-cream trucks going north so that someone else can guard them there'. In other words, US strategy in Iraq had collapsed into 'don't get the soldiers killed'. And frankly, if not getting killed was the only strategic objective, it could have been accomplished better by moving the troops to Colorado or Texas.

'Day-tripping like a tourist in hell' was how one counterinsurgency expert described the armoured sorties from the FOBs. Operating from such isolation, US forces were able to do little more than sweep through cities such as Tal Afar, hoping to kill some bad guys. Not many of these sweeps backfired as badly as the Haditha massacre, but few produced any valuable results. The trouble was that the insurgents could vanish simply by dropping their weapons and walking into any crowd. The people of Tal Afar may have known the difference, but the American soldiers did not, and the people of Tal Afar were not about to tell them.

One American counterinsurgency guru, John Nagl, who served in Iraq in 2003 and 2004, quickly discovered how little cooperation he could expect. On his first day in Iraq, Major Nagl sent one of his captains down to the police station to befriend the local police. Seeing the American coming, the police deserted the building, leaping out of the rear windows and scurrying in all directions as though somebody had discovered a bomb in the basement. Assuming the young captain must have blundered, Nagl went there himself the next day and earned the same reaction. Nagl eventually got his wish for a joint patrol: a policeman walked a couple of yards ahead with Nagl's rifle in his back. Despite all his expertise in counterinsurgency – Nagl has a doctorate from Oxford in the subject – it was only later that he figured out why the police wouldn't cooperate.

So why didn't locals help the American forces? The conventional wisdom was that the Americans were simply losing a popularity contest with the insurgents. Even experienced American commanders such as General Abizaid – who by then was responsible for all US forces in the Middle East – believed that the fundamental problem was that US forces were like an organ transplant that was being rejected. There could be no peace until the US forces withdrew, probably not even then.

It took a while for the penny to drop: although some Iraqis did hate the Americans, most weren't refusing to collaborate out of hatred. They were refusing to collaborate out of fear. Anyone who helped the American soldiers on one of their sweeps would be murdered when the soldiers withdrew. That was why Major Nagl could get 'help' only at gunpoint. It was why Iraqi teachers made excuses when American soldiers suggested that the Iraqi

elementary schools set up pen-pal relationships with American
elementary schools – it was too risky, no matter how enthusias-
tically the Iraqi children penned their friendly letters. And it was
why while the Americans restricted themselves to temporary
sweeps through Iraq's cities, they would help no one and be
helped by no one.

So Tal Afar remained an insurgent stronghold, and with
Sunnis running the streets while Shia policemen sallied forth in
murder squads at night, it was also a microcosm of Iraq's growing civil war.

Into this mess walked the 3rd Armored Cavalry Regiment,
3500 men led by an officer we'll call Colonel H. The Colonel is
affable company: his short muscular frame and leathery bald
pate might make him look thuggish, if that impression wasn't
continually undermined by a cheeky wit and an impish smile
that keeps bursting out during conversation.

Col. H. had quite a reputation. He was a war hero, having
captained American tanks in a celebrated battle during the Gulf
War in 1991. But Col. H. also had a record as a thinker, and a
courageous thinker at that. And as he prepared to turn the tide
in Tal Afar, Col. H. was thinking that the US strategy in Iraq
made no sense.

Victory in Tal Afar was going to require that Col. H.'s men
adapted quickly. Before they had even left American soil, Col. H.
had been training them, buying pocket histories of Iraq in bulk,
instructing his men to behave more respectfully towards Iraqis,
and role-playing difficult social interactions at a mocked-up
checkpoint in Fort Carson, Colorado. His soldiers would pre-
tend to deal with drunks, pregnant women, suspected suicide
bombers, and then watch videos of the encounters and discuss
how to learn from the mistakes they had made. 'Every time you
treat an Iraqi disrespectfully, you are working for the enemy,'
Col. H. told his men.

Arriving at Tal Afar, Col. H.'s regiment moved slowly into the
city, securing it block by block. His lieutenants organised

repeated, painstaking discussions with the local power-brokers. They tried to reconcile moderate Sunni nationalists with the Shia, to reform the Shiite police force and make it representative of the entire city. They brought in a new mayor, a Baghdadi who didn't even speak the local language, but at least he had no axe to grind. They established twenty-nine small outposts throughout the city; no ice-cream or swimming pools, and indeed no hot water or regular cooked meals. But Col. H.'s men refused to cede those little bases, no matter how ruthlessly they were attacked.

For the more extreme end of Tal Afar's warring factions, no act seemed too evil to contemplate. 'In one case,' recalls Col. H., 'terrorists murdered a young boy in his hospital bed, booby-trapped the body, and when the family came to pick up the body they detonated the explosives to kill the father.'

Police recruits were murdered when somebody with explosives strapped all over their body walked into their midst. It wasn't a suicide bomber, but a mentally disabled thirteen-year-old girl, accompanied by a toddler whose hand she had been asked to hold as she walked towards the line of recruits.

For a few weeks, Col. H.'s men took heavy casualties in tough conditions. But then, an apparent miracle: the people of Tal Afar began to cooperate with the Americans and – slowly, reluctantly – to talk with each other. The more moderate among the warring factions put down their weapons. The true terrorists fled, or were killed or captured when local townsfolk turned them in. Few people, after all, really wish to harbour men who use disabled girls as bombs and toddlers as camouflage. 'It happened with astonishing speed', said Col H., but the truth is that it happened the moment most people became convinced that the Americans weren't going to abandon them to the revenge of Al Qaeda in Iraq.

It would be hard to exaggerate quite how far Col. H. stuck his neck out when he pacified Tal Afar. His strategy was little short of a rebellion against his own commanding officers, General

Casey and General Abizaid. He apparently had little time for
Donald Rumsfeld's Orwellian epiphany, bluntly telling journalists that 'militarily, you've got to call it an insurgency, because
we have a counterinsurgency doctrine and theory that you want
to access.' He also short-circuited the chain of command, speaking freely to senior officers who were not his immediate
superiors. Those immediate superiors gave him little backing.
One of them warned him 'to stop thinking strategically' – that
is, to shut his big mouth and stop thinking above his rank.
When he asked for 800 men as reinforcements, he received no
response at all, and later figured out that his request had never
been passed up the chain of command. And later, according to
one account, when General Casey was pinning a medal on Col.
H.'s chest in recognition of his achievements at Tal Afar, he
warned him that he was making too many enemies among his
commanding officers – for his own sake, Col. H. needed to
listen more and argue less.

Think back to the idealised organisation, and you see that
Col. H. succeeded by violating every one of its principles. He
ignored strategic direction from his superiors if he felt it was
poor strategy. If the hierarchy suppressed his views, he commu-
nicated by turning to journalists. He didn't rely on 'big-picture'
information, focusing instead on the specifics of the situation on
the ground in Tal Afar and delegating authority to the junior
officers who commanded his urban outposts.

Col. H. improvised one of the few successful responses to the
Iraqi insurgency at great physical risk to himself and his men.
(When I first spoke to him, he was recuperating after a hip
replacement, the consequence of injuries sustained courtesy of a
bomb in Iraq.) What is more amazing is that he did so by
shrugging off the weight of every link in the chain of command
above him. He paid a price for his courageous independence.
Despite his early promise, a PhD in history, and his proven
achievements both in Desert Storm and at Tal Afar, Col. H. was
twice passed over for promotion to Brigadier-General – the

junior general's rank – first in 2006 and again in 2007. His superiors focused not on his performance, but on what they saw as a troublemaker's attitude. As early retirement beckoned for Col. H., a growing band of counterinsurgency geeks began to grumble that this was no way for the Army to treat its most brilliant colonel.

It is a rare soldier – indeed a rare character altogether – who takes such risks with his own career. But there was a simple explanation: Col. H. was H.R. McMaster, the author of *Dereliction of Duty*, the definitive account of how faulty leadership from the President, the secretary of defense and the senior Army generals had led to disaster in Vietnam. He literally wrote the book on how an organisation can fail from the top down. And if he had any say in the matter, he wasn't going to let the US Army defeat itself a second time.

6 'How to win the war in al Anbar by Cpt. Trav'

McMaster's achievements in Tal Afar were a rare bright spot in a dismal year for the Americans in Iraq. But they were not the only bright spot. Several other commanders either imitated McMaster's experiment or came to similar conclusions independently. The most important was Col. Sean MacFarland. MacFarland's men started in Tal Afar, where they saw what McMaster had achieved. Then they were moved to the city of Ramadi in al Anbar province, 60 miles west of Baghdad.

MacFarland immediately grasped that the official strategy – keep out of harm's way, train the Iraqi army, and then go home – was in desperate trouble. At a graduation ceremony for almost 1000 Iraqi soldiers, just before MacFarland had arrived, many ripped off their uniforms and deserted on the spot when they heard they were to be deployed outside al Anbar. MacFarland's own official Iraqi army support had also mutinied. Ramadi wasn't suffering from sectarian fighting as Tal

Afar had, because Ramadi was largely Sunni. But just as in Tal Afar, Al Qaeda in Iraq (AQI) had moved in and was all but running the city. Locals were terrified of being seen anywhere near the Americans.

MacFarland learned from McMaster's approach, despite a sceptical response from his superior officers, and he adapted it as necessary to deal with local circumstances. Through the summer of 2006, he pushed into Ramadi and gradually established eighteen small bases. AQI was immediately put on the defensive; rather than watching the front gates of a huge Forward Operating Base to learn when the next American patrol was to show up, AQI now had to cope with the fact that they were sharing Ramadi with their enemies. The response was violent, as AQI poured efforts into attacking the outposts, US convoys, and especially the sheikhs whom MacFarland was beginning to win round as allies. At the time the ferocity of the response was alarming; in retrospect, it was a sign of desperation. Emboldened by the solidity of the American presence on the ground, the local sheikhs turned against AQI, and within months, the terrorist organisation in Anbar province had collapsed.

No matter how determined Donald Rumsfeld was to learn nothing from the implosion of the US strategy, on the ground, US soldiers were adapting. Good advice was passed around like a girlie magazine among schoolboys. There was David Kilcullen's '28 Articles: Fundamentals of Company Level Insurgency', a spiky set of tips that Kilcullen said he wrote with the aid of a bottle of whisky and which was widely circulated by email. (Kilcullen, an Australian soldier and anthropologist hired by the Pentagon, evidently enjoyed his semi-detached status from the US Army and was even more of a maverick than McMaster. One of his notorious pronouncements: 'If I were a Muslim, I'd probably be a jihadist'; another: 'Just because you invade a country stupidly doesn't mean you have to leave it stupidly.')

It should be no surprise that soldiers on the front line were far quicker to seek out good advice, and far more eager to adapt, than their senior officers. 'We willingly implement lessons learnt at the bottom end, because changing and adapting low-level tactics saves lives,' one British general told me with an air of resignation. 'But we rarely adapt and implement lessons learned at the top end.'

Another famous piece of bottom-up advice was 'How to win the war in al Anbar by Cpt. Trav' – an eighteen-slide PowerPoint presentation which conveys more insight than the top brass picked up in the first three years of the occupation, using stick figures and explanations that would suit an eight-year-old. ('On the right is an insurgent. He is bad. On the left is an Iraqi Man, who is not an insurgent but who is scared of them . . . There's Joe and Mohammed! They don't know if these are good Iraqis or bad Iraqis. What to do?') 'Cpt. Trav' is a witty counterinsurgency mentor, but he also – like McMaster and Kilcullen – displays a streak of sedition. One slide shows one of the sheikhs, leaders of the local people 'for approximately 14,000 years', coping with the rules that cut them out of government – courtesy of the incompetently led US civilian authorities in Iraq, or as Cpt. Trav puts it, '25 year olds from Texas, and Paul Bremer'.

Cpt. Trav was Captain Travis Patriquin, one of Sean MacFarland's men, a young Arabic-speaking special forces officer who befriended the sheikhs of al Anbar. Like all good kids' stories, there's a happy ending to Cpt. Trav's tale: 'The Sheik brings more Sheiks, more sheiks bring more men. Joe realizes that if he'd done this three years ago, maybe his wife would be happier, and he'd have been home more . . . Joe grows a moustache, because he realizes that Iraqis like people with moustaches and have a hard time trusting people without one.'

Captain Patriquin, of course, sported his own moustache. But there was to be no happy ending for him. He was killed by a roadside bomb three weeks before Christmas 2006, leaving behind his wife and three young children. At his memorial service, the local sheikhs turned out in force.

7 'It's my job to run the division, and it's your job to critique me'

The conventional story of how the US military recovered from a near-impossible situation in Iraq is a simple one. The problem was that the US had a bad strategy and bad leaders: President Bush and Donald Rumsfeld. The solution came when President Bush – with a little nudge when the voters gave his party a kicking in the 2006 elections – replaced Rumsfeld with Robert Gates, and Robert Gates appointed General David Petraeus to replace General Casey. Good leaders replace bad leaders; good strategy replaces bad strategy; problem solved.

This is not only the story we tell ourselves about Iraq, but the story we tell ourselves about how change happens: that the solution to any problem is a new leader with a new strategy, whether it's the new coach of a football team, the new chief executive of a failing business, or a new president. The truth, both in Iraq and more widely, is more subtle and far more interesting.

General Petraeus didn't invent the successful strategy while out for one of his eight-mile runs, and then hand out the orders as though promulgating the Ten Commandments. He did something far rarer and more difficult: he looked further down the ranks, and outside the armed forces entirely, searching for people who had already solved parts of the problem that the US forces were facing.

It's not that David Petraeus was an empty vessel for the ideas of others. He commanded American forces in Mosul, the largest city in northern Iraq, in 2003. Like McMaster, he ignored much of what he was being ordered to do by his superiors – in particular, when the order came to sack anyone associated with Saddam Hussein's Baath party, he dodged it, leaving the newly elected governor of Mosul, a Baathist, in his post. Petraeus then figured out a legal fudge that gave him the authority to open the border with Syria – ignoring the State Department's attempts to freeze out the Syrians. (The joke was that under Petraeus, 101st Airborne was the only division in the US military with its own foreign policy.) Then he shrugged off the objections of the US civilian authorities in Baghdad by raising prices for locally grown wheat. Petraeus figured that a free market approach might sound attractive, but his own price floor would create supporters because farmers would be better off than they had been under Saddam Hussein.

General Petraeus was the only divisional commander to run a successful campaign in the first year of the war. He was rewarded for his success – and his borderline insubordination – by being passed over for the combat appointment he craved, and instead handed first the job of training the Iraqi police, and then a back-water job: training and education at Fort Leavenworth, 7000 miles from Iraq. It was like Peter Palchinsky being assigned to a consultant's role in Siberia, and the pedigree was unpromising. Petraeus's predecessor at Leavenworth had been sent there, apparently as a punishment, after guilelessly remarking to a reporter that the US had been caught by surprise during the invasion of Iraq.

But Petraeus realised that from Fort Leavenworth, he had the opportunity to influence American strategy in the most pro-found way possible: from the bottom up. He set himself the task of rewriting Army doctrine on counterinsurgency. Such doctrine rewrites were usually non-events, merely writing down whatever tactics the Army had adopted. On rare occasions, though, they transformed the Army, with soldiers in the field reading the new doctrine and changing the way they thought and acted.

Petraeus was determined that this would be one of those doc-trine rewrites that mattered. And he realised what Donald Rumsfeld, Robert McNamara and President Johnson did not: that the right decisions are more likely when they emerge from a clash of very different perspectives. Petraeus had already been a high-ranking evangelist for David Kilcullen's '28 Articles'. Now he asked the loud-mouthed Kilcullen to join him at a conference in Fort Leavenworth to help develop the Army's counterinsurgency doctrine. He also invited a British officer, Brigadier Nigel Aylwin-Foster, who had excoriated the American Army, accusing it of a cultural insensitivity bordering on institutional racism. (The *Guardian* commented that 'What is startling is the severity of his comments – and the decision by *Military Review*, a US army magazine, to publish them.' But *Military Review* was the Fort Leavenworth magazine – under the control of General Petraeus.) There was John Nagl, who'd learned the counterinsurgency trade in Oxford and then Baghdad, and Kalev Sepp, another counterinsurgency expert who was an outspoken critic of the US strategy. Petraeus didn't just seek out internal dissidents, but also officials from the State Department and the CIA, journalists, academics, and even human rights advocates. After opening the conference, Petraeus made a point of sitting next to Sarah Sewall, the director of a human rights centre at Harvard. One of the journalists at the conference commented that he had never seen such an open transfer of ideas in any institution.

H.R. McMaster – Colonel H. – was still in Tal Afar as the doctrine began to be drafted, but Petraeus's team sought his advice via email. 'H.R. was conducting counterinsurgency in Tal Afar and we used Tal Afar as a case study in real time,' says John Nagl. 'So we're writing the Tal Afar case study and emailing it to him and he's "Wikipedia-ing" it. Correcting it as we go along. And he's also saying, "Car bomb, gotta go."' While Rumsfeld had closed his eyes to what was going on in the front line, Petraeus managed to get a ringside seat from 7000 miles away.

This openness to new ideas might have seemed surprising. General Petraeus had a reputation for arrogance, as well as having much to be arrogant about. Petraeus famously described his experience in Mosul as 'a combination of being the president and the pope', and one colleague told the journalist Thomas Ricks that 'David Petraeus is the best general in the U.S. Army, bar none. He also isn't half as good as he thinks he is.'

But Petraeus received an education in the importance of feed-back back in 1981, when as a lowly captain he was offered a job as an aide to Major General Jack Galvin. Galvin told Petraeus that the most important part of the job was to criticise his boss: 'It's my job to run the division, and it's your job to critique me.' Petraeus protested but Galvin insisted, so each month the young captain would leave a report card in his boss's in-tray. It was a vital lesson for an officer unwilling to admit mistakes. Galvin himself had learned the hard way about the importance of feed-back: a Vietnam vet, he had been relieved from his first assignment after his commander had instructed him to inflate an enemy body count, and Galvin had refused. Later, Galvin was asked to be one of the writers of a confidential – and, it turned out, explosive – history of the US involvement in Vietnam. It was leaked to the *New York Times* and became known as the *Pentagon Papers*. Galvin was a man who understood that organ-isations which ignore internal criticism soon make dreadful errors, and he made sure that Petraeus learned that lesson.

Jack Galvin also taught Petraeus that it is not enough to tol-erate dissent: sometimes you have to demand it. Galvin ordered Petraeus to speak frankly to him despite Petraeus's reluctance to criticise a superior officer. This was absolutely the right example, because there are many instances where leaders have failed to get a frank discussion going, despite being far more open to dis-agreement than Donald Rumsfeld or Lyndon Johnson.

The classic example is the Bay of Pigs disaster, which required an extraordinary level of self-delusion on the part of President Kennedy. Irving Janis's classic analysis of the Bay of Pigs and other foreign policy fiascos, *Victims of GroupThink*, explains that a strong team – a 'kind of family' – can quickly fall into the habit of reinforcing each other's prejudices out of simple team spirit and a desire to bolster the group. Janis details the way in which John F. Kennedy fooled himself into thinking that he was gath-ering a range of views and critical comments. All the while his team of advisers were unconsciously giving each other a false sense of infallibility. Later, during the Cuban Missile Crisis, Kennedy was far more aggressive about demanding alternative options, exhaustively exploring risks, and breaking up his advisory groups to ensure that they didn't become too comfortable. It was a lesson that David Petraeus – another historian – had grasped.

Once Petraeus had a robust, usable doctrine, properly tested by a range of contrasting views, he launched his own guerrilla campaign to get the US Army to pay attention to it. The media-savvy Petraeus had already scored a coup when he appeared on the cover of *Newsweek* under the caption 'Can this man save Iraq?' *Newsweek* reckoned that Petraeus was 'the closest thing to an exit strategy the United States now has'. Rumsfeld had been incandescent: passing through Dublin Airport, an aide had run ahead of him rearranging the airport magazine racks so that Rumsfeld wouldn't have to face a reminder of his own insurgent general.

The diversity of opinions that had helped produce the manual became Petraeus's main weapon in disseminating the ideas. The heavy-hitting journalists who'd been invited along were impressed by the doctrine – and perhaps just a little flattered at their involvement – and were happy to write about it. The human rights expert Sarah Sewall wrote a foreword to the counterinsurgency manual *FM 3-24*. John Nagl appeared on chat shows such as *Charlie Rose* and even Jon Stewart's *Daily Show*. The manual was reviewed in the *New York Times Book Review* and made front-page news in most of the quality newspapers. It was posted on the internet and downloaded more than 1.5 million times in the first month, having already been open to comments from the 'six hundred thousand editors' of the Army and Marine corps. As the new book was circulated at the front line, it mattered less and less what Donald Rumsfeld thought about whether there was, or was not, an insurgency.

While all this was happening, Petraeus was also one of several high-ranking officers trying to change the strategy from the top down. Several generals, some active and some retired, bypassed the traditional chain of command in Washington to lobby for a new approach to the war. H.R. McMaster was in Washington, too – Petraeus had recommended that he be appointed to a panel of colonels reviewing the US strategy in Iraq.

In Vietnam, Lyndon Johnson's insistence that all information flow through approved channels doomed America to disaster. In Iraq, the Army discovered that if the official hierarchy was on a disastrous course, it was vital to bypass it in order to adapt. Petraeus himself was using the media as a way of talking to everyone from the greenest private to the commander in chief. Others used their influence to whisper in the ear of the President himself. It wasn't that the hierarchy was always useless, simply that it got in the way of change when change was needed. By the time President Bush and the new defense secretary, Robert Gates, decided to put General Petraeus in command in Iraq, an internal revolution at every level of the US Army had already profoundly changed its direction.

For an organisation that needs to quickly correct its own mistakes, the org. chart can be the worst possible road map.

8 Drawing the wrong lessons from history

There was a dramatic improvement both in US military strategy and in the situation for ordinary Iraqis between 2006 – the nadir of the occupation – and 2008 or 2009, and we've seen that a surprising amount of trial and error was involved. It wasn't simply a matter of replacing one general with another, or even one defense secretary with another, but of learning from hard experience on the ground, and comparing the successful approaches pioneered by David Petraeus in Mosul, H.R. McMaster in Tal Afar, and Sean MacFarland in Ramadi, with awful failures elsewhere. The US Army stumbled its way to a successful strategy.

But was such a painful process of experimentation really necessary? Certainly, the learning process could have been quicker – if H.R. McMaster had been promoted, David Petraeus not banished to Fort Leavenworth, and Donald Rumsfeld more willing to listen to the warnings he was receiving. But could the US military have skipped the 'mistakes were made' part of the war entirely and figured out a better strategy from the start?

That was the view of John Nagl, the historian of counterinsurgency who fought in Baghdad and was on the team Petraeus assembled to write the counterinsurgency doctrine, when I suggested that the US military had solved its problem in Iraq through trial and error.

'We weren't just trying stuff at random,' he objected, and pointed to the need to learn lessons from history, as any good historian would. H.R. McMaster and David Petraeus both had history doctorates, too. But while nobody would suggest that pure random experimentation is a good idea, history is also an imperfect guide. A few minutes later, Nagl all but admitted as much when he reflected on the actions of General Abizaid.

'Abizaid drew the wrong lessons from Lebanon in 1983,' Nagl explained. 'Abizaid was convinced that Western forces were a foreign presence that inspired the creation of antibodies in Arab societies. And therefore his conclusion from that was that we need to hand over responsibility for Iraq as soon as we possibly can.' The result of that lesson was the 'draw down' strategy which left the Iraqi army and police underprepared as US troops withdrew to the FOBs, their concrete cocoons in the desert. It was a serious mistake.

But this example simply highlights the fact that it is impossible to know in advance what the correct strategy will be. Remember that General Abizaid, who a few months after the start of the war had been given command of all US forces in the Middle East and central Asia, was an expert on the region. He had lived in Jordan and performed a brilliant peacekeeping role in the aftermath of the first Gulf War. He was a sensitive and intelligent man who had correctly warned that de-Baathification would lead to disaster. If you were looking for one man with the experience and track record to set the right course in Iraq, you'd have had trouble looking further than John Abizaid. If he, of all men, drew the wrong lesson from history, drawing the right lesson cannot be a simple process. That is what Philip Tetlock's study of expert judgement revealed. And that is why trial and error will always be a part of how any organisation solves a complex, ever-shifting problem.

Another example of history's uncertain guidance came from the first Gulf War in 1990–1. Desert Storm was an overwhelming defeat for Saddam Hussein's army: one day it was one of the largest armies in the world; four days later, it wasn't even the largest army in Iraq. Most American military strategists saw this as a vindication of their main strategic pillars: a technology-driven war with lots of air support and above all, overwhelming force. In reality it was a sign that change was coming: the victory was so crushing that no foe would ever use open battlefield tactics against the US Army again. Was this really so obvious in advance?

Even had the basic US strategy been correct after the invasion, local adaptation would have been necessary. The nature of the problem kept changing as the insurgents changed their methods. Tactics that had worked yesterday were a liability today. Nagl, again, discovered this when putting to the test his Oxford doctorate in the history of counterinsurgency. Iraq was full of surprises. If he tried to respond to a tip-off about someone planting roadside bombs, it wasn't so easy simply to go and arrest the suspect. Iraq has no addresses: no street names, signs or house numbers. The informant couldn't be seen with soldiers, and if Nagl were to disguise himself and drive past in an unmarked car, Nagl would lose his rights under the Geneva Convention. These local difficulties weren't easy to anticipate in the Pentagon, even if the secretary of defense had tried to do so. Some degree of local adaptation was always going to be needed.

The lesson of the Iraq war was that the US Army should have had much better systems for adapting a failing strategy, and should have paid far more attention to successful local experiments. But perhaps there is a broader lesson, too. Donald Rumsfeld was by no means alone in believing he knew better than the soldiers on the ground. His mistakes have been made by many leaders before – in the military, politics and business.

9 'It was hard enough teaching computers to play chess'

As a seventeen-year-old boy, I was surely the perfect audience for 'Stormin'' Norman Schwarzkopf's no-nonsense briefings during the Gulf War. I remember distinctly the foggy grey aerial images of Iraqi buildings, perspective shifting as the camera moved with the stealth fighter that carried it. Cross-hairs fixed on a bridge or a bunker, giving the viewer a couple of seconds' warning before the target was obliterated by a laser-guided bomb. As the camera struggled to adjust, there was a screen-wiping blaze of white, then black. I stood in front of the common-room television at school with my classmates, and we were unanimous: precision bombing was cool.

Almost twenty years later, I sat in the late spring sunshine in the courtyard of London's Royal Academy, listening to Andrew Mackay, a British general who had served in Iraq, and been one of the UK's most successful commanders in Afghanistan, explain what the images had been supposed to advertise. Allied forces would have superb, real-time information about potential targets – ideally, 'information dominance', in which the allies had also destroyed the enemy's computers, telephone lines and radar. Not only that, but the information would be fed into supercomputers, capable of centralising and processing all the data, which could be distilled into usable form so that a three- or four-star general could perceive the entire theatre of war and adjust tactics and strategy on the fly. The computer could even calculate the likely impact of different strategies, including second-order and third-order knock-on effects. Using 'effects-based operations' or EBO, the general could choose a precise tactical strike, knowing that it would disrupt enemy logistics, manoeuvring, perhaps even morale, in a predictable way. It was the third pillar of the ideal organisation, the 'big picture', Robert McNamara's analytical fantasy from Vietnam made reality: a vision of war in which information was so rich and ubiquitous that it could deliver an optimal strategy to a single, all-powerful decision maker.

General Mackay cuts a tall, commanding figure, but this is offset by white hair and eyebrows, soft features, and a magpie fascination with different ideas. He put down his coffee and pointed over my shoulder. 'So, using effects-based operations, a computer might calculate that destroying that pot plant behind you would achieve precisely the desired strategic outcome. We would launch a missile from fifty miles away, accurate to within a couple of feet, and destroy the pot plant.' Wow. Suddenly I was recalling those Stormin' Norman briefings, but with an extra eighteen years of technological sophistication.

Mackay picked up his coffee. 'The only trouble is, it was hard enough teaching computers to play chess. And chess only has sixty-four squares and thirty-two pieces.'

With a healthy dose of scepticism, Andrew Mackay was describing the planner's dream: a huge leather swivel-chair, a wall full of screens, infinity in the palm of your hand. It is a vision so seductive that it refuses to die.

Earlier versions of the planner's dream, of course, pre-date supercomputers. Originally the idea was that with a careful enough plan and a room full of bean-counters, a decentralised system could be centralised and rationalised. For example, Leonid Kantorovich, the only Soviet economist ever to win the Nobel Memorial Prize in economics, was asked to apply his mathematical skills to the problem of production scheduling in the Soviet steel industry in the 1960s. His efforts did lead to a more efficient production process, but gathering the data necessary for the calculations took six years – by which time, of course, the needs of the Soviet economy were different.

At much the same time, Robert McNamara had the same faith in the ability of centralised quantitative analysis to solve a complex problem. His problem was not steel production but the bombing of Vietnam. US bombers dropped three times as much explosive on Vietnam as was used in the entire Second World War. The high explosives weighed more in total than the citizens of Vietnam did. Some districts suffered more than 1200 bomb strikes per square mile. And every bombing raid was meticulously recorded and analysed at Robert McNamara's request. McNamara's centralised analytical approach did not bring victory.

It is tempting to conclude that both Kantorovich and McNamara could have prospered if only they had had better computers. That seems to have been the belief of their respective successors, Salvador Allende and Donald Rumsfeld.

Allende was elected President of Chile in 1970 on a Marxist platform, and went on to sponsor one of the most surreal examples of the planner's dream, Project CyberSyn. CyberSyn used a 'supercomputer' called the Burroughs 3500, and a network of telex machines, in an attempt to coordinate decision-making in an increasingly nationalised economy.

Allende recruited the cybernetic theorist Stafford Beer, a larger-than-life character with socialist sympathies and huge enthusiasm for the project, but who still demanded $500 a day and a steady flow of wine, cigars and chocolate. Workers – or more usually, managers – would telex reports of production, shortages and other information at 5 o'clock each morning. Operators would feed the information into the Burroughs 3500, and by 5 p.m. a report could be presented to Allende for his executive input. As with the effects-based operations it predated, CyberSyn would allow for feedback and second-order effects. Some CyberSyn defenders argue that the system was designed to devolve decision-making to the appropriately local level, but that does not seem to be what Allende had in mind when he said that, 'We are and always shall be in favour of a centralised economy, and companies will have to conform to the Government's planning.'

The project was not a success. Chile's economy collapsed, thanks to a combination of the chaos brought on by an ambitious programme of nationalisation, industrial unrest, and overt and covert economic hostility from the United States. Allende died during a coup led by General Pinochet, who then tortured and murdered many of his political opponents. Stafford Beer had the good fortune to be in London on the day of the coup. Shortly afterwards, tormented by survivor's guilt, he left his family and moved to a cottage in rural Wales.

The Burroughs 3500 was an impressive machine by the standards of the day, but that is not saying much. My father worked for Burroughs in those days – he tells me tales of hard drives the size of washing machines, with eight platters on a spindle storing a total of a few megabytes, less than a simple cell phone has today. Testing a computer was a great way to work out, hauling massive drive spindles and tape spools from one location to another. One of the attractions of the Burroughs 3500 was that memory could be expanded in discrete, reasonably priced chunks – 10,000 bytes at a time, just enough to store a few pages of this chapter. The Burroughs 3500 was never really regarded as a supercomputer, but it was an effective piece of corporate kit that, with the help of piecemeal upgrades, lasted for decades in the back rooms of banks. The 3500s ended their days as controllers for cheque-sorting machines.

CyberSyn is interesting not because it proves that computerised centralisation is a disaster – it does not, since Chile's economy was under so much internal and external stress that it would surely have collapsed anyway – but because it shows the way in which our critical faculties switch off when faced with the latest technology. Western newspapers were giddily reporting that Chile's economy was run by a computer that, by today's standards, was a toy. But CyberSyn seemed sophisticated at the time, which was enough. Its iconic operations room looked tailor-made for Captain Kirk and Mr Spock, with chairs whose arm rests contained screens and control panels. This control room came to represent CyberSyn to the project's supporters and to its opponents. Yet the control room itself never became operational.

Donald Rumsfeld had better computers at his disposal than Salvador Allende, but the dream was much the same: information delivered in detail, real-time, to a command centre from which computer-aided decisions could be sent back to the front line. Rumsfeld pored over real-time data from the theatre of war and sent memos about minor operational questions to generals such as Abizaid and Casey. But even had Rumsfeld been less of a control freak, the technology was designed to empower a centralised decision maker, be it the secretary of defense or a four-star general. In the Iraq war, the control centre, an air-conditioned tent inside a metal shell in Qatar, provided minute-by-minute updates on the movement of troops and aircraft.

These systems are not useless. Allende's CyberSyn worked well enough to allow him to coordinate a response when Chile was racked by strikes and industrial sabotage. The opening phases both of the Gulf war and of the Iraq war were astonishing examples of the power of a coordinated, computer-aided attack plan. But such systems always deliver less than they promise, because they remain incapable of capturing the tacit knowledge that really matters.

CyberSyn was designed to bring problems to the attention of the President and his economic planners, but it succeeded only in reporting the issues that local factory managers wanted to report. Problems that they wanted to conceal, they had no difficulty in concealing. And when times were good it was hard to persuade them to telex any useful information at all, a state of affairs anticipated by Friedrich Hayek in an article published in 1945. What Hayek realised, and Allende and Beer did not seem to, was that a complex world is full of knowledge that is localised and fleeting. Crucially, the local information is often something that local agents would prefer to use for their own purposes. Hayek's essay pre-dated modern computers, but his argument will retain its force until the day that computers can read our minds.

Rumsfeld's computerised revolution in military affairs, like CyberSyn, often provided the illusion of information without really penetrating the fog of war. In February 2002 in Afghanistan, coalition commanders spent two weeks planning Operation Anaconda, focusing satellites and unmanned surveillance aircraft on a section of the Shah-i-Kot valley before attacking with helicopter-borne infantry. The helicopters dropped the soldiers almost directly on top of Taliban forces who had remained completely undetected. Apache helicopters were shot down by unknown assailants, precision bombers were unable to locate Taliban targets, and the entire operation was nearly a catastrophe for the coalition. Similar problems plagued coalition forces in the early stages of the war in Iraq. They often bumped into enemy forces of which they had received no warning from the 'information-dominant' command centre.

An early example of the limitations of 'dominant battlespace knowledge' came, not in the narrow streets of Tal Afar or the wooded hills of Kosovo, but in the best possible theatre for computer-aided warfare, the open deserts of Iraq during the first Gulf war. A group of nine US tanks, Eagle Troop, was speeding across the desert in a sandstorm when it stumbled upon a much larger force of Iraqi armour.

'We had been moving through what was a relatively flat and featureless desert, and what I didn't realise is that my tank was moving up a very slight rise in the terrain,' recalls Eagle Troop's captain. 'After we crested that rise and came down on the other side, the whole enemy position really came into view.' Because of the storm, the Americans had no air support, and they suddenly discovered that they were heavily outnumbered by the tanks and armoured cars of Saddam Hussein's elite Republican guard, dug into defensive emplacements.

Both sides were caught by surprise. Eagle Troop's captain had to make a snap decision: there was no time to discuss the situation with his superiors, or plug it into the 'information-dominant' computers. He realised at once that it would be more dangerous to try to retreat than to attack quickly and attempt to catch the Iraqis off balance. He yelled the order for his gunner to start firing anti-tank rounds – 'Fire, fire sabot!' – and an Iraqi tank was instantly destroyed. Reloading and firing every three seconds, his tank destroyed two more enemy tanks in the few seconds before the rest of Eagle Troop crested the ridge and opened fire. Nine American tanks destroyed almost ninety Iraqi vehicles without suffering any casualties themselves, thanks to their captain's quick thinking, their training, and their superior weapons. No thanks at all were due to 'information dominance' or 'effects-based operations'.

The spectacular engagement, swift and skilful, is now studied in war colleges as The Battle of 73 Easting. It earned Eagle Troop's captain a write-up in a Tom Clancy book, and he is the subject of the opening pages – indeed the very first sentence – of the Army's official history of the Gulf War. The author of this book, titled *Certain Victory*, gushes that Eagle Troop 'dramatically illustrates the transformation of the American Army from disillusionment and anguish in Vietnam to confidence and certain victory in Desert Storm'.

Maybe so. It also dramatically illustrates the limits, even with the very best technology, of what a general's command centre can know about the shape of the battlefield. American planes dominated the theatre of war with their precision bombs, but in the middle of that sandstorm, Eagle Troop was all on its own.

The name of Eagle Troop's captain was H.R. McMaster.

10 'Knowledge of the particular circumstances of time and place'

It is still tempting to think that the US Army would have had no problems if only men like H.R. McMaster, Sean MacFarland, and David Petraeus had been in charge from the beginning. That conclusion misses the real lesson that McMaster was trying to teach the US Army. Long before Tal Afar, he had been arguing that the celebrated technology behind Effects-Based Operations was simply not as effective as military doctrine of the day assumed. Not only was the picture always incomplete, as the Battle of 73 Easting and Operation Anaconda demonstrated, but sometimes it was completely irrelevant. If you are talking to a man at a checkpoint in Tal Afar, no amount of data from a satellite or a surveillance drone will tell you whether he is friendly or hostile. As the British General Andrew Mackay puts it: 'Insurgents do not show up on radar screens.'

If you are fighting a counterinsurgency campaign, the important decisions will be made by men on the ground, and the challenge is to make sure that the decisions look more like those made at Tal Afar and less like those at Haditha. Even if David Petraeus had been the chairman of the Joint Chiefs of Staff, and H.R. McMaster the head of US operations in the Middle East, someone would have had to develop the strategy in Tal Afar, paying close attention to the local situation. Eagle Troop's captain would still have had to make an instant decision, no matter who he was. Petraeus and McMaster could have created a more accommodating space for local adaptation, but they could not have made local adaptation unnecessary.

Any large organisation faces a basic dilemma between centralisation and decentralisation. Hayek, back in 1945, argued that the dilemma should be resolved by thinking about information. Decisions taken at the centre can be more coordinated, limit wasteful duplication, and may be able to lower average costs because they can spread fixed resources (anything from a marketing department to an aircraft carrier) across a bigger base. But decisions taken at the fringes of an organisation are quick and the local information will probably be much better, even if the big picture is not clear. Hayek believed that most people overestimated the value of centralised knowledge, and tended to overlook 'knowledge of the particular circumstances of time and place'. For H.R. McMaster, knowledge of the particular circumstances of time and place was precisely what was necessary to win many wars, and above all to conduct a successful counterinsurgency campaign.

Hayek's argument was for decades largely ignored in mainstream economics, even after he won the Nobel Memorial Prize in 1974. But more recently, economists have been gathering the detailed data necessary to evaluate how successful organisations actually organise themselves. Julie Wulf and the former chief economist of the International Monetary Fund, Raghuram Rajan, examined large US firms from the mid-1980s throughout the 1990s. They found that these companies were flattening their bureaucracies, with junior executives facing fewer levels of hierarchy than fifteen years previously, and many more managers reporting directly to the top. Rajan and Wulf also gathered evidence on salaries and performance pay which suggests that the changes reflect a real delegation of decision-making power.

One reason for these changes is that businesses are operating in a different environment. Thanks to globalisation, businesses have ventured into new and varied markets, where they face intense competition. The traditional purpose of centralisation is to make sure every business unit is coordinated and nobody is duplicating anyone else's effort. That might work for a business like Tesco or Wal-Mart, businesses with such control over their supply chains and shop floors that experiments with new products or marketing ideas can be delegated to a computer. But a centralised organisation doesn't work so well when confronted with a diverse, fast-moving range of markets. The advantage of decentralisation, rapid adaptation to local circumstances, has grown.

Meanwhile, information technology has improved at a famously staggering pace. Kantorovich, Allende, McNamara and Rumsfeld all seemed to operate on the assumption that better computers and better communication links would help the process of centralisation, gathering everything into one place where a planner could make the key decisions. The exact opposite is true: the evidence suggests that more technologically advanced firms are also more decentralised. Typically, new equipment (anything from software to a large machine tool) is superior not because it does the same things faster, but because it is more flexible. To get the most out of that flexibility requires well-trained, adaptable workers with authority to make their own decisions, which is precisely the kind of workforce successful firms seek out or train when they upgrade their machinery or their software. In the organisation of the future, the decisions that matter won't be taken in some high-tech war-room, but on the front line.

This is a lesson the Army is beginning to learn. When John Nagl served in Baghdad in 2003, he found that while his young, inexperienced soldiers had the authority to kill, he – a major with a doctorate and a decade of experience – didn't have the authority to print his own propaganda pamphlets to counteract the clever PR campaign that the local insurgents were running. The commander of US forces in Baghdad in 2004 found that he couldn't tap into the massive USAID budget to provide electricity, clean water, jobs and other assistance to the locals. The budget had been assigned in Washington DC to the Bechtel Corporation, which had been commissioned to carry out a few very large, long-term projects instead. The commander could see immediate needs but had no authority to act.

Over time, the Army learned to decentralise these essential decisions to the same extent that they had decentralised the authority to shoot people. In al Anbar, Sean MacFarland's men broadcast news from loudspeakers six evenings a week, mixing information from locally trusted sources such as the Al Jazeera network, sports news, helpful advice – for instance, about food aid arriving at the UN warehouse – and just a sprinkling of propaganda attacking Al Qaeda in Iraq.

The Bechtel problem was partly allayed when decentralised aid in the form of the Commander's Emergency Response Program was introduced. CERP provided cash to local officers, who had the authority to spend it on whatever local reconstruction seemed needed. A careful statistical analysis later found that CERP spending was effective at reducing violence. Spending $200,000 in a district containing 100,000 citizens could be expected to prevent about three violent acts – and since the definition of 'violent act' was something an exhausted and battle-hardened field commander felt was worth taking twenty minutes to log in the official records, the bar for inclusion was high.

But perhaps the most significant sign that the Army was learning to give authority to more junior officers came from the career of H.R. McMaster himself. It was a career that, by 2007, looked to be over. Returning from Tal Afar, he was passed over for promotion in 2006. In 2007 he was passed over for promotion again. After his successes in the field and outspoken comments to journalists, H.R. McMaster was the most famous colonel in the US Army. When he was snubbed, people noticed.

'Every officer I spoke with knew about it and had pondered its implications,' wrote the journalist Fred Kaplan in the *New York Times*. One officer told Kaplan that promotion 'communicates what qualities are valued and not valued'; another that 'When you turn down a guy like McMaster that sends a potent message to everybody down the chain.' In this case the message was clear: if you want to get promoted, respecting your superiors is more important than setting the example that saves the US Army from defeat.

In 2008, it was rumoured that McMaster was about to be passed over yet again, quite possibly pushing him into premature retirement. David Petraeus took the unprecedented step of flying back to the Pentagon, at the height of the surge, to chair the Army's promotion board. Among those he promoted to the rank of one-star general were Sean MacFarland and H.R. McMaster. Petraeus overruled the complaints of the men who had commanded McMaster in Iraq. Once again, the one-time micromanager Petraeus had demonstrated that what really counted was identifying the more junior officers who were capable of thinking for themselves.

11 Mission command and 'the enduring uncertainty of war'

H.R. McMaster's study of the Vietnam war revealed disastrous flaws in the way decisions were taken at the highest levels of the military and political establishment. Lyndon Johnson and Robert McNamara enforced a strictly defined hierarchy, insisted on unanimity, and put too much faith in the idea that information was best centralised and analysed using the latest quantitative techniques.

In Iraq, the US military achieved more success than most observers thought was possible, given how bad the situation had become by 2006. They had good leaders in Robert Gates and General David Petraeus, and a good strategy, but the real story of success was the way more junior officers, including H.R. McMaster himself, improvised new ways to win the war on the front line. The key to learning from mistakes was not to stick blindly to the official chain of command but to subvert it where necessary, not to seek unanimity but to listen to dissenters, and above all, not to rely on a top-down strategy but to decentralise and trust that junior officers would adapt, learning from each other and figuring out the best response to fast-changing local conditions.

In 2001, Army doctrine declared that 'unmanned systems

with artificial intelligence will augment human action and decision making ... improved command and control systems will
enable leaders to know more than ever before about the nature
of activities in their battlespace'. That didn't impress H.R.
McMaster, a man whose formative combat experience involved
stumbling upon a large enemy force in a sandstorm, and whose
lasting achievement was to supervise a highly political, house-
by-house and family-by-family campaign of counterinsurgency
in Tal Afar.

'We tended to believe, you know, that situational understanding could be delivered on a computer screen,' says McMaster,
who in an echo of Petraeus's career, spent his first assignment as
a general redeveloping Army doctrine as the Army's head of
'experimentation'. His new approach emphasises cultural
understanding, local knowledge, urban environments, and
the 'enduring uncertainty of war'. McMaster is an evangelist
for the old Army concept of mission command: senior officers
set the aims, but junior officers decide how those aims are to be
achieved, adapting flexibility to local information. Under mission
command, air support and heavy artillery isn't allocated by a
three-star general sitting in a push-button swivel-chair, but is
called in by a colonel or a major who actually understands the
local situation and can be trusted to make the right decisions. It
is an idea whose time has come again – and not just for the Army.

The painful process by which the US military learned from its
mistakes in Iraq offers lessons for any organisation with a failing
strategy in a fast-moving world. Experimentation mattered. But
there is a limit to how much experimentation – how much variation, to use the Darwinian term – is possible for a single
organisation, or desirable on the battlefield.

Sometimes, far more experimentation and far more variation
are required – more than any one organisation, no matter how
flexible, can provide. In such cases a far more radical approach to
promoting new ideas is called for. It is to this problem of creating wild variation that we now turn.

Three

Creating new ideas that matter or: Variation

'Nothing we design or make ever really works ... Everything we design and make is an improvisation, a lash-up, something inept and provisional.'

– David Pye

'The end of surprise would be the end of science. To this extent, the scientist must constantly seek and hope for surprises.'

– Robert Friedel

1 'A most interesting experiment'

In 1931, the British Air Ministry sent out a demanding new specification for a fighter aircraft. It was a remarkable document for two reasons. The first was that throughout its existence the Royal Air Force had been dismissive of fighters. The conventional wisdom was that bombers could not be stopped. Instead, foreshadowing the nuclear doctrine of mutually assured destruction, the correct use of air power was widely presumed to be to build the largest possible fleet of bombers and strike any enemy with overwhelming force. The second reason was that the specification's demands seemed almost impossible to meet.

Rather than rely on known technology, the bureaucrats wanted aviation engineers to abandon their orthodoxies and produce something completely new.

The immediate response was disappointing: three designs were selected for prototyping, and none of them proved to be much use. The Air Ministry briefly went so far as to consider ordering aircraft from Poland.

Even more remarkable than the initial specification was the response of the ministry to this awkward failure. One of the competing firms, Supermarine, had delivered its prototype late and well below specification. But when Supermarine approached the ministry with a radical new design, an enterprising civil servant by the name of Air Commodore Henry Cave-Brown-Cave decided to bypass the regular commissioning process and order the new plane as 'a most interesting experiment'. The plane was the Supermarine Spitfire.

It's not hard to make the case that the Spitfire was one of the most significant new technologies in history. A brilliant, manoeuvrable and super-fast fighter, the Spitfire – and its pin-up pilots, brave to the point of insouciance – became the symbol of British resistance to the bombers of the Nazi air force, the Luftwaffe. The plane, with its distinctive elliptical wings, was a miraculous piece of engineering.

'She really was a perfect flying machine,' said one pilot. A Californian who travelled to Britain to sign up for the Royal Air Force agreed: 'I often marvelled at how this plane could be so easy and civilized to fly and yet how it could be such an effective fighter.'

'I have no words capable of describing the Spitfire,' testified a third pilot. 'It was an aircraft quite out of this world.'

It wasn't just the Spitfire pilots who rated the plane. The top German ace, Adolf Galland, was asked by Hermann Göring, head of the Luftwaffe, what he required in order to break down the stubborn British resistance. 'I should like an outfit of Spitfires,' was the terse reply. Another German ace complained,

'The bastards can make such infernally tight turns. There seems to be no way of nailing them.'

Thanks to the Spitfire, Britain's tiny Royal Air Force defied overwhelming odds to fight off the Luftwaffe's onslaught in the Battle of Britain. It was a dismal mismatch: Hitler had been single-mindedly building up his forces in the 1930s, while British defence spending was at historical lows. The Luftwaffe entered the Battle of Britain with 2600 operational planes, but the RAF boasted fewer than 300 Spitfires and 500 Hurricane* fighters. The wartime Prime Minister himself, Winston Churchill, predicted that the Luftwaffe's first week of intensive bombing would kill 40,000 Londoners. But thanks in large part to the Spitfire's speed and agility, the Germans were unable to neutralise the RAF.

This meant the Germans were unable to launch an invasion that could quickly have overwhelmed the British Isles. Such an invasion would have made D-Day impossible, denying the United States its platform to liberate France. It would likely have cost the lives of 430,000 British Jews. It might even have given Germany the lead in the race for the atomic bomb, as many of the scientists who moved to the United States to work on the Manhattan Project were living in Britain when the Spitfires turned back the Luftwaffe. Winston Churchill was right to say of the pilots who flew the Spitfires and the Hurricanes, 'Never in the field of human conflict has so much been owed by so many to so few.'

It is only a small exaggeration to say that the Spitfire was the plane that saved the free world. The prototype cost the government roughly the price of a nice house in London: £10,000.

---

*Supporters of the Hurricane grumble to this day that the Spitfire grabbed too large a share of the glory. The cheap, easy-to-build and effective Hurricanes did indeed outnumber Spitfires in the early months of the war, but it was the Spitfire's design that won the plaudits.

2 Lottery tickets, positive black swans and the importance of variation

When we invest money now in the hope of payoffs later, we think in terms of a return on our investment – a few per cent in a savings account, perhaps, or a higher but riskier reward from the stock market. What was the return on Henry Cave-Brown-Cave's investment of £10,000? Four hundred and thirty thousand people saved from the gas chambers, and denying Adolf Hitler the atomic bomb. The most calculating economist would hesitate to put a price on that.

Return on investment is simply not a useful way of thinking about new ideas and new technologies. It is impossible to estimate a percentage return on blue-sky research, and it is delusional even to try. Most new technologies fail completely. Most original ideas turn out either to be not original after all, or original for the very good reason that they are useless. And when an original idea does work, the returns can be too high to be sensibly measured.

The Spitfire is one of countless examples of these unlikely ideas, which range from the sublime (the mathematician and gambler Gerolamo Cardano first explored the idea of 'imaginary numbers' in 1545; these apparently useless curiosities later turned out to be essential for developing radio, television and computing) to the ridiculous (in 1928, Alexander Fleming didn't keep his laboratory clean, and ended up discovering the world's first antibiotic in a contaminated Petri dish).

We might be tempted to think of such projects as lottery tickets, because they pay off rarely and spectacularly. They're rather better than that, in fact. Lotteries are a zero-sum game – all they do is redistribute existing resources, whereas research and development can make everyone better off. And unlike lottery tickets, bold innovation projects do not have a known payoff and a fixed probability of victory. Nassim Taleb, author of *The Black Swan*, calls such projects 'positive black swans'.

Whatever we call them, such ventures present us with a headache. They are vital, because the payoff can be so enormous. But they are also frustrating and unpredictable. Usually they do not pay off at all. We cannot ignore them, and yet we cannot seem to manage them effectively either.

It would be reassuring to think of new technology as something we *can* plan. And sometimes, it's true, we can: the Manhattan Project did successfully build the atomic bomb; John F. Kennedy promised to put a man on the Moon inside a decade, and his promise was kept. But these examples are memorable in part because they are unusual. It is comforting to hear a research scientist, corporation or government technocrat tell us that our energy problems will soon be solved by some specific new technology: a new generation of hydrogen-powered cars, maybe, or biofuels from algae, or cheap solar panels made from new plastics. But the idea that we can actually predict which technologies will flourish flies in the face of all the evidence. The truth is far messier and more difficult to manage.

That is why the story of how the Spitfire was developed against the odds offers a lesson for those of us who hope technology will solve the problems of today. It was developed in an atmosphere of almost total uncertainty about what the future of flying might be. In the previous war with Germany, which ran from 1914 to 1918, aeroplanes were a brand-new technology and were used mainly for scouting missions. Nobody really knew how they could most effectively be used as they matured. In the mid-1920s, it was widely believed that no aeroplane could exceed 260 miles per hour, but the Spitfire dived at over 450 mph. So it is hardly surprising that British air doctrine failed for such a long time to appreciate the potential importance of fighter planes. The idea of building fighters that could intercept bombers seemed a fantasy to most planners.

The Spitfire seemed especially fantastical as it fired directly forward, meaning that in order to aim at a target, the entire plane needed to change course. A design that struck many as much more plausible was a twin-seater plane with a gunner in a turret. Here are the words of one thoughtful and influential observer in 1938, one year before Germany and Britain went to war:

> We should now build, as quickly and in as large numbers as we can, heavily armed aeroplanes designed with turrets for fighting on the beam and in parallel courses ... the Germans know we have banked upon the forward-shooting plunging 'Spitfire' whose attack ... if not instantly effective, exposes the pursuer to destruction.

The name of this Spitfire sceptic was the future Prime Minister, Winston Churchill. The plane he demanded was built all right, but few British schoolboys thrill to the legend of the Boulton-Paul Defiant. No wonder: the Defiant was a sitting duck.

It is easy to say with hindsight that official doctrine was completely wrong. But it would also be easy to draw the wrong lesson from that. Could ministers and air marshals really have predicted the evolution of aerial combat? Surely not. The lesson of the Spitfire is not that the Air Ministry nearly lost the war with their misconceived strategy. It is that, given that misconceptions in their strategy were all but inevitable, they somehow managed to commission the Spitfire anyway.

The lesson is *variation*, achieved through a pluralistic approach to encouraging new innovations. Instead of putting all their eggs in what looked like the most promising basket – the long-range bomber – the Air Ministry had enough leeway in its procedures that individuals like Air Commodore Cave-Brown-Cave could fund safe havens for 'most interesting' approaches that seemed less promising, just in case – even approaches, like the Spitfire, that were often regarded with derision or despair.

3 Skunk Works and 'freak machines'

In September 1835, Charles Darwin was rowed ashore from *The Beagle* and stepped into the breakers of the Galapagos Islands. He soon discovered some remarkable examples of how safe havens provide space for new things to develop – examples that would later lead him towards his theory of evolution through natural selection. Darwin, a meticulous observer of the natural world, noted the different species of finch that inhabited the islands. Not a single one was found anywhere outside the Galapagos archipelago, which lies in the Pacific Ocean 600 miles west of Ecuador in South America. Even more intriguingly, each island boasted a different selection of finches, all of similar size and colour but with very different beaks – some with thin, probing bills to grab insects, others with large powerful bills to crack seeds, still others adapted to eat fruit. The famous giant tortoises, too, had different species for different islands, some with a high-lipped shell to allow browsing on cactuses, those on the larger, grassier islands with a more conventional high-domed shell. This caught Darwin so unawares that he mixed up his specimens and had to ask the island's vice-governor to unscramble them; Galapagos tortoises are like no other tortoise on earth, so it took Darwin a long time to figure out that there were several distinct species. When Darwin turned his attention to Galapagan plants he discovered the same story yet again. Each island had its own ecosystem.

The Galapagos Islands were the birthplace of so many species because they were so isolated from the mainland and, to a lesser degree, from each other. 'Speciation' – the divergence of one species into two separate populations – rarely happens without some form of physical isolation, otherwise the two diverging species will interbreed at an early stage, and converge again.

Innovations, too, often need a kind of isolation to realise their potential. It's not that isolation is conducive to having ideas in the first place: gene mutations are no more likely to happen in the Galapagos than anywhere else, and as many people have observed, bright ideas emerge from the swirling mix of other ideas, not from isolated minds. Jane Jacobs, the great observer of urban life, looked for innovation in cities, not on Pacific islands. But once a new idea has appeared, it needs the breathing space to mature and develop so that it is not absorbed and crushed by the conventional wisdom.

This idea of allowing several ideas to develop in parallel runs counter to our instincts: we naturally tend to ask, 'What is the best option?', and concentrate on that. But given that life is so unpredictable, what seemed initially like an inferior option may turn out to be exactly what we need. It's sensible in many areas of life to leave room for exploring parallel possibilities – if you want to make friends, join several social clubs, not just the one that appears most promising – but it is particularly true in the area of innovation, where a single good idea or new technology can be so valuable. In an uncertain world, we need more than just Plan A; and that means finding safe havens for Plans B, C, D and beyond.

The Spitfire was a long way down the alphabet from Plan A, not least because the Galapagan isle from which it emerged was populated by some highly unlikely characters. There was Noel Pemberton Billing, a playboy politician most famous as a campaigner against lesbianism. Billing successfully provoked a sensational libel trial in 1918 by accusing the exotic dancer Maud Allan of spreading this 'Cult of the Clitoris', and then used the trial to publicise his rather unconventional view that almost 50,000 'perverts' had successfully been blackmailed by German spies into undermining the British war effort.

When not whipping the media into a frenzy about seditious sapphists, Billing was running Supermarine, a ragtag and notoriously disorganised aeronautical engineering company which in 1917 had employed a second unlikely character: a shy but bloody-minded and quite brilliant young engineer by the name of Reginald Mitchell. On his first job, the foreman complained that Mitchell had served him a cup of tea that 'tastes like piss'. For the next brew, Mitchell steeped the tea leaves in his own boiling urine. 'Bloody good cup of tea, Mitchell,' was the response.

No surprise, then, that Mitchell reacted furiously when the large defence engineering company Vickers bought Supermarine, and tried to place him under the supervision of the great designer Barnes Wallis – who later became famous as the creator of the bouncing bomb used by the Dambusters. 'It's either him or me!' Mitchell fumed. Whether by good judgement or good fortune, the board of Vickers Aviation decided Barnes Wallis should be moved elsewhere, and Mitchell's team continued to enjoy Galapagan isolation from the committees of Vickers.

Then there was the most unexpected escape of all. In 1929 and 1930, Mitchell's planes – the direct ancestors of the Spitfire – held the world record for speed, winning the Schneider Trophy set up to test competing designs. But the government, which was providing much of the funding for these record attempts, decided that they were frivolous in a time of austerity. Sir Hugh Trenchard, Marshal of the Royal Air Force at the time, called high-speed planes 'freak machines'. Without the development money for the latest world record attempt – and with Henry Cave-Brown-Cave not yet on the scene to pay for an 'experiment' – Supermarine was set to abandon the project.

Rescue came from the most unlikely character: Dame Fanny Houston, born in humble circumstances, had become the richest woman in the country after marrying a shipping millionaire and inheriting his fortune. Lady Houston's eclectic philanthropy knew few bounds: she supported oppressed Christians in Russia, coalminers and the women's rights movement. And in 1931 she wrote a cheque to Supermarine that covered the entire development costs of the Spitfire's predecessor, the S6. Lady Houston was furious at the government's lack of support: 'My blood boiled in indignation, for I know that every true Briton would rather sell his last shirt than admit that England could not afford to defend herself against all-comers.' The S6 flew at an astonishing speed of 407.5 mph less than three decades after the Wright Brothers launched the Wright Flyer. England's pride was intact, and so was the Spitfire project. No wonder the historian A.J.P. Taylor later remarked that 'the Battle of Britain was won by Chamberlain, or perhaps by Lady Houston.'

The lone furrow ploughed by Mitchell pre-dated by over a decade the establishment of the celebrated 'Skunk Works' division of Lockheed. The Skunk Works designed the U2, the high-altitude spy plane which produced photographs of nuclear missile installations in Cuba; the Blackbird, the fastest plane in the world for the past thirty-five years; and radar-invisible stealth bombers and fighters. The value of the 'skunk works' model – a small, unconventional team of engineers and innovators in a big corporation, deliberately shielded from a nervous corporate hierarchy – has since become more widely appreciated. Mitchell's team, like the Skunk Works, was closely connected with the latest thinking on aeronautical engineering: Mitchell tested his designs against the world's best each year in the Schneider Trophy races. But the team *was* isolated from bureaucratic interference. In a world where the government was the only likely customer, this was no small feat.

Protecting innovators from bureaucrats won't guarantee results: on the contrary: we can confidently expect that most of the technological creations that stumble out of these Galapagan islands of innovation will prove singularly ill-equipped to thrive in the wider world. But if the occasional Spitfire also results, the failures will be worth it.

4 The burden of knowledge

If such amazing results can emerge when new ideas are protected and nurtured, one might think that there is no problem encouraging innovation in the modern world. There have never been more universities, more PhDs, or more patents. Look at the world's leading companies and consider how many of them – Google, Intel, Pfizer – make products that would either fit into a matchbox, or have no physical form at all. Each of these large islands of innovation is surrounded by an archipelago of smaller high-tech start-ups, all with credible hopes of overturning the established order – just as a tiny start-up called Microsoft humbled the mighty IBM, and a generation later Google and Facebook repeated the trick by outflanking Microsoft itself.

This optimistic view is true as far as it goes. Where it's easy for the market to experiment with a wide range of possibilities, as in computing, we do indeed see change at an incredible pace. The sheer power and interconnectedness of modern technology means that anyone can get hold of enough computing power to produce great new software. Thanks to outsourcing, even the hardware business is becoming easy to enter. Three-dimensional printers, cheap robots and ubiquitous design software mean that other areas of innovation are opening up, too. Yesterday it was customised T-shirts. Today, even the design of niche cars is being 'crowd-sourced' by companies such as Local Motors, which also outsource production. Tomorrow, who knows? In such fields, an open game with lots of new players keeps the innovation scoreboard ticking over. Most ideas fail, but there are so many ideas that it doesn't matter: the internet and social media expert Clay Shirky celebrates 'failure for free'.

Here's the problem, though: failure for free is still all too rare. These innovative fields are still the exception, not the rule. Because open-source software and iPad apps are a highly visible source of innovation, and because they can be whipped up in student dorms, we tend to assume that *anything* that needs innovating can be whipped up in a student dorm. It can't. Cures for cancer, dementia and heart disease remain elusive. In 1984, HIV was identified, and the US health secretary Margaret

Heckler announced that a vaccine preventing AIDS would be available within a couple of years. It's a quarter of a century late. And what about a really effective source of clean energy – nuclear fusion, or solar panels so cheap you could use them as wallpaper?

What these missing-in-action innovations have in common is that they are large and very expensive to develop. They call for an apparently impossible combination of massive resources with an array of wildly experimental innovative gambles. It is easy to talk about 'skunk works', or creating safe havens for fledgling technologies, but when tens of billions of dollars are required, highly speculative concepts look less appealing. We have not thought seriously enough about how to combine the funding of costly, complex projects with the pluralism that has served us so well with the simpler, cheaper start-ups of Silicon Valley.

When innovation requires vast funding and years or decades of effort, we can't wait for universities and government research laboratories to be overtaken by dorm-room innovators, because it may never happen.

If the underlying innovative process was somehow becoming cheaper and simpler and faster, all this might not matter. But the student-startup successes of Google and Facebook are the exceptions, not the rule. Benjamin F. Jones, an economist at the Kellogg School of Management, has looked beyond the eye-catching denizens of Silicon Valley, painstakingly interrogating a database of 3 million patents and 20 million academic papers.

What he discovered makes him deeply concerned about what he calls 'the burden of knowledge'. The size of teams listed in patent citations has been increasing steadily since Jones's records began in 1975. The age at which inventors first produce a patent has also been rising. Specialisation seems sharper, since lone inventors are now less likely to produce multiple patents in different technical fields. This need to specialise may be unavoidable, but it is worrying, because past breakthroughs have often depended on the inventor's sheer breadth of interest, which allowed concepts from different fields to bump together in one creative mind. Now such cross-fertilisation requires a whole team of people – a more expensive and complex organisational problem. 'Deeper' fields of knowledge, whose patents cite many other patents, need bigger teams. Compare a typical modern patent with one from the 1970s and you'll find a larger team filled with older and more specialised researchers. The whole process has become harder, and more expensive to support in parallel, on separate islands of innovation.

In academia, too, Jones found that teams are starting to dominate across the board. Solo researchers used to produce the most highly cited research, but now that distinction, too, belongs to teams of researchers. And researchers spend longer acquiring their doctorates, the basic building blocks of knowledge they need to start generating new research. Jones argues that scientific careers are getting squashed both horizontally and vertically by the sheer volume of knowledge that must be mastered. Scientists must narrow their field of expertise, and even then must cope with an ever shorter productive life between the moment they've learned enough to get started, and the time their energy and creativity starts to fade.

This is already becoming true even in some areas of that hotbed of dorm-room innovation, software. Consider the computer game. In 1984, when gamers were still enjoying *Pac-Man* and *Space Invaders*, the greatest computer game in history was published. *Elite* offered space combat depicted in three dimensions, realistic trade, and a gigantic universe to explore, despite taking up no more memory than a small Microsoft Word document. Like so many later successes of the dot-com era, this revolutionary game was created by two students during their summer vacation.

Twenty-five years later, the game industry was awaiting another gaming blockbuster, *Duke Nukem Forever*. The sequel to a runaway hit, *Duke Nukem Forever* was a game on an entirely different scale. At one stage, thirty-five developers were working on the project, which took twelve years and cost $20 million. In May 2009, the project was shut down, incomplete. (As this book was going to press, there were rumours of yet another revival.)

While *Duke Nukem Forever* was exceptional, modern games projects are far larger, more expensive, more complex and more difficult to manage than they were even ten years ago. Gamers have been eagerly awaiting *Elite 4* since rumours of its development surfaced in 2001. They are still waiting.

Outside computing, this trend is even starker. The £10,000 that the Spitfire prototype cost is the equivalent of less than a million dollars today, and the plane took seven years to enter service. The US Air Force's F-22 stealth fighter, made by the real Skunk Works of Lockheed, was an equally revolutionary aircraft in a different technological era. It required government development funds of $1400 million in today's terms, plus matching funds from Lockheed Martin and Boeing, just to produce the prototype. The plane took a quarter of a century to enter service.

The proliferation of iPhone and Android apps has hidden the uncomfortable truth, which is that innovation has become slower, harder and costlier, and in most areas we have fallen far short of the hopes of our predecessors. Flip through a report penned in 1967 by the influential futurist Herman Kahn, and you will discover that by the year 2000 we were expected to be flying around on personal platforms, curing hangovers with impunity and enjoying electricity that was too cheap to meter, beamed down from artificial moons. Kahn was no idle fantasist. He was accurate in his ideas about progress in communications and computing. He predicted handheld communicators, colour photocopying and the digitisation of financial transactions, and he was right. But this is exactly the sector of the economy where pluralism is alive and well.

Another sector of the economy that must have seemed set for never-ending improvement at the time Kahn was writing is long-haul air travel. Who would have expected in the late 1960s, when the Boeing 747 was designed, that the same plane would still dominate the industry over forty years later? If we had asked business travellers of the 1960s to predict what their counterparts in the 2000s would vote as 'the travel innovation of the decade', they would surely have thought of jet packs or flying cars. Half a century later and the real winner of the vote was 'online check-in'.

Cars have comfier interiors, better safety systems, and louder sound systems, but fundamentally they are not much more efficient than in 1970. Nuclear fusion is three decades away, as it has been for three decades; China instead depends on the less than revolutionary technology of coal-fired electricity plants, while clean energy from the sun or the wind is expensive and sporadic. As for the pharmaceutical industry, the number of highly successful 'blockbuster' drugs has stopped rising over the past decade and fell for the first time ever in 2007; the number of new drugs approved each year in the US has also fallen sharply.

Over the past few decades, the number of people employed in research and development in the world's leading economies has been rising dramatically, but productivity growth has been flat. Yes, there are more patents filed – but the number of patents produced per researcher, or per research dollar, has been falling. We may have booming universities and armies of knowledge workers, but when it comes to producing new ideas, we are running to stand still.

This is particularly worrying because we are hoping that new technology will solve so many of our problems. Consider climate change: Bjorn Lomborg, famous as 'the sceptical environmentalist' who thinks we worry too much about climate change and not enough about clean water or malaria, argues that we should be spending fifty times *more* on research and development into clean energy and geoengineering. If that's the demand from someone who thinks climate change is overhyped, we are entering a world in which we expect much, much more from new technology.

5 The problem with patents

The obvious place to turn for solutions is to the market, where countless companies compete to bring new ideas into profitable shape, from start-ups to giant innovation factories such as Intel, General Electric and GlaxoSmithKline. As we've seen, the market is tremendously innovative – as long as the basic setting is fierce competition to develop super-cheap ideas, such as new software.

But when it comes to the more substantial, expensive innovations – the kind of innovations which are becoming ever more important – the market tends to rely on a long-established piece of government support: the patent. And it's far from clear that patents will encourage the innovations we really need.

The basic concept is sound: patents entice inventors by awarding them a monopoly on the use of their idea, in the hope that the cost of this monopoly is offset by the benefits of encouraging innovation in the first place. Whether patents actually get this balance right is an open question. They have been discredited by the appearance of absurdities such as US patent 6,004,596, for a 'sealed crustless sandwich', or patent 6,368,227, 'a method of swinging on a swing', which has been granted to a five-year-old boy from Minnesota. These frivolous patents do little harm in their own right, but they exemplify a system where patents are awarded for ideas that are either not novel, or require little or no research effort.

Consider IBM's patent for a 'smooth-finish auction', where the auction is halted at an unpredictable moment – unlike an eBay auction, which is vulnerable to opportunistic last-second bids. The patent office's decision to grant the patent is puzzling, because the idea is not new. In fact, it is very old indeed: the auction expert Paul Klemperer points out that Samuel Pepys, London's most famous diarist, recorded the use of such auctions in the seventeenth century. (A pin was pushed into a melting candle. When it dropped, the auction ended.) Such mistakes happen, but there is no simple way to correct them: to do so requires going into direct competition with IBM, hiring an army of lawyers, and taking your chances. A cheaper way of fixing errors is essential.

Or take the idea of using a smart phone to scan bar codes in stores, and immediately reading reviews and checking whether the product is available more cheaply nearby. The concept of the scanner-phone popped into the head of a young Canadian economist called Alex Tabarrok while he was taking a shower one morning, at the height of the dot-com boom. Alas for Tabarrok, it had popped into other people's heads too, and he soon discovered that patent 6,134,548 had been awarded for the same proposal just a few months earlier. That might seem like a misfortune for Tabarrok alone, but in fact we all suffer: a patent given out as a reward for random moments of inspiration delivers all the costs of intellectual monopoly without any of the benefits.

Worse, patents also fail to encourage some of the really important innovations. Too strong in the case of the scanner phone and the smooth-finish auction, they are too weak to inspire a vaccine for HIV, or important breakthroughs in clean energy. Part of the problem is the timescale: many important patents in, say, solar power, are likely to have expired by the time solar energy becomes competitive with fossil fuels, a technology which has been accumulating a head start since the industrial revolution began.

A second, ironic, problem is that companies fear that if they produce a truly vital technology, governments will lean on them to relinquish their patent rights or slash prices. This was the fate of Bayer, the manufacturer of the anthrax treatment Cipro, when an unknown terrorist began mailing anthrax spores in late 2001, killing five people. Four years later, as anxiety grew about an epidemic of bird flu in humans, the owner of the patent on Tamiflu, Roche, agreed to license production of the drug after very similar pressure from governments across the world. It is quite obvious why governments have scant respect for patents in true emergencies. Still, if everybody knows that governments will ignore patents when innovations are most vital, it is not clear why anyone expects the patent system to encourage vital innovations.

The cheese sandwich patent problem could be fixed with some simple administrative improvements, but questions remain about whether any reform to the patent system can encourage companies to focus on truly large-scale, long-term projects. The innovation slowdown is likely to continue.

If patents can't encourage the market alone to unleash the scale of innovations we need, the obvious alternative is governments. Governments, after all, are supposed to have the long time horizons, and the interest in solving our collective problems. But so far, government grants have failed to deliver their full potential. A clue as to why emerges from one of the most remarkable lives of the twentieth century.

6 'We are glad you didn't follow our advice'

Mario Capecchi's earliest memory is of German officers knocking on the door of his mother's chalet in the Italian Alps, and arresting her. They sent her to a concentration camp, probably Dachau. Mario, who had been taught to speak both Italian and German, understood exactly what was being said by the SS officers. He was three and a half.

Mario's mother Lucy was a poet and an antifascist campaigner who had refused to marry his abusive father, Luciano, an officer in Mussolini's air force. One can only imagine the scandal in prewar, Catholic, fascist Italy. Expecting trouble, Lucy had made preparations by selling many of her possessions and entrusting the proceeds to a local peasant family. When she disappeared, the family took Mario in. For a time he lived like an Italian farmer's son, learning rural life at an apron hem.

After a year, his mother's money appears to have run out. Mario left the village. He remembers a brief time living with his father, and deciding he would rather live on the streets: 'Amidst all of the horrors of war, perhaps the most difficult for me to accept as a child was having a father who was brutal to me.' Luciano was killed shortly afterwards in aerial combat.

And so Mario Capecchi became a street urchin at the age of four and a half. Most of us are content if, at the age of four and a half, our children are capable of eating lunch without spilling it or confident enough to be dropped off at nursery without tears. Mario survived on scraps, joined gangs, and drifted in and out of orphanages. At the age of eight he spent a year in hospital, probably suffering from typhoid, passing in and out of feverish oblivion each day. Conditions were grim: no blankets, no sheets, beds jammed together, nothing to eat but a crust of bread and some chicory coffee. Many Italian orphans died in such hospitals.

Mario survived. On his ninth birthday, a strange-looking woman arrived at the hospital asking to see him. It was his mother, unrecognisable after five years in a concentration camp. She had spent the last eighteen months searching for him. She bought him a suit of traditional Tyrolean clothes – he still has the cap and its decorative feather – and took him with her to America.

Two decades later Mario was at Harvard University, determined to study molecular biology under the great James Watson, co-discoverer of DNA. Not a man to hand out compliments easily, Watson once said Capecchi 'accomplished more as a graduate student than most scientists accomplish in a lifetime'. He had also advised the young Capecchi that he would be 'fucking crazy' to pursue his studies anywhere other than in the cutting-edge intellectual atmosphere of Harvard.

Still, after a few years, Capecchi had decided that Harvard was not for him. Despite great resources, inspiring colleagues and a supportive mentor in Watson, he found the Harvard environment demanded results in too much of a hurry. That was fine, if you wanted to take predictable steps along well-signposted pathways. But Capecchi felt that if you wanted to do great work, to change the world, you had to give yourself space to breathe. Harvard, he thought, had become 'a bastion of short-term gratification'. Off he went instead to the University of Utah, where a brand-new department was being set up. He had spotted, in Utah, a Galapagan island on which to develop his ideas.

In 1980, Mario Capecchi applied for a grant from the US National Institutes of Health, which use government money to fund potentially life-saving research. The sums are huge: the NIH are twenty times bigger than the American Cancer Society. Capecchi described three separate projects. Two of them were solid stuff with a clear track record and a step-by-step account of the project deliverables. Success was almost assured.

The third project was wildly speculative. Capecchi was trying to show that it was possible to make a specific, targeted change to a gene in a mouse's DNA. It is hard to overstate how ambitious this was, especially back in 1980: a mouse's DNA contains as much information as seventy or eighty large encyclopedia volumes. Capecchi wanted to perform the equivalent of finding and changing a single sentence in one of those volumes – but using a procedure performed on a molecular scale. His idea was to produce a sort of doppelganger gene, one similar to the one he wanted to change. He would inject the doppelganger into a mouse's cell, and somehow get the gene to find its partner, kick it out of the DNA strand and replace it. Success was not only uncertain but highly improbable.

The NIH decided that Capecchi's plans sounded like science fiction. They downgraded his application and strongly advised him to drop the speculative third project. However, they did agree to fund his application on the basis of the other two solid, results-oriented projects. (Things could have been worse: at about the same time, over in the UK, the Medical Research Council flatly rejected an application from Martin Evans to attempt a similar trick. Two research agencies are better than one, however messy that might seem, precisely because they will fund a greater variety of projects.)

What did Capecchi do? He took the NIH's money, and ignoring their admonitions he poured almost all of it into his risky gene-targeting project. It was, he recalls, a big gamble. If he hadn't been able to show strong enough initial results in the three to five-year timescale demanded by the NIH, they would have cut off his funding. Without their seal of approval, he might have found it hard to get funding from elsewhere. His career would have been severely set back, his research assistants looking for other work. His laboratory might not have survived.

In 2007, Mario Capecchi was awarded the Nobel Prize for Medicine for this work on mouse genes. As the NIH's expert panel had earlier admitted, when agreeing to renew his funding: 'We are glad you didn't follow our advice.'

7 '... even if it means uncertainty or the chance of failure'

The moral of Capecchi's story is not that we should admire stubborn geniuses, although we should. It is that we shouldn't require stubbornness as a quality in our geniuses. How many vital scientific or technological advances have foundered, not because their developers lacked insight, but because they simply didn't have Mario Capecchi's extraordinarily defiant character?

But before lambasting the NIH for their lack of imagination, suppose for a moment that you and I sat down with a blank sheet of paper and tried to design a system for doling out huge amounts of public money – taxpayers' money – to scientific researchers. That's quite a responsibility. We would want to see a clear project description, of course. We'd want some expert opinion to check that each project was scientifically sound, that it wasn't a wild goose chase. We'd want to know that either the applicant or another respected researcher had taken the first steps along this particular investigative journey and obtained some preliminary results. And we would want to check in on progress every few years.

We would have just designed the sensible, rational system that tried to stop Mario Capecchi working on mouse genes.

The NIH's expert-led, results-based, rational evaluation of projects is a sensible way to produce a steady stream of high-quality, can't-go-wrong scientific research. But it is exactly the wrong way to fund lottery-ticket projects that offer a small probability of a revolutionary breakthrough. It is a funding system designed to avoid risks – one that puts more emphasis on forestalling failure than achieving success. Such an attitude to funding is understandable in any organisation, especially one funded by taxpayers. But it takes too few risks. It isn't right to expect a Mario Capecchi to risk his career on a life-saving idea because the rest of us don't want to take a chance.

Fortunately, the NIH model isn't the only approach to funding medical research. The Howard Hughes Medical Institute, a large charitable medical research organisation set up by the eccentric billionaire, has an 'investigator' programme which explicitly urges 'researchers to take risks, to explore unproven avenues, to embrace the unknown – even if it means uncertainty or the chance of failure'. Indeed, one of the main difficulties in attracting HHMI funding is convincing the institute that the research is sufficiently uncertain.

The HHMI also backs people rather than specific projects, figuring that this allows scientists the flexibility to adapt as new information becomes available, and pursue whatever avenues of research open up, without having to justify themselves to a panel of experts. (General H.R. McMaster would surely recognise the need to adapt to changing conditions on the ground.) It does not demand a detailed research project – it prefers to see the sketch of the idea, alongside an example of the applicant's best recent research. Investigators are sometimes astonished that the funding appears to be handed out with too few strings attached.

The HHMI does ask for results, eventually, but allows much more flexibility about what 'results' actually are – after all, there was no specific project in the first place. If the HHMI sees convincing signs of effort, funding is automatically reviewed for another five years; it is only after ten years without results that HHMI funding is withdrawn – and even then, gradually rather than abruptly, allowing researchers to seek out alternatives rather than sacking their staff or closing down their laboratories.

This sounds like a great approach when Mario Capecchi is at the forefront of our minds. But is the HHMI system really superior? Maybe it leads to too many costly failures. Maybe it allows researchers to relax too much, safe in the knowledge that funding is all but assured.

Maybe. But three economists, Pierre Azoulay, Gustavo Manso and Joshua Graff Zivin, have picked apart the data from the NIH and HHMI programmes to provide a rigorous evaluation of how much important science emerges from the two contrasting approaches. They carefully matched HHMI investigators with the very best NIH-funded scientists: those who had received rare scholarships, and those who had received NIH 'MERIT' awards, which, like other NIH grants, fund specific projects, but which are more generous and are aimed only at the most outstanding researchers. They also used a statistical technique to select high-calibre NIH researchers with a near-identical track record to HHMI investigators.

Whichever way they sliced the data, Azoulay, Manso and Zivin found evidence that the more open-ended, risky HHMI grants were funding the most important, unusual and influential research. HHMI researchers, apparently no better qualified than their NIH-funded peers, were far more influential, producing twice as many highly-cited research articles. They were more likely to win awards, and more likely to train students who themselves won awards. They were also more original, producing research that introduced new 'keywords' into the lexicon of their research field, changing research topics more often, and attracting more citations from outside their narrow field of expertise.

The HHMI researchers also produced more failures; a higher proportion of their research papers were cited by nobody at all. No wonder: the NIH programme was designed to avoid failure, while the HHMI programme embraced it. And in the quest for truly original research, some failure is inevitable.

Here's the thing about failure in innovation: it's a price worth paying. We don't expect every lottery ticket to pay a prize, but if we want any chance of winning that prize then we buy a ticket. In the statistical jargon, the pattern of innovative returns is heavily skewed to the upside; that means a lot of small failures and a few gigantic successes. The NIH's more risk-averse approach misses out on many ideas that matter.

It isn't hard to see why a bureaucracy, entrusted with spending billions of taxpayer dollars, is more concerned with minimising losses than maximising gains. And the NIH approach does have its place. Recall the work by the Santa Fe complexity theorists Stuart Kaufman and John Holland, showing that the ideal way to discover paths through a shifting landscape of possibilities is to combine baby steps and speculative leaps. The NIH is funding the baby steps. Who is funding the speculative leaps? The Howard Hughes Medical Institute invests huge sums each year, but only about one twentieth of 1 per cent of the world's global R&D budget. There are a few organisations like the HHMI, but most R&D is either highly commercially-focused research – the opposite of blue-sky thinking – or target-driven grants typified by the NIH. The baby steps are there; the experimental leaps are missing.

We need bureaucrats to model themselves on the chief of Britain's air staff in the 1930s: 'firms are reluctant to risk their money on highly speculative ventures of novel design. If we are to get serious attempts at novel types ... we shall have to provide the incentive.' That is the sort of attitude that produces new ideas that matter.

Unfortunately, such bureaucrats are rare. So far, we have discovered two vital principles for promoting new technology. First, create as many separate experiments as possible, even if they appear to embody contradictory views about what might work, on the principle that most will fail. Second, encourage some long-shot experiments, even though failure is likely, because the rewards to success are so great. The great weakness of most government-funded research is that both these goals are the antithesis of government planning. Bureaucracies like a grand plan, and they like to feel reassured that they know exactly how that plan is to be achieved. Exceptions, such as the Spitfire, are rare.

Traditional government funding has an important part to play in encouraging ideas that matter, especially if more money can be awarded following the failure-tolerant model of the Howard Hughes Medical Institute. The market also clearly plays a critical role in developing new ideas and bringing ideas out of government-funded labs and into practical products we enjoy in everyday life.

Yet the problem of encouraging expensive, world-changing innovations remains daunting. Government officials will always tend to avoid risks when spending large sums of public money, while the patent system will rarely inspire costly, long-term research efforts from private firms. Neither approach is likely to combine the two elements essential to encourage significant innovation in a complex world: a true openness to risky new ideas, and a willingness to put millions or even billions of dollars at risk. These two elements are fundamental to twenty-first-century innovation, yet they seem mutually incompatible. They are not. In fact the way to combine them has been around, if often forgotten, for more than three centuries.

8 '... for such person or persons as shall discover the Longitude'

The year 1675 marked the foundation of one of the first and most famous government agencies for research and design. The Royal Observatory was founded with the aim of improving navigation at sea, and in particular of solving the 'longitude' problem of figuring out how far east or west a ship at sea was. (The latitude problem was far more easily solved, by measuring the length of the day, or the elevation of the sun or stars.) For a great naval power such as Great Britain, with trade routes stretching across the world, the significance of a ship's captain being unable to figure out his location could hardly be overstated. And the Royal Observatory today gladly associates itself with the sensational breakthrough that solved the conundrum. Its original site in Greenwich, East London, is bisected by what the Observatory still proudly describes as 'the Prime Meridian of the World' – Longitude 0° 0' 0".

There is an inconvenient tale behind this happy association, however. The Royal Observatory's own astronomers failed hopelessly to solve the problem for almost a century, while ruthlessly undermining the man who did.

Dissatisfaction with the Royal Observatory's performance had come to a head in 1707, with its experts still apparently clueless after more than three decades of research. One foggy night Admiral Sir Clowdisley Shovell, wrongly believing that his fleet was further west of the English mainland, wrecked four ships on the Isles of Scilly. Sir Clowdisley's miscalculation led to more deaths than the sinking of the *Titanic*. The British parliament turned to Sir Isaac Newton and the comet expert Edmond Halley for advice, and in 1714 passed the Act of Longitude, promising a prize of £20,000 for a solution to the problem. Compared with the typical wage of the day, this was over £30 million pounds in today's terms.

The prize transformed the way that the problem of longitude was attacked. No longer were the astronomers of the Royal Observatory the sole official searchers – the answer could come from anyone. And it did. In 1737, a village carpenter named John Harrison stunned the scientific establishment when he presented his solution to the Board of Longitude: a clock capable of keeping superb time at sea despite the rolling and pitching of the ship and extreme changes in temperature and humidity. While it was well known that knowing the correct time back in London could enable a navigator to calculate longitude using the sun, the technical obstacles to producing a sufficiently accurate clock were widely thought to be beyond human ingenuity. Harrison, spurred on by a fabulous prize, proved everyone wrong.

It should have been a salutary lesson that prizes could inspire socially beneficial ideas from unexpected sources. Unfortunately, the Royal Observatory's experts took it as a lesson that prizes could embarrass the likes of them. The Astronomer Royal, James Bradley, and his protégé Nevil Maskelyne, went to extraordinary lengths to deny Harrison his prize while they struggled to make progress with an alternative, astronomical method of determining longitude. Bradley used his authority first to delay sea trials of Harrison's latest clock, and then to send the clock – along with Harrison's son William – into a war zone. When the clock passed this test with flying colours, losing a mere five seconds in an eighty-one-day journey to Jamaica, they insisted on more tests. After Maskelyne himself became Astronomer Royal in 1765, he impounded Harrison's clocks for 'observation and testing', transporting them on a rickety wagon over London's cobblestones to Greenwich. Oddly, they didn't work so well after that.

It is true that Harrison did himself few favours – he was not so much a stubborn genius as an irascible one – but it is hard to avoid the conclusion that he was unfairly rebuffed and perhaps even cheated.* Harrison's clocks did eventually become the standard way to find longitude, but only after his death.

Still, the longitude prize had inspired a solution, and the prize methodology was widely imitated. In 1810 Nicolas Appert, a chef and confectioner also credited with the invention of the bouillon cube, was presented with a 12,000-franc prize by Napoleon for inventing a method of preserving food that is still used in canning factories today. Unfortunately, the prickly reaction of the Observatory's scientific establishment was widely imitated, too. In 1820 a French aristocrat, Baron de Montyon, bequeathed his fortune to the Académie des sciences with instructions that it be used to fund two annual prizes, one for 'making some industrial process less unhealthy', and one for 'improving medical science or surgery'. The Académie was less than impressed with these irksome stipulations. If prizes were to be given out, they reasoned at first, surely some of de Montyon's money should be spent on administrative support for those prizes, not to mention printing costs? In years when no prize was handed out, they started to use the money to buy library books and experimental equipment – all of which 'might be necessary in the judging of competitions'.

A decade after De Montyon's death, the Académie was scarcely even pretending to respect his will, looting his legacy to fund whatever projects it pleased. Ultimately the Académie

---

*The Board of Longitude never gave Harrison his prize, but it did give him some development money. The British parliament, after Harrison petitioned the King himself, also awarded the inventor a substantial purse in lieu of the prize that never came. The sad story is superbly told by Dava Sobel in her book *Longitude*, although Sobel perhaps gives Harrison too much credit in one respect: it is arguable that by producing a seaworthy clock, albeit a masterpiece, he did not solve the longitude problem for the Royal Navy or society as a whole. To do that, he needed to produce a blueprint that a skilled craftsman could use to produce copies of the clock.

began to turn down bequests for prizes, insisting on its right to make grants to favoured projects or people instead.

France was not alone. Across Europe and the United States, scientific societies shifted from chiefly awarding prizes to mostly handing out grants, or even employing researchers directly. What prizes remained tended to be handed out retrospectively and on a subjective basis – the most famous being the Nobel prizes – rather than, as with the Longitude prize and the Food Preservation prize, pre-announced with the aim of encouraging some future solution. Despite their early successes, innovation prizes were firmly supplanted by direct grants. Grants, unlike prizes, are a powerful tool of patronage. Prizes, in contrast, are open to anyone who produces results. That makes them intrinsically threatening to the establishment.

Finally, after almost two centuries out of fashion, prizes are now enjoying a renaissance – thanks to a new generation of entrepreneurs and philanthropists who care more about getting solutions than about where they come from.

9 Seekers and solvers

Netflix is a mail-order film rental company which recommends films to its customers based on what they've previously rented or reviewed on the company website. The better the recommendations, the happier the customer, so in March 2006 the founder and chief executive of Netflix, Reed Hastings, met some colleagues to discuss how they might improve the software that made the recommendations. Hastings had been inspired by the story of John Harrison, and suggested offering a prize of $1m to anyone who could do better than Netflix's in-house algorithm, Cinematch.

The Netflix prize, announced in October 2006, struck a chord with the Web 2.0 generation. Within days of the prize announcement, some of the best minds in the relevant fields of computer science were on the case. Within a year, the leading entries had reduced Cinematch's recommendation errors by more than 8 per cent – close to the million-dollar hurdle of 10 per cent. Over 2,500 teams from 161 countries and comprising 27,000 competitors entered the contest. The prize was eventually awarded in September 2009 to a team of researchers from AT&T.

The use of prizes is catching on again, and quickly. Another company, Innocentive, has for the last decade provided an exchange where 'seekers' can offer cash to 'solvers'. Both sides are anonymous. The problems are like the small ads on the world's least romantic lonely-hearts website: 'A technology is desired that produces a pleasant scent upon stretching of an elastomer film' ($50,000); 'Surface chemistry for optical bio-sensor with high binding capacity and specificity is required' ($60,000).

Then there are more glamorous prizes, such as those under the aegis of the non-profit X Prize Foundation. The Archon X Prize for genomics will be awarded to the team that can sequence 100 human genomes within ten days at a cost of $10,000 per genome. That is unimaginably quicker and cheaper than the first private genomic sequencing in 2000, which took nine months and cost $100m for a single human genome. (Craig Venter, the director of that effort, is one of the backers of the new prize.) But it is the kind of leap forward that would be necessary to usher in an era of personalised medicine, in which doctors could prescribe drugs and give advice in full knowledge of each patient's genetic susceptibilities. Another prize will be awarded to the manufacturer of a popular mass-production car that has a fuel efficiency of 100 miles per gallon.

The prize-giving model is the same each time. The X Prize Foundation identifies a goal and finds sponsors; it announces a prize and whips up the maximum possible enthusiasm, with the aim of generating far more investment than the prize itself; the prize achieved, it hands out the award with great fanfare and moves on to set other challenges. The prize winner is left with intellectual property intact, and may capitalise on the commercial value of that intellectual property, if any commercial value exists.

'One of the goals of the prize is to transform the way people think,' says Bob Weiss, vice-chairman of the X Prize Foundation. 'We were trying to create a sea-change.'

They have certainly made an impact. And others have trodden a similar path. There is, for example, an 'Mprize' for creating long-lived mice, with the hope, eventually, of lengthening human life too. And the Clay Mathematics Institute, a non-profit body set up in 1998 by a Boston businessman, is offering million-dollar prizes for the solution of seven 'Millennium' problems in mathematics. (Not everybody responds to such incentives. The first such prize was awarded to the reclusive Russian genius Grigory Perelman. He ignored it.)

But all these prizes are dwarfed by an ambitious scheme that promises to unleash the true potential of innovation prizes. Five national governments and the Bill and Melinda Gates Foundation have put $1.5 billion into a prize called an 'advanced market commitment' to reward the developers and suppliers of a more effective vaccine against pneumococcal diseases such as pneumonia, meningitis and bronchitis. The reason a prize is needed is because even with a patent, no pharmaceutical company could expect to reap much reward from a product that will largely benefit the very poor. Pneumococcal infections kill nearly a million young children a year, almost all of them in poor countries.

As John Harrison could have attested, the problem with an innovation prize is determining when the innovator has done enough to claim his reward. This is especially the case when the prize is not for some arbitrary achievement, such as being the fastest plane on a given day – remember the Schneider Trophy, which inspired the development of the Spitfire – but for a practical accomplishment such as finding longitude or creating immunity to pneumococcal meningitis. Harrison was caught up in an argument between proponents of the clock method and the astronomical method. Similar arguments could emerge today. One pneumococcal vaccine might be cheap and fastest to market; another might be more reliable and have fewer side-effects. Who is to decide who wins the prize? Or have both won, or neither?

For this reason the vaccine prize takes the form of an agreement to subsidise heavily the first big orders of a successful vaccine. The developers do not reap their rewards unless they can persuade governments or citizens of poor countries to buy the vaccine – albeit at a bargain price – and they will receive their money slowly or quickly, in part or in full, depending on how the market responds. The prize also partly replaces the pricing-power that comes with any patent, because if the drug company wants to collect the prize it has to agree to offer the drug cheaply.

Given that only the very largest pharmaceutical companies spend more than $5 billion per year on research and development, a $1.5 billion prize should be taken seriously on hard-nosed commercial grounds alone. And it has worked: at the end of 2010, children in Nicaragua received the first prize-funded vaccines for pneumococcal disease.

There is more to come. The next target is a vaccine for malaria, which might require a prize of $5 billion to generate commercial interest. Prize enthusiasts think that even an HIV vaccine may be possible, and speculate about a fund of $10 billion to $20 billion, three times the total annual research spending of the largest drugs companies. This is serious money. But the wonderful thing about prizes is that they don't cost a penny until success is achieved. This allows the ultimate combination: a completely open field, where failures are tolerated and the boldest, riskiest idea could succeed, alongside huge sums of money that are spent only when the problem is solved.

10 'There's nothing else to do in Mojave'

On 21 June 2004 – seven decades after Reginald Mitchell was overturning the conventional wisdom about what flying machines could do – an outlandish-looking aeroplane with a single, impossibly long thin wing and the name 'White Knight One' taxied down a runway in the Mojave Desert. White Knight One had been developed by the brilliant aircraft designer Burt Rutan, a genius in the mould of Mitchell, in the Galapagan isolation of a tiny desert town with a scattering of fast-food joints and gas stations and a vast parking lot for disused commercial airliners. (Says Rutan, 'Innovation is what we do because there's nothing else to do in Mojave.') Slung under that eggshell-wing, between White Knight's catamaran-style twin hulls, was a stubby little appendage, SpaceShipOne. Inside it sat a 63-year-old man named Mike Melvill. The age of private space flight – and with it the potential for space tourism – was about to dawn.

On the face of it, innovation prizes deserve credit for this epochal event. White Knight was one of two dozen competitors trying to win the Ansari X Prize, created by a non-profit foundation. (Some were unlikely challengers: one team was proudly sponsored by 'the Forks Coffee Shop in downtown Forks'.) A few months later, when White Knight had flown two qualifying missions in quick succession, Rutan's team secured the $10 million prize.

But that's far from the whole story. We can also credit philanthropy: Paul Allen, the co-founder of Microsoft and one of the world's richest men, bankrolled Rutan's work for reasons reminiscent of the HHMI: he liked the idea and believed in the experimenter's talent. Or we could equally thank hard-nosed commercialism: Rutan teamed up with Sir Richard Branson's Virgin Group, which is determined to turn space tourism into a profitable business. Virgin Galactic has since commissioned a larger ship, SpaceShipTwo, with bigger windows and room to float around.

Take a longer view, and it's government that deserves a pat on the back for the dawn of private space flight. Back in the 1950s, the X-15 plane funded by NACA – the short-lived predecessor of NASA – flew at a height of 106 km, at the edges of space itself, after hitching a lift on a B-52 bomber. This method of getting things into space fell into disuse, however, after President Kennedy focused attention on the goal of getting to the Moon, a task for which multi-stage, ground-launched rockets were the obvious choice. The price we paid was a loss of pluralism: a promising avenue for reliable, low-cost satellite launches – air-launched satellites – was largely abandoned until the combination of profit, prizes and philanthropy came along to revive the technology and turn it into something with real-world value.

In short, the whole unlikely project of putting a man into space with private money succeeded on the back of an untidy jumble of intellectual influences and a tangled web of funding sources. It's a jumble we should embrace, because it has delivered many other good things. The internet resulted from a project funded by Pentagon pen-pushers, but it took dorm-room innovators to unleash its potential; satellites and GPS, the Global Positioning System, were devised with government backing, but it's unlikely that any bureaucrat would ever have brought in-car navigation systems to market.

The lesson is that pluralism encourages pluralism. If you want to stimulate many innovations, combine many strategies. Prizes could, in theory, replace the patent system – governments could scrap patent protection but offer prizes for desirable inventions. But to explain that idea is to see its limitations. How could the government know enough about the costs, benefits and even the very possibility of an innovation to write the rules and set the prize money for a competition? We know we need an HIV vaccine, but nobody knew we needed the internet until we had it. We couldn't have established a prize for inventing the World Wide Web.

Prizes go a long way towards plugging the inevitable gaps left by bureaucrats less wise than Henry Cave-Brown-Cave and scientists less brave than Mario Capecchi, but they should add to rather than replace other methods of funding and encouraging innovation. The Millennium prizes are likely to be awarded to mathematicians who are already receiving public funding. The Schneider Trophy didn't fund the development of the Spitfire, but it proved Reginald Mitchell's quality and inspired Lady Houston's contribution at just the right moment. The pneumococcal vaccine funding may impose pricing conditions on pharmaceutical firms, but it does not invalidate their patents, which can still earn money in other markets or royalties from subsequent technologies. Trial and error can be messy, and so, too, can the tangle of institutions needed to encourage it.

However we hand out the credit for Mike Melvill's flight, it must have been a journey to remember. White Knight took off at 6.47 a.m. and over the next hour climbed to a height of almost nine miles, higher than any commercial airliner could reach. White Knight then released Melvill and his craft, which glided for a moment before Melvill fired its rocket engine. SpaceShipOne curved sharply upwards until travelling nearly vertically. It accelerated past the speed of sound within ten seconds; after seventy-six seconds, the engine shut down automatically. The ship, already over 30 miles or 50 kilometres up, continued to hurtle through the ever sparser atmosphere at over 2000 miles an hour until it reached, just barely, the 100-kilometre mark that is accepted to be the point at which space begins. When first reaching the brink of space, weightless for a few moments at the top of his craft's arc above the desert, Mike Melvill fumbled past his oxygen tubes to pull a handful of M&Ms out of his left breast pocket. He released them and they drifted and bounced in all directions, floating around his head, breaking the silence as they clicked against the portholes of the ship.

Four

Finding what works for the poor or: Selection

'An empiricist, I was willing to learn by my mistakes and those of others.'

– Muhammad Yunus

'The barrier to change is not too little caring; it is too much complexity.'

– Bill Gates

1 If at first you don't succeed, try again

When starving refugees from the countryside began to pour into his more affluent suburb in the capital city, the young professor of economics was struck by how the young and the old, men and women, were all so skeletal it was impossible to tell them apart. 'They were everywhere, lying very quiet. They did not chant any slogans. They did not demand anything from us. They did not condemn us for having delicious food in our homes while they lay down quietly on our doorsteps.' Starvation, he concluded, was the worst of all ways to die.

The young professor, who had gained a Fulbright scholarship and a PhD from Vanderbilt University before returning to his homeland, knew he had to do something. But what? Observing that fields around the capital city were lying idle during the dry winter season, due to lack of money to operate irrigation pumps, he gathered together local landowners and farm workers and proposed a way of planting a winter crop: the landowners would contribute their land, the farm workers their labour, and the professor would buy high-yielding seeds, fertiliser, and fuel for the water pumps. The three parties to the deal would split the crop three ways. After some haggling, all sides agreed. The professor had launched his first development project.

It was a disaster, at least for the professor. Despite bumper harvests, the farmers didn't repay him. He lost almost $600, a substantial sum for a young Bangladeshi academic in the mid-1970s. Nor did the benefits accrue to those who were most in need. The professor was appalled by how paltry were the sums paid to the destitute women who laboured to separate the rice grains from their stalks.

Undeterred, the professor started to think about how else he might be able to help the desperately poor. He noticed that craftswomen in the environs of Chittagong University had to borrow from local moneylenders to buy their raw materials, and the local moneylenders charged up to 10 per cent interest per day; at such rates, a debt of a single cent would balloon to the size of the US economy in just over a year. In 1976, the professor began lending to these women – less than a dollar each to a first group of forty-two families, far less than he had lent to the local farm owners. The professor, of course, was Muhammad Yunus, and those forty-two tiny loans were the start of what would become the Grameen Bank, now the world's most famous microfinance organisation.

The story of how Yunus built Grameen is widely known, especially since he was awarded the Nobel Peace Prize for it in 2006. But its prologue – Yunus's costly farming project – is not. Few people realise that the world's most famous development success story began with trial and error.

2 'As soon as the foreigner with a camera comes out . . . kids get excited'

At its most basic, adapting requires variation and selection. If the previous chapter emphasised the importance of variation, this one is about the importance of selection. It can be surprisingly difficult to distinguish between what is working and what is not, and nowhere is this more true than in the area of economic development – and particularly, of development aid. This is partly because when the challenge is as big as the problem of poverty, our desire for simple stories seems to go into overdrive: we don't ask what works, we simply gravitate to what sounds miraculous.

One example is the way in which Yunus himself has been all but beatified as the Patron Saint of Development. This is odd on a number of levels. Yunus is a charismatic and admirable man, certainly – even before Grameen, as the high-flying young head of economics at Chittagong University, he had made quite an impact. He vacated his spacious office to create a staff common room, kicked up a stink in the national press about absurd bus schedules that meant the university was empty every day after 2 p.m., and circulated an influential petition calling on the government to show more leadership in dealing with the famine. (His facility for pragmatic problem-solving was apparent even at a young age, when Yunus hit upon a sneaky way to secure copies of his favourite magazine, *Shuktara* – stealing the identity of a subscriber.) But it's not as if Yunus was the only person ever to have had the idea of non-profit small loans (ACCION International was making microloans in Brazil in 1973, and Opportunity International was making non-profit loans in Colombia in 1971). Nor is Grameen the world's largest microfinance lender, or even the largest lender in Bangladesh; BRAC, the Bangladesh Rural Advancement Committee, is gigantic.

Yunus stumbled upon microfinance because he was willing to

experiment and to accept his early missteps. He was in a good position to do that. Like Peter Palchinsky he had travelled widely, picking up his PhD in the US, but he returned to his roots to experiment in a local context he understood far better than any foreign adviser would have been able to. Yunus advocates what he calls the 'worm's-eye view'.

'I thought I should rather look at things at close range and I would see them sharply,' he explains. 'If I found some barrier along the way, like a worm I would go around it, and that way I would certainly achieve my aim and accomplish something.'

There is something very striking about the 'worm's-eye view'. Partly it's about humbly adjusting to obstacles, changing course until the path to success is clear. But it's also about seeing those obstacles 'sharply ... at close range'. That is unusual. Development is currently the business of national governments, who are often rather distant, unaccountable and ideological, and international donors, who are even more so. Development is a field that is full of surprises. Many apparent successes are not what they seem, and the people who fund them are often poorly placed to spot the failures and close them down. In the foreign aid business, we rarely get to check out the truth with our own eyes.

Consider the PlayPump, a clever-sounding idea in which a deep well is connected to a pump powered by a children's roundabout as a way of bringing fresh water to isolated communities. As the children play, the roundabout spins, and the pump fills a large tank that can be tapped as needed. The PlayPump removes the need both for unreliable electrical pumps and for hours of labour from hardworking women: clean water simply appears as a by-product of innocent play.

Or does it? Because it's a pricey and mechanically inefficient alternative to a hand-pump, the PlayPump justifies itself only if the village children really do spend much of their time playing on it. From the pictures sent back from rural Africa, it seems that they do. But rural Africa is a place where few of us spend much time, so it's hard to be sure. Owen Scott, a young

Canadian engineer, does spend his time in rural Africa. He lives in Malawi and works for Engineers Without Borders, so he can easily see what really happens when a PlayPump is installed:

'Each time I've visited a PlayPump, I've always found the same scene: a group of women and children struggling to spin it by hand so they can draw water. I've never found anyone playing on it,' he explains. But then comes the Kodak moment: 'As soon as the foreigner with a camera comes out ... kids get excited. And when they get excited, they start playing. Within five minutes, the thing looks like a crazy success.'

Sometimes the PlayPump replaces a traditional hand-pump. Scott compared how long it took to fill a 20-litre bucket with a traditional hand-pump (28 seconds) versus a PlayPump (3 minutes 7 seconds of strenuous and faintly humiliating running around). Scott also asked the locals, in sparsely populated Malawian villages, whether they preferred the new PlayPumps or their old, traditional hand-pumps. They were unambiguous: the hand-pumps did the job much better.

The trouble is, not everyone is as inquisitive as Owen Scott. And those photos the foreigners take after five minutes do look convincing, not to mention heart-warming. Soon the PlayPumps won a prestigious award from the World Bank. They were swiftly backed by the US aid agencies USAID and PEPFAR, private foundations, the then-President's wife Laura Bush and the rap entrepreneur Jay-Z.

Owen Scott is up against quite a set of cheerleaders, but has managed to make an impact by posting video interviews with Malawian teachers on YouTube – 'the message is stop immediately ... play pumps are causing problems for Malawi'.

One of the funders of PlayPumps, the Case Foundation, now says it's discovered that the pumps 'perform best in certain community settings, such as at large primary schools, but they are not necessarily the right solution for other communities' and is looking at other approaches – an excellent example of adapting to failures.

Success and failure in development are often separated by subtle distinctions. Yunus lent money to farmers for raw materials and lost several months' income. Then he lent money to craftswomen for raw materials, inspired a global movement, and won a Nobel Prize. PlayPumps may work in townships but not villages; or perhaps they would work better linked to seesaws rather than merry-go-rounds. The challenge is to figure this out in a world where much of the cash is coming from foreign governments, millionaire musicians, and millions of well-meaning Westerners who have nothing to guide them except a few well-chosen words and photographs as they try to make the best use of their donations.

But there is another field in which its practitioners have been trying to help those in need for far longer. Like development experts, they struggle with complex problems that they barely understand, and like development experts they are capable of doing serious damage with the best of intentions. They are doctors.

3 'We shall see how many Funerals both of us shall have'

I don't recall it myself, but I am told that like most babies born in 1973, I slept face-down in my cot. This was the standard advice, made famous by Benjamin Spock in the 1950s. In the 1956 edition of his parenting bible *Baby and Child Care* he advised against putting a baby to sleep on its back: 'If he vomits he's more likely to choke on the vomitus . . . I think it is preferable to accustom a baby to sleeping on his stomach from the start.' *Baby and Child Care* was one of the bestselling books in history. Tens of millions of people read this pronouncement and countless others received it second-hand.

We now know that for many unlucky families, this well-meaning advice was fatal. Front-sleeping is rarely deadly – I survived it, after all, and most babies do. But because of this low overall death rate, it took years to work out the truth about putting babies to sleep face-down: it's dangerous, tripling the likelihood of cot death. Tens of thousands of babies died as a result of being placed to sleep on their tummies.

It would be unfair to blame Dr Spock himself for this, partly because he was only the most influential voice of many paediatricians who advised front-sleeping, but mostly because in 1956 the evidence was patchy either way. Paediatricians were hotly disputing the issue from the mid-1940s and it wasn't unreasonable for an expert such as Spock to make his best guess. But it took too long to review all the evidence systematically, which would have conclusively pointed to the dangers of front-sleeping as early as 1970. It was only in 1988 that new parents began to be advised that back-sleeping was best. The delay between 1970 and 1988 killed about 60,000 babies.

These days, doctors care about rigorous evidence, because they know that bad advice can kill, and good intentions save nobody. And doctors have also come to realise that selecting treatments based only on theory or conventional wisdom can be dangerous: rigorous evidence often overturns years of received practice.

The medical profession has come a long way since the seventeenth century, when a Belgian scientist called Jan Baptist van Helmont challenged the quacks of the day to prove that bloodletting and purging actually did any good. He proposed a fair trial, and was even prepared to wager 300 florins on the outcome:

> Let us take out of the Hospitals, out of the Camps, or from elsewhere, 200, or 500 poor People, that have Fevers, Pleurisies, etc. Let us divide them in Halfes, let us cast lots, that one half of them may fall to my share and the other to yours; I will cure them without bloodletting and sensible evacuation; but do you do as ye know ... we shall see how many Funerals both of us shall have.*

---

*Van Helmont's trial is not even the earliest recorded. Ben Goldacre points out that there is a clinical trial described in the Bible (Daniel 1:16).

History does not record whether anyone took van Helmont up on the bet, though as bloodletting continued for three further centuries, it seems that they did not. But more than a century later, the naval surgeon James Lind did conduct a careful trial – perhaps the first significant example of its kind. Lind wanted to find a decent treatment for scurvy, a nasty illness that leads first to spots and gum disease but then to open wounds, internal bleeding, and eventually, death. The disease, which still afflicts malnourished people around the world, was then especially common among sailors. Various cures had been proposed. The Admiralty, which commanded the Royal Navy, favoured vinegar. The Royal College of Physicians took a different view: in its expert opinion, sulphuric acid was just the tonic. Other suggestions included sea water, nutmeg, cider and citrus fruit.

In the spring of 1747, after eight weeks at sea on the warship *Salisbury*, Lind chose a dozen sailors out of the three dozen then suffering from scurvy. To make his test as fair as he could, he tried to pick men whose illness seemed to be at about the same stage. Then he divided them into six pairs and gave each pair a different treatment. The pair being given oranges and lemons made a good recovery; those taking cider, acid or brine did not fare so well. It was not a perfect randomised clinical trial by today's standards, but it did the job. Scurvy, we now know, is caused by lack of vitamin C, so oranges and lemons are a sensible treatment. Ships started to carry greater stores of them, and many sailors on subsequent voyages owed their lives to Lind's experiment.

Lind's trial highlights, however, some of the difficulties with collecting and reviewing evidence. For a start, if Lind had been tempted to rely on data collected by someone else for some other purpose – which is quicker and cheaper than organising a bespoke trial – he might have come unstuck. Good data are often just not available: we know from Lind's account that thirty or forty sailors suffered from scurvy and six men died during that voyage, but official records note only two illnesses. Sometimes there is no choice but to perform an experiment yourself.

Even with better data, the truth is not always apparent. For example, Lind had speculated that scurvy was connected with beer, because he noticed that scurvy often struck when a ship's supply of beer ran out. But this was coincidence: both were the result of a long voyage, but scurvy has nothing to do with a deficiency of beer. Correlation is a treacherous guide to causation.

There is, naturally, an ethical question over all this. Ten of Lind's twelve scurvy sufferers saw their illnesses deteriorate as they took salt water, sulphuric acid and various other substances that proved to be useless as cures for scurvy. When we really have no idea what the right treatment is, there is little downside here: with the possible exception of the pair taking sulphuric acid, the ten sick sailors would have been no worse off without Lind on board. But once we have a fairly strong suspicion of what the best treatment is, ethical problems arise. If someone had wanted to double-check Lind's result by repeating the experiment on another voyage, the scurvy-stricken sailors denied lemons and oranges to be fed vinegar or cider would have had cause to feel aggrieved.

The ethical agonising over such experiments continues today, but it is surprising that the scales remain heavily loaded against trials, even when there are two apparently equivalent treatments. A doctor who wants to run a properly controlled trial to test these two options needs approval from an ethics committee. A doctor who prescribes one or the other arbitrarily (there being no other basis for the decision), and who makes no special note of the results, needs to satisfy no higher authority. He's simply regarded as doing his job.

4 'You must stop the trial at once . . . '

Few people have railed against this double standard with more determination than Archie Cochrane, a remarkable Scottish epidemiologist who, when not battling fascism in the Spanish civil war, campaigned tirelessly for better standards of evidence in medicine. Cochrane complained of the 'God complex' of doctors who didn't need to carry out trials because they *knew* the correct course of treatment – even when some of their fellow doctors were issuing contradictory advice with equal confidence. The criticism Cochrane took from these doctors was often harsh, frequently unfair, and sheds light on some strong passions currently being aroused in debates about aid to the poor.

In the 1970s, Cochrane published an influential book entitled *Effectiveness and Efficiency*. He inspired the creation of the Cochrane Library, which today relies on the voluntary efforts of 28,000 medical researchers to gather together the best available evidence on effective treatments. But it was Archie Cochrane's very first clinical trial, carried out under desperate conditions in the Second World War, that remains one of his most telling achievements.

Cochrane, who spoke fluent German, was a prisoner of war in a German camp in Salonica when the prisoners were struck by a severe outbreak of pitting oedemas – a horrible swelling up of fluid under the skin in the legs. Not knowing what illness he was dealing with, and himself suffering terribly, Cochrane did not hold out much hope. Nonetheless he improvised a trial with the only two potential treatments at his disposal: his personal store of vitamin C tablets and some Marmite he had managed to buy on the black market. (Beloved of many Britons, Marmite is a tangy, salty spread that looks like crude oil and is made from yeast.) He had no idea if either would do any good. He divided twenty severe cases into two groups of ten, and after four days, eight out of ten in the Marmite group felt better; nobody in the vitamin C group did. Cochrane was not sure why the Marmite was helping, but he could see that it was. He meticulously graphed his data and took it to the Germans who ran the camp.

He was not optimistic that he would get much response. Relations between guards and prisoners had been very bad. Some of the guards were in the habit of shooting into the camp with the slightest pretext. One guard had recently tossed a grenade into the prisoners' latrine, packed with sick men, because he heard 'suspicious laughter'. Cochrane had been among those to clear away the horrific consequences.

But one young German doctor looked beyond the jaundiced, half-starved, swollen, flame-bearded Scot who stood before him, and studied the data. He was deeply impressed by the care of the clinical trial and the incontrovertible results. As Archie Cochrane returned to his room and wept with the hopelessness of it all, he did not know that the young German was insisting it would be a war crime not to take action, and demanding that generous supplies of yeast be delivered to the camp. They were, and the prisoners started to recover.

It was the beginning of a lifelong enthusiasm for rigorous evidence in medicine. But as he pushed for controlled experiments, Cochrane's motives were often misunderstood. On one occasion, he proposed a randomised trial to test the most effective way of punishing schoolboys for misbehaviour – a stern talking to, detention, or flogging with a cane. He couldn't persuade anyone to incorporate flogging schoolboys into a controlled experiment, and the idea does seem disturbing at first. Cochrane saw things differently: across the country schoolboys were caned daily anyway and Cochrane sincerely doubted that the beatings were effective deterrents. He wasn't hoping to prove that this brutality was a good idea; he suspected that he could discredit it by producing rigorous evidence that it did not work. (Incidentally, the other parts of the trial did go ahead: it turns out that verbal reprimands are more effective than detentions at preventing lateness.)

On another occasion, Cochrane had been trying to run a randomised trial on coronary care units in hospitals. He wondered whether they really did patients any good, compared with recuperating at home. Consultants in one city blocked the trial on 'ethical' grounds, but it went ahead in a different city. Noticing that his medical colleagues seemed to insist that he adhere to much higher moral standards than they did, he played an impish prank on them when reporting the early results. He showed them evidence that the home-care arm of the trial was leading to more deaths – not statistically significant yet, but a worrisome development.

'"Archie", they said, "we always thought you were unethical. You must stop the trial at once ..."' Archie Cochrane recalled. 'I let them have their say for some time.' Then Cochrane revealed that he had reversed the statistics. It was the coronary care units that were showing signs of being more dangerous, and the home care that was starting to look safer. Would the coronary consultants now clamour for their own units immediately to be closed? 'There was dead silence and I felt rather sick because they were, after all, my medical colleagues.'

It's easy to see why the idea of controlled experiments on coronary care patients might make people queasy. What Archie Cochrane had the courage to understand is that the alternative to controlled experiments is uncontrolled experiments. These are worse, because they teach us little or nothing.

Later in the war, after his impromptu trial with vitamin C and Marmite, Cochrane was interned at Elsterhorst, a hospital for prisoners of war. A young Russian soldier was brought to his ward late one night. The man was in an awful condition and was screaming incessantly; Cochrane took him into his own room because he didn't want him to wake the rest of the ward. But he felt he could do nothing for the man's pain, which he blamed on pleurisy, an agonising deterioration of his lungs and lung cavity.

'I had no morphia, just aspirin, which had no effect. I felt desperate. I knew very little Russian then and there was no one in the ward who did. I finally instinctively sat down on the bed and took him in my arms, and the screaming stopped almost at once. He died peacefully in my arms a few hours later. It was not the pleurisy that caused the screaming but loneliness. It was a wonderful education about the care of the dying.'

Archie Cochrane insisted on gathering evidence of what works rather than bowing to the 'God complex' claims of authority figures. That wasn't because he didn't care. It was because he did.

5 'If we don't know whether we are doing any good, then we are not any better than the medieval doctors and their leeches'

The idea of using randomised trials in foreign aid has a much shorter history than it does in medicine – not least because the history of foreign aid is itself a short one. (The World Bank made its first loan as recently as 1949 – to France.) But controlled experiments in international development have recently been taking off thanks to a group of young researchers, now dubbed the randomistas. 'If we don't know whether we are doing any good, then we are not any better than the medieval doctors and their leeches,' says Esther Duflo, a leading randomista. 'Sometimes the patient gets better, sometimes the patient dies. Is it the leeches? Is it something else? We don't know.'

A fascinating trio of experiments carried out in Kenya in the late 1990s show why randomised trials can be so useful in development. A Dutch charity, International Christelijk Steunfonds, funded a 'school assistance programme' for the Kenyan government in the Busia and Teso regions of Kenya. ICS paid for twenty-five schools to receive official government textbooks in English, Science and Maths. However, rather than simply choosing the twenty-five most deserving schools – or perhaps the twenty-five best-connected schools – ICS did something smarter, under the guidance of three randomistas: Harvard's Michael Kremer, Paul Glewwe of the University of Minnesota, and Sylvie Moulin of the World Bank. They chose twenty-five schools at random from a list of 100 deserving schools provided by the Kenyan government.

All the traditional statistical methods suggested that textbooks provide a big boost to kids' test scores. But like James Lind's hypothesis that scurvy is a disease caused by lack of beer, such a conclusion might well have been due to tricks of the data. Schools with textbooks may also have richer parents or better-connected teachers, which – if some of these factors were invisible to the statistician – would produce a spurious connection between textbooks and academic achievement.

Sure enough, when Glewwe, Kremer and Moulin analysed the randomised trial they found little evidence that textbooks were helpful, at least in this context. The very brightest children enjoyed some benefits, but most did not. Perhaps this was because the textbooks were aimed to suit the needs of the more privileged kids back in Nairobi, and were written in English, the third language of most of these poorer children.

Most development organisations would never have carried out such careful work. They would instead have pointed to the research which showed that textbooks looked promising, and produced glossy brochures explaining how many textbooks had been distributed. ICS actually bothered to ask whether the textbook programme was worth backing and discovered that it was not.

Rather than give up, or produce the glossy brochures anyway, ICS launched a second experiment in which teachers were given illustrated flip charts as visual aids to use in lessons. The flip charts covered science, health, mathematics, geography and agriculture, and provided a much more promising approach than textbooks: with bold graphics the flip charts offered something for students who could not read well, or who took in information in a visual way. Standard statistical methods also suggested that they would be a big success. ICS took a list of 178 schools and distributed flip charts to half of them, chosen at random. The flip charts flopped.

Undaunted, ICS funded a third experiment in Kenyan classrooms. This time, they provided the money for children to be treated for intestinal worms. This is not everyone's idea of education promotion, but – as with the flip charts and the text-books – there was a logic to the idea. Intestinal worms are parasites that cause malnourishment and stunted growth. Children are particularly prone to infection because – in villages where latrines are scarce – they often play barefoot in areas that other children have used as a bathroom. This time ICS phased in the worming treatments across seventy-five schools. The first twenty-five received treatment immediately, the next twenty-five after two years, and the final third another two years later. The programme was a huge success, boosting children's height, reducing re-infection rates, and also reducing absenteeism from school by a quarter. And it was cheap.

Even better, it was also cheap for ICS to make the deworming experiment rigorous. Lacking the cash to provide worming tablets to every Kenyan school in Busia and Teso, ICS was always going to have to roll the project out gradually. Simply ensuring that the gradual roll-out was done randomly created the perfect data for Michael Kremer and his colleague Edward Miguel to produce a fair test of whether the deworming project was a tremendous success or, like previous plausible-sounding projects, an unexpected disappointment.

Nevertheless, like Archie Cochrane's medical colleagues, some people are made deeply uneasy by this kind of thing. ICS and the randomistas were *experimenting* on people, indeed experimenting on children. Can that really be ethical? After all, if we have some reason to believe that some policy or treatment is beneficial, shouldn't we be giving it to everybody? And if we have no reason to believe that some policy or treatment or hand-out is beneficial, what on earth are we doing ramming it down the throats of vulnerable people?

One high-profile abstention from the randomised trial methodology is Jeffrey Sachs, a hugely influential development economist based at Columbia University. Sachs is the charismatic force behind the 'Millennium Development Villages', a pilot scheme designed to demonstrate a complex package of local aid interventions in agriculture, health, education and renewable energy, in over a dozen clusters of around 40,000 people, sprinkled across Africa. Sachs says this is necessary not only because poor people have many needs, but also because there will be 'important synergies'.

The effectiveness of this multi-faceted approach could in principle have been tested on a randomised basis, with some receiving the full package of interventions and others, chosen randomly, put into a control group. That is not the decision Jeffrey Sachs made. Sachs questions whether it is ethical to have control groups who are questioned and evaluated but receive nothing. 'It pains me to be in a village that doesn't have bed nets,' he told the *New York Times*.

Yet randomised trials don't usually work in that way. The control group need not be people who get nothing. It is far more common for a medical trial to compare a new drug against the best existing treatment. A randomised trial for the Millennium Villages could have compared the full package against an aid transfer of a similar cost (the sums are substantial), but in a much simpler form – the logical limit being to give the villagers the money to spend as they wished.

Everybody participating in such a trial would surely benefit, and the world would see whether the results were driven simply by the cash injection, or whether the expertly crafted, multi-faceted approach is essential, as Sachs claims. It is hard to see what is troubling about this, except to people who have convinced themselves – like Cochrane's 'God complex' colleagues – that they already know the answer.

All this matters because of the PlayPump problem: there is a strong incentive in development to focus on projects that look good and sound good. As Madeleine Bunting of the *Guardian* points out, 'Model villages of all kinds everywhere have always had an appeal to donors; at its crudest, they often look good. You can tidy up a place by concentrating resources. There's stuff to see. But the reality is that they have not proved sustainable.'

A recent example of that is China's SouthWest project. This was a village-level package of interventions supported by the World Bank in the 1990s. At the time, it seemed to be working brilliantly. Five years after the project ended, other villages in the region had caught up with the project villages: the benefits had been transient.

We cannot take the effectiveness of complex aid projects for granted, and for this reason evaluation experts such as Esther Duflo and Edward Miguel have criticised the evaluation of the Millennium Villages. They may be working brilliantly and they may not, but without a randomised trial it's going to be difficult to know.

It is disturbing to advocate flipping a coin to see who receives a fancy new programme. But the sad truth is that unlike Western clinical trials, which take place in an environment of relative plenty, randomised trials of development projects run against a backdrop of widespread deprivation. Most people will not get the help they need, whether the trial exists or not. In fact the very scarcity of development aid makes it easy to run informative trials: ICS dished out worming tablets to Kenyan school kids twenty-five schools at a time, not because they wanted to run an experiment but because there wasn't enough money to help everyone at once. The experiment simply made a virtue of necessity. Without ICS's willingness to experiment, of course, it might never have got around to giving any children the deworming pills in the first place. All the cash might have gone into foisting useless textbooks and flip charts onto more and more schools.

6 'Our kids were abducted, helicopters overhead, but we had a very nice Christmas'

The ethical objection to using randomised trials in international development is real, but looks puny compared to the objection to ploughing on with little knowledge of what works. But there's another powerful obstacle to the randomised trial approach. This is the existence of 'fundamentally unidentified questions', or as the econometrician Josh Angrist indelicately puts it, 'questions that are completely FUQed'. A FUQed question is one that cannot be answered by an experiment – for instance, the effect of carbon dioxide emissions on the world's climate. We can measure and calculate, extrapolate from our existing knowledge, but one thing we can't do is run a controlled experiment. We won't know exactly what our carbon dioxide emissions will do to the climate until they've already done it; even then we won't know for sure whether a different course of action would have had a different effect.

Some development experts argue that the randomistas' approach is fatally limited because too many questions in development are 'FUQed'. Poverty, they argue, has a complex mix of causes – corruption, oppression of women, lack of credit, broken social ties – which can be fixed only by a complex package of aid. The knot is simply too tangled to be picked apart by randomised trials.

Any social science researcher will ultimately come up against such questions. But many development questions that once appeared fundamentally unidentified have been succumbing to the remarkable ingenuity and ambition of researchers. The key to unpicking a tangled knot is known as an 'identification strategy' – how you identify what causes what. If crops grow better in the shade of a rook-infested tree, is that because they prosper from the shade or the bird droppings?* Econometricians, the statistical wing of the economics profession, ask each other 'What's your identification strategy?' in the same way that teenagers ask 'Did you get to second base?' While Steven Levitt is famous to a wider audience as the *Freakonomics* researcher

---

*This example comes from a celebrated article on the subject, Ed Leamer's 'Let's take the con out of econometrics', from the *American Economic Review*, 1983.

who did the research about the drug dealers and the sumo wrestlers, to other economists he is famous for the brilliance of his identification strategies. (The most famous looked at crime rates and the legalisation of abortion, assembling evidence by looking both at individual US states over time but also the changing relationship between states.) Yet the clearest identification strategy of all is a randomised trial, which hard-wires identification into the design of the experiment itself. And the randomistas are now carrying out experiments that would once have seemed impossible.

Corruption seems like an example of a 'FUQed' question. Everyone agrees that corruption significantly holds back development, but for obvious reasons it is hard to measure precisely how much public money – or aid money – ends up in somebody's back pocket. This is why corruption is typically measured indirectly, by asking visitors to a country whether they think it's corrupt or whether anyone demanded a bribe from them. In 2003, a young Harvard economist named Benjamin Olken organised an astonishingly ambitious experiment to directly measure how much money was being stolen from a large project – funded by the World Bank and the UK's Department for International Development – to build over 600 roads connecting remote Indonesian villages to the existing road network. It was a logical choice: road projects are especially notorious for being plagued by corruption, and among the world's emerging giants Indonesia is perceived to be one of the most corrupt.

Olken recruited a team of expert surveyors and engineers to check the roads. They took core samples to check the quality of materials used, estimated the local cost of labour and supplies, and handed him an estimate of the cost of building each and every road. From the World Bank, Olken obtained what the project's managers *claimed* to have spent on the road. The gap was an objective measure of corruption – a very rough measure, to be sure, but with over 600 separate roads Olken could be confident that the optimistic and pessimistic estimates were likely to cancel each other out. He also checked the accuracy of his engineering teams' estimates by getting them to estimate the costs of roads whose cost he already knew. Olken discovered that in a typical Indonesian village road project, over a quarter of the money was going missing.

Olken also wanted to figure out whether there was any cure for this endemic corruption. He experimented with two main approaches: top-down and bottom-up. In the top-down system, villagers were told that their project would certainly be audited by the government's anti-corruption watchdog, rather than the normal probability 1 in 25 chance of an audit. In the bottom-up approach, Olken's team organised village meetings in which everyone was invited to share their views on how road construction was going. In some of the bottom-up villages, the villagers were also given anonymous comment cards to express their concerns. (Most villagers could write.) Top-down and bottom-up villages were chosen randomly before any of the roads were built.

Perhaps surprisingly, the bottom-up approach was almost entirely useless, comments or no comments. Village meetings rarely took serious action to deal with corruption, perhaps because it was easy for crooks to steal something the villagers didn't much care about, materials, rather than something they did, wages. The top-down approach, on the other hand, was strikingly effective. It reduced missing expenditures by almost a third, making the project as a whole 8–9 per cent more efficient. Given the expense of road-building projects, this is well worth knowing about. Olken achieved something remarkable: a vast, rigorously evaluated and fair test of two plausible ways to fight graft.

(His result might sound unexpected: we've already seen that bottom-up often beats top-down, and we'll see even more powerful examples of that tendency later. But this is the point: the world is complicated. What works in the US Army may not work in a rural Javanese village. The lesson is to keep experimenting and adapting, because a single success may or may not replicate in other contexts.)

An equally ingenious identification strategy shed light on corruption in a quite different setting. Four randomistas, Marianne Bertrand, Simeon Djankov, Rema Hanna and Sendhil Mullainathan, approached Indians who were learning to drive: to some they offered cash bonuses if they passed their driving test, while others were given subsidised driving lessons. After the subjects had sat their tests, the researchers surprised them by sending them out for a drive with a second, independent examiner. The students who'd had subsidised driving lessons were less likely to have passed their tests, but more likely to be actually able to control a car. Somehow – and it's not hard to imagine how – the group given a cash bonus for obtaining a licence had managed to persuade government examiners to grant them licences despite not being able to drive.

Or consider another age-old debate: do moneylenders exploit or help the poor? The question seems imponderable, but economists Dean Karlan and Jonathan Zinman teased out an answer by persuading a South African consumer finance company to randomly grant loans to half the applicants who would otherwise have been narrowly rejected. Compared with the rejected half, the borrowers were more likely to be better off even after paying back a loan at interest rates (200 per cent APR) that are punitive by Western standards. By interviewing the borrowers, Karlan and Zinman figured out why: many had used the credit for one-off expenses that prevented them losing their jobs, like buying some smart new clothes or fixing the family moped.

There appear to be few limits to what the randomistas will attempt. Duflo and Hanna conducted a trial to deal with the problem of absentee teachers in rural India, showing that a solution was to send cameras with tamper-proof time stamps to half the schools. Pupils photographed the teacher with the class at the beginning and the end of each school day. Teacher absenteeism plummeted and the class test scores improved markedly.

Another experiment asked, How good are the investment opportunities available to small-scale entrepreneurs in Sri Lanka, opportunities that remain untapped for lack of funds? It seems a mysterious and elusive question to explore, but it was strikingly simple to produce a clear answer. The researchers found over 400 very small businesses – such as bicycle repairers or small stalls – and used a randomisation process to give $200 to some, $100 to others, and nothing at all to yet others. They concluded that the return on investment was about 6 per cent per month, which is almost 90 per cent a year.

Other randomistas have teamed up with a bank in the Philippines to help rural villagers save more – by sending text-message reminders. And randomly selected villagers in Rajasthan are enjoying plays with live music, puppets and a political message about female leadership. The question is whether attitudes to women improve in the villages which have seen the play. 'If it has a positive effect, it means we can educate people,' Esther Duflo has explained. 'It if has no effect, then it will be interesting, too, because then it will show that you have to get them to experience women in action.'

There are many other equally inventive examples, but few more ambitious than those being organised in war-ravaged countries by the political scientist Macartan Humphreys and his colleagues.

Liberia is one such country: a place with a hopeful name and a hateful history. Founded by former American slaves in the first half of the nineteenth century on the southern edge of Africa's western bulge, Liberia now is mired in desperate poverty – Liberians have one sixth the paltry income that is the average for sub-Saharan Africa – and slowly recovering from a particularly vicious pair of civil wars. When former rebel-turned-president Charles Taylor stood trial for war crimes in The Hague, his former lieutenant 'ZigZag' Marzah accused him of ordering outrageous acts such as eating the organs of enemies 'with salt and pepper', or cutting open pregnant women. Five years after hostilities ended, a quarter of Liberians still considered themselves displaced from their homes. In Lofa County in Northern Liberia, fully 85 per cent of people had fled from their villages at least once; one in ten people were killed or injured during the civil wars, and one in twenty were combatants, many forced to fight against their will.

How can communities such as those in Lofa, which have been ripped apart by war, be stitched back together? An approach called community-driven reconstruction (CDR) is increasingly popular in development circles; the World Bank alone is estimated to have lent over $2 billion for CDR in 2003, the year the last Liberian civil war ended, and CDR is touted as the only way to make development work in places like Afghanistan. The idea is simple enough: a development charity first engages with a community to solicit cooperation, then gives the community substantial grants to which one simple set of conditions is attached – a council must be democratically elected by the community to decide on how the money is spent. In theory, this ensures that locals will make informed decisions about their needs and be able to keep a close eye on corruption; it should not only regenerate the local economy but above all rebuild community spirit by giving people an incentive to participate in decision-making. If communities can't demonstrate some ability to come together, they'll miss out on the money. And it encourages institutions to grow from the bottom up, not the top down.

The policy is plausible and fashionable, but so were many other policies that didn't work out so well. So can these CDR projects promote good will, or are they just another development fad that will be dropped again in due course? It sounds much too nebulous a question to be answered by anything other than anecdote and guesswork. But Macartan Humphreys, with his colleagues James Fearon and Jeremy Weinstein, has devised an experiment to produce a more rigorous answer.

The three researchers teamed up with International Rescue Committee, a major development charity which was running community-driven projects in Liberia funded by DFID, the UK aid agency. They persuaded IRC to randomly allocate their scarce funds through a lottery at which local chiefs of equally deserving communities were represented. If the winning villagers first set up a 'community development council' with elected members, IRC gave them grants that could reach up to $17,000 – one hundred times the annual income of an average Liberian. (This was some incentive. In a rich country, a project of one hundred times the average person's annual income would be in the range of $2 million to $5 million.)

With randomly chosen communities getting the grants – and a control group to compare them with – Fearon, Humphreys and Weinstein then needed a way of measuring whether the project had made any difference. They recruited a team of local Liberian researchers, entirely separate from the IRC operation, to carry out the kind of game theory experiment one might expect in the research labs of MIT. They chose, at random, twenty-four people from each village, a total of almost 2000 individuals across Lofa County. Each person was offered a choice; they could have 5 dollars for themselves (actually three 100 Liberian dollar notes, a good week's wages) or could contribute some or all of that money to the community – and for every dollar they decided to give up, the community would receive either twice or five times as much. Individuals were given an envelope that they could hand back to the research team, without anyone seeing whether or not any of the banknotes were inside. It was a test of how self-sacrificing, community-minded and cooperative people were. And it was meaningful: researchers into aid effectiveness often find that villagers quickly learn to say whatever it is the donors want to hear, but in this case, acting cooperatively would cost a week's income, so it was a sign of more than just pandering to donors.

Macartan Humphreys is a chatty Irishman with a rainbow of academic credentials: the top prize in Oxford's intensive master's degree in economics, a PhD in Government from Harvard, plus qualifications in history and politics from Dublin and Lille.

When I spoke to him about this experiment, he was very impressed with IRC's willingness to learn. 'Increasingly when organisations approach you, it's because they're under pressure from donors to prove that they can do the job', he explained. 'IRC is an honourable exception. They really wanted to improve the way they worked.'

But Humphreys was also frankly sceptical that the IRC project would have much effect. He had a pleasant surprise in store: the community development projects actually changed the way people acted towards their community. In the communities which had received no IRC money, there was still an impressive show of community spirit: over 60 per cent of these very poor individuals gave up everything they had been offered so that their community could benefit. (War-torn they may be, but not lacking in generosity and solidarity.) But in the villages which had experienced setting up an elected council to spend the IRC's grant, that figure rose to above 70 per cent. This improvement in cooperation was statistically robust and big enough to be important. It was good news for proponents of community-driven reconstruction: the IRC project seemed to be working.

Humphreys is now embarking on even more ambitious research with IRC in the Democratic Republic of Congo. This is currently requiring teams of brave and dedicated local researchers to visit the remote villages in Eastern Congo that will be randomly assigned to receive, or not, another IRC community development project. First they must locate the villages, which is no easy task: the researchers have four separate and largely inconsistent lists of where the villages might be, sometimes on the other side of a river they need to bridge, or a shoulder-high swamp they need to spend a day wading through. And all this in a country termed the 'rape capital of the world' by senior UN official Margot Wallstrom, where around 5 million people are thought to have died in a war that sucked in most of Congo's neighbours and ended only in 2003.

'There are hot areas,' says Humphreys, which is something of an understatement. People get killed a lot in Congo, and sometimes they get killed in villages which have received money. That will be something to investigate as the surveys and field experiments continue. But 'People get very excited simply because at last they have a voice. We'll receive comments like, "Our kids were abducted, helicopters overhead, but we had a very nice Christmas."'

Such experiments are enormously ambitious and very important. But the Congolese experiment is particularly amazing. Even without the difficulties of operating in the heart of Africa, it is a controlled experiment on a colossal scale. Almost 2 million people live in communities that will receive grants, another 2 million in communities that will not. Archie Cochrane had far more modest proposals 'laughed out of court', such as comparing two philosophies for medical schooling by randomly assigning students to universities in nearby British cities. If Cochrane were alive today, even he might be amazed by the projects the randomistas are now managing to launch.

7 'We should not try to design a better world. We should make better feedback loops'

Looking at the US Army's adaptation in Iraq, and the development of vital innovations such as Mitchell's Spitfire, Capecchi's knockout genes, and Harrison's clock, we've put a great deal of emphasis on creating space for new ideas to emerge – for 'variation'. But adapting also requires selection, the winnowing out of bad approaches from good ones.

The selection problem – answering the question 'What works?' – is ever present in a complex world. Nowhere is this more true than in development, where much money is spent by well-meaning outsiders as far from the 'worm's-eye view' as anyone can imagine. Doctors persisted with bloodletting for three hundred years after Van Helmont challenged them to prove that their technique worked. In the business of development aid, there are even more lives at stake, and the feedback between the ultimate recipients of aid and the ultimate donors is extremely weak. There are many ways to experiment and pick out successes, and a randomised trial is one of the most powerful tools available.*

Yet randomised trials only take us part of the way. When we know what ideas work, we still have to ensure those ideas are taken up more widely. In many other walks of life this isn't a problem. If one café is offering a better combination of service, range of food, prices, décor, coffee blend, and so on, then more customers will congregate there than at the café next door – which will inevitably end up either copying the techniques of the rival, or closing down and seeing the rival take over its premises.

When we get into public services, it's not so straightforward. The development expert Owen Barder – once an adviser to the British Prime Minister of the day, Tony Blair – points out that while a market provides a short, strong feedback loop, in public services the feedback loop is longer and looser. If parents don't like the local school, they can complain to local politicians, or lobby the headmaster directly. They can also move to a different school, but this act has fewer direct consequences for the school than for a café.

In development aid, the feedback loops are longer still, and very fragile. Whereas in a school the taxpayers paying for the school are much the same people as the parents relying on it, in development aid the taxpayers and charitable donors providing the money will probably never meet the beneficiaries. If the aid project is misfiring for any reason, it's hard for the intended

---

* Randomisation is not the only way to create a controlled trial. It may sometimes be better to vary treatment and control groups systematically rather than randomly. In using 'randomised trial' to stand for any carefully controlled trial, I am speaking loosely and I hope the technically-minded will excuse me.

beneficiaries to complain up a long chain of intermediaries – the PlayPump problem. And as long as some benefit is getting through, the beneficiaries have little reason to object, for fear the project will be halted entirely – even if much of the money is being wasted or stolen. Owen Barder concludes that if development aid is to adapt and evolve, 'We should not try to design a better world. We should make better feedback loops.'

Jakob Svensson, a development economist at the University of Stockholm, has been examining such feedback loops for years in Uganda. In one influential study with Ritva Reinikka of the World Bank, he investigated a cash grant programme for schools: the Ugandan government provided a grant to schools on a per-pupil basis, but Reinikka and Svensson discovered that 80 per cent of the money was going missing somewhere between the central government and the classroom, typically because local officials were stealing it.

When the scale of the theft became clear, the Ugandan government responded with a quite brilliant experiment: it began to publish details in two newspapers of exactly how much money was being sent to each school, each month. Quickly, the situation began to change. Armed with information about the money that should have arrived, parents began to complain vociferously. Within six years, the percentage of grants making it through to the school itself had risen from 20 per cent to 80 per cent. The newspaper campaign seems to be largely responsible: although Reinikka and Svensson couldn't conduct a randomised trial, they were able to show that the schools where parents had the best access to newspapers were also those that showed the largest fall in theft.

A second Svensson investigation, with Martina Björkman, used a randomised trial to study the introduction of community monitoring in Ugandan clinics. As with Benjamin Olken's study of Indonesian road building, Björkman and Svensson organised a way for local communities to report back on whether they were getting decent healthcare from these clinics. But they got a different result. In this context, community monitoring was very effective, probably because anyone knows whether the doctor has shown up for work or not. (Olken's stolen construction materials were harder to spot.) Clinics were cleaner, far fewer doctors and nurses skipped work, and fewer medicines were stolen. Most notably, vaccination rates rose by almost a half, and one third fewer young children died in the areas where community monitoring had been introduced. These are dramatically effective results. Feedback matters, and if we can improve feedback loops in development, we can create much stronger incentives for development aid to improve, evolve and adapt.

8 Explorations in 'product space'

But while foreign aid should be tested more often through randomised trials, and improved through more robust feedback from the people who are supposed to benefit, there is a larger question looming. The economic processes now taking place in China and India, or which previously industrialised Korea and Japan, Europe and North America, seem far more complex and wide-ranging even than the most ambitious foreign aid projects can stimulate.

Perhaps they are not. Many economists believe that small steps are enough, if a country takes enough of them in the right direction. In a lecture of 1755, Adam Smith declared that 'little else is requisite to carry a state to the highest degree of opulence from the lowest barbarism but peace, easy taxes and a tolerable administration of justice: all the rest being brought about by the natural order of things.' In other words, if the government can just get the basics right, everything else will gradually follow in time, and foreign aid can help – if only it is properly tested.

But what was true in 1755 may not be true today. Imagine an executive from the web-retailer Amazon considering whether to set up a subsidiary in a new country. She would ask focused questions about what kind of economy it was: How many people have credit cards? How many have internet connections? Do postal workers routinely steal the mail? Do people even have meaningful street addresses? With the right set of economic building blocks, the Amazon business model is feasible. Otherwise, it is not. And worse, if several building blocks are missing, there may be no straightforward political mechanism for providing them. If a single regulation was blocking its entry into a new market, Amazon might make representations to the government. But if there were half a dozen diverse problems, the company would probably just shrug and look elsewhere.

If this is true not just for web-retailing but for many different industries, some poor countries may be stuck in a trap: there may be no gradual progression from what they do now to what they need to do to be rich. Government or donors may need to step in and coordinate progress – a 'big push', in the development jargon, simultaneously fixing the mail, the banking system and the internet infrastructure, or enabling private firms to do so in concert. How can that gigantic coordinating effort ever be subject to the forces of trial and error?

But we're getting ahead of ourselves. Before asking how a suitably 'experimental' big push could be possible, we should first ask whether it is necessary. It is perfectly possible that each of these economic building blocks could develop gradually, and separately, without government help. The answer to whether a big push is needed comes from an unexpected source: a young physicist fascinated by the nature of connections.

César Hidalgo has never studied economics, but he knows more about how economies develop than most economists. Hidalgo is a curious character: a physicist whose computer-generated networks have been exhibited as art.

'While it is trivial that everything is connected,' he says, 'the structure and nature of connected systems is not trivial.' Hidalgo's art creates visual representations of medical records, cell-phone calls, migration – and even the expression of genes in nematode worms. 'All of them are spin-offs of figures produced for scientific publications,' he adds. Hidalgo's long hair and goatee beard are practically standard issue for a physicist under the age of thirty, but in other ways he has broken the mould. Teaming up with the economists Ricardo Hausmann and Bailey Klinger, and the great network physicist Albert-László Barabási, Hidalgo has been producing remarkable and revealing ways of visualising the process of economic development.

The groundwork was laid by the National Bureau of Economic Research, which has broken down each country's exports into 775 distinct products such as: 'Meat of bovine animals, frozen' and 'Fans and cooker hoods incorporating a fan'. Exports are a meaningful measure, because if you export a product it means someone else is willing to pay for it. Ricardo Hausmann and Bailey Klinger then used that data to map the 'product space' of every country in the world, estimating how similar each product is to each other product. The idea is that if every major apple exporter also exports pears, and every major pear exporter also exports apples, then the data are demonstrating apples and pears to be similar. Presumably, both economies would have fertile soil, agronomists, refrigerated packing plants, and ports.

Then César Hidalgo and Albert-László Barabási stepped in to turn the Hausmann-Klinger data into a map of the relationships between different products, not geographically but in an abstract economic space. Apples and pears appear close together on the product map because many countries export both products and many countries export neither. Oil production is a long way away from anything else in the abstract product space, because whether a country exports oil tells you very little about what else it might export.

César Hidalgo was responsible for producing the visualisation itself. His maps of product space look at first glance a little like a Jackson Pollock painting, with a web of lines connecting a scattering of large and small blobs, with blobs of the same colour clustered together as if by the flick of the artist's wrist. These clusters actually indicate large subsets of product space, such as textiles, vehicles or fruit; the blobs are more specific products.

The researchers weren't just interested in the product space for its own sake but for what it showed them about the capabilities of countries. Hidalgo uses a mathematical trick that he calls 'the method of reflections' to infer capabilities from the space of products by programming a computer to circle backwards and forwards between the products and the countries that make them.

Hidalgo starts by observing that some products are ubiquitous: many countries make them and so presumably they are not especially challenging to produce. Countries that export *only* ubiquitous products, such as socks, can be presumed to lack many complex capabilities. Countries that also export products that are made by few others, such as helicopter components or memory chips, probably have more sophisticated capabilities. The method of reflections then carries that information back to the product space: products produced in simple economies tend to be simple products, while those produced only in sophisticated economies are likely to be sophisticated products. It sounds like circular reasoning, but it isn't: a particular product (say, gold) might at first seem sophisticated because only a select list of countries produce it, but as the mathematical process bounced back and forth between products and economies, it would become clear that there's no correlation between being a sophisticated economy and being a gold producer.

The method of reflections eventually converges on a list of simpler and more complex products, and a ranking of the simpler and more complex economies that produce them. Economic sophistication is closely related to income, but not exactly so. Some countries have more sophisticated capacities than income, suggesting they have 'room to grow'. An example, from data collected in 2000, is South Korea: the world's eighteenth most sophisticated economy, but not yet quite as rich as that sophistication would suggest it could become. China and India also have plenty of room to grow. Conversely, there are relatively rich but simple economies, which are in a less sustainable position. Intriguingly, they include Greece and the United Arab Emirates, home to Dubai.

Because Hidalgo's beautiful network maps show how economies develop in a way that no researcher has previously been able to see, they provide new insight into the way that economies grow. By highlighting the products a particular country exports on the universal product map, Hidalgo shows each economy in this network of products. Rich countries have larger and more diversified economies, and produce lots of products – especially products close to the densely connected heart of the network. East Asian 'tiger' economies look very different, with their more recent spurts of growth illustrated by big clusters around textiles and electronics manufacturing, and – contrary to the hype – not much activity in the products produced by the richest countries. African countries tend to produce a few scattered products with no great similarity to any others. And that could be a big problem.

The network maps show that economies tend to develop through closely related products. Colombia is an example of a country that already makes products that are well connected on the network. That suggests that if Colombia could achieve peace, easy taxes and justice, then wealth would follow just as Adam Smith promised, because there are plenty of opportunities for private firms to pursue. A contrasting example is South Africa. Many of its current exports – diamonds, for example – are not very similar to anything. If South Africa is to develop new products, it will mean making a big leap in this abstract product space.

The data suggest that such leaps are uncommon: as Hidalgo clicks through product-map images on his laptop, he reveals that economies tend to evolve by spreading from one cluster to a nearby cluster. For some countries, the necessary leaps across product space may be simply too far without some kind of big push.

It is possible to find examples where governments have launched very successful forays across product space. In 1982, Chile's government sponsored an effort to learn more about salmon farming and attract the best international companies to Chilean waters; over the next twenty-five years, Chile's salmon industry grew tenfold – with domestic firms also growing strongly – and it became the world's largest salmon exporter bar Norway. (This growth may have been too fast – in 2007 Chile's progress was set back by an outbreak of disease, blamed by some on lax standards.) Taiwan's government identified orchids as a possible crop for some of the agricultural land previously devoted to sugar – a smarter response to the cheapness of Brazilian sugar than slapping a trade tariff on it, as the EU and US did. They built the infrastructure – packing areas, electricity hook-ups, roads, an exhibition hall and even a genetics laboratory – and invited private firms to show up and plug into it. Taiwan is now the world's largest orchid exporter.

But there is a real dilemma here. The lesson of Hidalgo's research is that a big push from government may sometimes be necessary. The experience of the Chilean salmon and Taiwanese orchid industry shows that the big push can also be effective. But the broader record of governmental attempts to steer the economy has often been catastrophic in countries with corrupt or dictatorial governments – and unimpressive even under wealthy democratic governments. For example, a government-backed venture capital fund in Denmark, designed to back exciting new businesses, lost 60 per cent of its value in short order. A regional development fund in the UK was an even more spectacular failure, somehow contriving to lose 94 per cent. The British average for such regional funds was a negative return of 15 per cent; across Europe, minus 0.4 per cent. Silicon Valley venture capitalists need lose little sleep.

The problem seems to be that governments love to back

losers: think about the big banks or car companies. The ideal candidate to receive government support seems to be a company that is very big and very unsuccessful. This is the perfect formula for sustained failure. Perhaps that is why historically, 'big-push' policies have often been ham-fisted – a shove off a cliff rather than a launch into orbit.

Yet if the gap from simple products to complex products is too wide to cross in small steps, what are policy makers to do? Somehow governments have to harness the resources and the patience that only they can access, without blundering in with crude white elephant projects. And that means finding a new tool of selecting policies that work, a tool which operates on a larger scale than anything the randomistas can provide.

9 'A formula for creating order out of chaos and prosperity amid backwardness'

Lübeck is now a small city on the north coast of Germany, but in 1158 it was little more than a castle on a pirate-infested coast. Henry the Lion, one of the local rulers, conquered the place, took over the castle, executed the local pirate chief, and began to turn Lübeck into the richest town in northern Europe. His method was simple: he established a different set of rules which would apply only in Lübeck. Would-be citizens were offered a charter of 'most honourable civic rights', feudal rulers were kicked out and replaced with a local council, an independent mint guaranteed sound money, excessive taxes were prohibited and a free-trade area was arranged from which Lübeck's traders could reach cities such as Münster, Magdeburg, Nuremberg and even Vienna. Henry then put out the word across northern Europe that commercially-savvy immigrants would be welcomed with open arms. They flocked to answer the call and Lübeck became the Hong Kong or Shanghai of its day – a sudden and astonishing success. The Holy Roman Emperor himself, Charles IV, rated Lübeck as one of the five 'glories of the Empire' alongside Rome, Pisa, Venice and Florence.

Lübeck was widely copied. City after city along the Baltic coast adopted some variant of Henry's charter, and ushered in an age of prosperity. Lübeck became the capital of the Hanseatic League, an alliance that ultimately numbered 200 cities and lasted into the seventeenth century. (Lübeck itself retained some independence into the twentieth century: the town senate refused to allow Adolf Hitler to campaign there in 1932. He took his revenge by turning it into an administrative suburb of Hamburg.)

With the world fast urbanising, perhaps the time has come to copy Lübeck again. As the journalist Sebastian Mallaby points out, Henry's project for Lübeck was 'a bit like trying to build a new Chicago in modern Congo or Iraq' – and that is pretty much what the economist Paul Romer now wants to do. Romer is the founder of the 'charter cities' movement, and he argues that the world needs entirely new cities with their own infrastructure and, in particular, their own rules on democracy, taxes and corporate governance. These cities, like Lübeck, would be governed by a set of rules designed to attract ambitious people. According to Mallaby, Lübeck represented 'a formula for creating order out of chaos and prosperity amid backwardness' in the Middle Ages. It is just such a formula that Paul Romer is now promoting.

There is plenty of evidence that charter cities could work in today's world. There's Singapore, long a successful independent city state off the coast of Malaysia; Hong Kong, for many years a British enclave on the South China Sea; more recently, Shenzhen, thirty years ago a fishing village not far from Hong Kong, now a city to rival Hong Kong itself after being designated China's first 'special economic zone'. Beyond South-East Asia, Dubai has proved – property bubble notwithstanding – that one can build a successful city anywhere. What all four cities have in common with Lübeck, along with their coastal settings, is that they have been governed by different rules from surrounding areas.

So we know that independent city states can survive and prosper in a globalised economy. We know it is physically possible to put together impressive infrastructure in a short space of time. We know that urbanisation is good for the planet (because it promotes compact living, smaller dwellings and the use of public transport), and that it is happening anyway. In other words, new city states with some degree of autonomy are economically, architecturally, environmentally and socially feasible.

But Romer has pushed the charter city concept to its limit by suggesting that the cities could be run by foreign countries. In one of his more fanciful examples, Cuba, the USA and Canada agree to transfer Guantanamo Bay to the Canadians, who establish a Hong Kong in the Caribbean: the Cubans gain a gateway to twenty-first-century capitalism; the Americans rid themselves of a public-relations problem; the Canadians gain influence and wealth. Economically this is plausible. Politically it is almost inconceivable.

Romer is not short of self-confidence: a brilliant and influential scholar of economic growth, he walked away from research to make a small fortune as an internet entrepreneur, before turning down the job of Chief Economist of the World Bank to evangelise for the idea of charter cities. But is his extreme version of the charter city idea necessary? Romer thinks so: he argues that foreign ownership could be a way for shaky governments to import credibility, in much the same way that democratically elected politicians sometimes hand control of interest rates to technocrats at the central bank, or cede some sovereignty to international institutions.

But perhaps that puts too much emphasis on the problem of credibility. After all, Lübeck – Sebastian Mallaby's example of the original charter city – was an entirely domestic affair: Henry the Lion didn't need to sign a treaty with the Pope or Henry II of England or anyone else. He just made a promise to prospective citizens, and that seemed to be enough.

Charter cities have an entirely different appeal, which Henry the Lion captured perfectly with Lübeck: they allow both variation and selection on a grand scale. The variation emerges because charter cities are zones in which the tariffs, laws and taxes are different from those in the rest of the country. This has nothing to do with foreign ownership as such. Shenzhen, for example, is an entirely Chinese affair, but the rules in Shenzhen have been different from the rules elsewhere in China.

Consider New Songdo City, a modest metropolis about the size of mid-town Manhattan that is being constructed from scratch on a landfill island about 40 miles away from Seoul in South Korea. The city is a for-profit project supported by the South Korean authorities but funded and managed by South Korea's POSCO, perhaps the world's most successful steel firm, and the US developer Gale. It boasts South Korea's tallest skyscraper, a Jack Nicklaus-designed golf course, canals (a Venetian inspiration), luxury networked apartments, digital infrastructure exclusively supplied by Cisco, and plenty of green space. It is due to be finished sometime around 2015.

What is really intriguing about New Songdo is not the blank-canvas architecture – this has often proved dysfunctional in the past – but that New Songdo exists in a legal and regulatory bubble. It's a free economic zone with less restrictive labour laws than the rest of South Korea and more attractive regulations for foreign corporations, such as the right to file official documents in English. The infrastructure is just the groundwork: New Songdo will live or die by its ability to act as a scaffolding for entrepreneurs. South Korean officials privately admit that reforming the country's regulations is a difficult process, but setting up a small city where simpler regulations apply is an easy way to try them out.

Shenzhen and New Songdo could be regarded as gigantic Skunk Works: just as Reginald Mitchell, Burt Rutan and Mario Capecchi needed protecting from the mainstream in order to develop their innovations, sometimes a city economy needs to be protected from its host country's own entrenched policies.

Charter cities, then, offer the ability to adapt on a promising scale: they are experiments which are big enough to make a difference, but small enough that dozens or hundreds can exist in parallel. As such, they offer a response to the development dilemma, which is that big pushes almost always fail, while small steps may not be enough.

There is a second key component to the charter idea: not only variation, but also selection. Henry the Lion set up his charter and threw open the doors to anyone who wished to come to Lübeck (none of the compulsion of Magnitogorsk, almost eight hundred years later). The same could be true of twenty-first-century charter cities: governments would establish the city and see if any of their citizens actually wanted to live and work under the new rules. It's the ultimate selection mechanism: if a city's rules, institutions and physical infrastructure can be designed so as to offer citizens a decent quality of life, freedom from the fear of crime, and the chance of a good income, then the cities will attract the people they need to prosper.

Charter cities are certainly a bold leap, but surprisingly, they satisfy the conditions for adapting. They allow new approaches to be tested out. They are on a small enough scale that if some cities flop, and fail to attract citizens or businesses, that failure is survivable. And there is a built-in mechanism for distinguishing the successes from the failures: ordinary people, voting with their feet. This final idea is, sadly, something which has been entirely missing from most development initiatives for the past sixty years.

But harnessing the power of ordinary people as a selection mechanism isn't limited to the idea of charter cities. It could also be an answer to one of the greatest global challenges of all: the challenge of climate change.

Five

Climate change or: Changing the rules for success

'I think we're going to find, with climate change and everything else – things like global warming and goodness knows what else and the cost of fuel for a start – that things are going to become very complicated.'

– Prince Charles

'Evolution is cleverer than you are.'

– Leslie Orgel

1 The Greenhouse Effect, 1859

John Tyndall had a problem. A dazzling lecturer at London's Royal Institution in its Victorian glory days, the extravagantly sideburned Irish scientist was a skilled experimenter who was famous for his public demonstrations of scientific principles using the latest technical equipment. (Tyndall had studied under Robert Bunsen, the inventor of the eponymous burner.) In 1859 his new experiment involved a vacuum pump, a long brass tube plugged with rock salt at either end, and a sensitive thermometer called a *thermomultiplicateur*.

Tyndall's aim was to solve a puzzle posed by the French scientist

Joseph Fourier three decades earlier. Fourier had calculated how much energy reached Earth from the sun, and how much was radiated into space by the Earth. The hotter the Earth, the more radiation would be given off, and Fourier had expected that Earth's radiation would balance the heat absorbed from the sun at a temperature of about 15°C (60°F). Fourier was in for a shock, because according to his careful calculations, the actual energy balance implied that the average temperature of the planet should be *minus* 15°C (5°F). In short, the planet should be a giant snowball.

Tyndall reckoned that the answer to this puzzle was that the Earth's atmosphere must be trapping heat like a greenhouse, and he decided to measure the effect. First he pumped air out of his brass tube and pointed his *thermomultiplicateur* through it, discovering, as he expected, that a vacuum absorbed no radiated heat. Then he added a mix of oxygen and nitrogen, the two gases that together make up over 99 per cent of the planet's atmosphere. And there his problem began – because oxygen and nitrogen do not absorb much radiated heat either. The atmosphere didn't seem to function as a greenhouse after all. So what was going on?

One of Tyndall's obsessions was the purity of air. (Another of his experiments included purifying air by coating the inside of a container with sticky glycerine. After a few days, impurities in the air had stuck to the glycerine, and the circulating air was now so pure that food would not decay inside the container, even after months. He also devised a way of measuring impurities in air by observing the way a bright light scattered as it passed through.) In this case, however, it was the very purity of Tyndall's air that was the problem, because Earth's atmosphere contains traces of other gases than oxygen and nitrogen. It is about 0.4 per cent water vapour and 0.04 per cent carbon dioxide, along with argon and some other trace gases. Tyndall guessed that these impurities, insignificant as they seemed, might be making the difference. He added a tiny amount of water vapour, methane and carbon dioxide into his tube, and suddenly the radiated heat was absorbed.

Tyndall was surprised because the effect was so large; despite the minute presence of water vapour and carbon dioxide, the tube was absorbing many times more radiated heat. He wrote, 'comparing a single atom of oxygen or nitrogen with a single atom of aqueous vapour, we may infer that the action of the latter is 16,000 times that of the former. This was a very astonishing result, and it naturally excited opposition.'

John Tyndall had discovered the greenhouse effect.

A century and a half later, the effect is not in serious doubt. What is up for dispute is how much we should care and what we should do. The first part of that question, as we saw in the last chapter, is 'fundamentally unidentified' or 'FUQed' – it simply can't be resolved by another lab experiment like Tyndall's. There are many complications: clouds may form in a warmer atmosphere, reflecting more heat; but white ice will melt, reflecting less; but when Arctic tundra melts and rots, it can release methane, a powerful greenhouse gas. Because of these feedback loops, some of which should dampen the effect while others are likely to increase it, the likely outcomes are uncertain. Some disastrous outcomes are plausible.

We know that the pre-industrial concentration of carbon dioxide was 280 parts per million (0.028 per cent); it's now around 390 ppm, and international negotiators are paying lip service to the idea of keeping the concentration below 450 ppm. But we don't know what level spells disaster. Some climate scientists reckon 450 ppm is far too high. There are a small minority who are far more relaxed: Richard Lindzen, a contrarian meteorologist at MIT, reckons that atmospheric concentrations of carbon dioxide could safely rise past 10,000 ppm. The large uncertainty is an argument for action rather than inaction: it's the very uncertainty that makes catastrophe possible.

This chapter asks a different question: What is to be done? Our journey will involve an apparent paradox: the problem of tackling climate change is far more complicated than we tend to think, and failing to appreciate that complexity is precisely what holds us back from pushing ahead with a relatively straightforward solution.

2 'It couldn't be simpler!'

This seeming paradox deceives many climate-change activists. A couple of years ago, after briefly addressing a convocation of environmental policy gurus, I was buttonholed by a climate-change activist who was almost speechless with rage. How could I say that dealing with climate change was complicated? 'It couldn't be simpler!' he declared, and he started reeling off statistics – about the population of the planet, its 'carrying capacity', ice melting at the north pole – that proved he had both mastered his subject matter and missed the point. He was determined to convince me that climate change was very important. He had confused the importance of the problem with the simplicity of the solution.

In much the same way, a great deal of the discussion on climate change confuses targets with policies. Climate-change negotiators discuss whether countries should commit to reducing emissions of greenhouse gases such as methane and carbon dioxide by 10 or 15 or 20 per cent. Activists demand much bigger cuts, and many scientists think they are right. Yet debating whether the targets should be 15 per cent or 50 per cent or 80 per cent makes the problem sound like one of sheer willpower, and sheer willpower is not nearly enough. We must also figure out how these targets are to be met. Even with modest reductions in greenhouse gases, what is being prescribed is a wholesale reorganisation of the economy that surrounds us every day. There are almost 7 billion people on the planet, many of whom make many dozens of daily choices that affect greenhouse gas emissions. An appreciable reduction in greenhouse gases is going to require billions of individual decisions every day across the world, billions of human actions each hour, to change. 'It couldn't be simpler!' Really?

Any answer is going to come either because individuals voluntarily change their behaviour, or because governments change the rules. Activists often point at big corporations, too. Certainly, some businesses have powerful lobbies that have successfully stymied government action on climate change. But that is still politics, rather than the everyday activity of business. There should be no confusion as to where the main responsibility for action lies. We drive cars not because ExxonMobil tell us to, but because we find cars convenient and vote out any politician who does too much to impinge on that convenience. Change will come either from the governments we elect, or through each of us voluntarily changing our ways.

Could individual voluntarism save the planet? It seems like a simple matter of willpower: we know what we must do and our challenge is to do it. This, at least, sounds like it couldn't be simpler. We shall see.

3 A day in the life of a born-again environmentalist

It's not every day that a film changes your life; especially not a film that is largely a PowerPoint presentation. But that is what has just happened to Geoff. Geoff is a straightforward kind of fellow: twenty-six, single, lives in London, works in an insurance office and until twelve hours ago, had very little interest in climate change. Last night, Geoff agreed to let a crush on his friend's new flatmate, Jude, influence his judgement. Jude is a tree-hugging environmentalist – albeit a very cute one – and she showed Geoff Al Gore's documentary *An Inconvenient Truth*. And this morning – having slept fitfully, amid dreams that he had set up home with Jude but the crumbling Antarctic ice sheet was about to submerge it in a terrifying wall of water – is the first day of the rest of his life: A life as a born-again environmentalist.

Geoff starts his day, as he always does, by filling the kettle for a coffee. But then he remembers that the kettle is an energy-guzzler, so he has a cold glass of milk instead. He saves more electricity by eating his usual two slices of bread untoasted. As he leaves the flat – pausing to unplug his mobile phone charger – he picks up his car keys, then thinks again and walks to the bus stop instead. By the time he hops off the bus by his office, the lack of morning coffee is getting to him so he pops into Starbucks for a cappuccino. At lunchtime, he quizzes the local deli owner about the provenance of ingredients and opts for a cheeseburger made with locally-reared beef. There's a slow period in the afternoon so he surfs the internet, ordering himself a brochure about the Toyota Prius and arranging for an installer of rooftop windmills to come round and give him a quote. He's tired at the end of the day and absent-mindedly leaves his office computer on standby before he heads for the bus stop.

Back at home late, after waiting ages for a bus, he drives to the supermarket – just a short trip, and he remembered to take his own plastic bags – where he buys a pack of energy-efficient light bulbs and a box of phosphate-free washing powder so that he'll be able to put tomorrow's work clothes through the washer-drier. He picks up some local organic lamb, local tomatoes and potatoes, and a bottle of wine (not shipped halfway round the world from Chile) for dinner. Having eaten, he saves more electricity by eschewing the dishwasher and doing the washing-up by hand. He decides to install his new energy-efficient bulbs, and then rethinks as that would involve throwing perfectly good light bulbs into the trash; so he puts them in a drawer, to replace the others as they fail. That night Geoff enjoys the sleep of the just, dreaming of Jude laughing happily, her hair tossed in the breeze of the open sunroof as she rides in the passenger seat of his new Prius.

You have no doubt guessed that Geoff's eco-friendly day was not quite as successful as he would like to think.

Let's start with the milk, which requires a critical piece of equipment to manufacture: a cow. Cows emit a lot of methane. (I put the matter delicately. If it is any consolation, most of the emission is through the cow's mouth, rather than the alternative route.) And methane is a more potent greenhouse gas than carbon dioxide: in producing about 250 ml of milk, a cow belches 7.5 litres of methane, which weighs around 5 grams, equivalent to 100 grams of carbon dioxide.* Add all the other inputs to the milk – feed for the cows, transport, pasteurisation – and the 250 ml that Geoff drank produced around 300 grams of carbon dioxide. By not boiling his kettle, on the other hand, he saved only about 25 g of carbon dioxide. His first planet-saving decision, eschewing a coffee in favour of a glass of milk, increased the greenhouse gas emissions of his morning drink by a factor of twelve. Dairy products are so bad for the planet that Geoff would have done better to toast his bread but not butter it rather than buttering it but not toasting it.

As beef relies on the same methane-emitting equipment as dairy products, it should be no surprise that Geoff's choice of a cheeseburger (2500 g of carbon dioxide for a quarter-pounder) was poor. The lamb chops he had for supper (say another 2500 g) were just as bad: sheep, too, produce methane. Geoff would have done better to choose pork or chicken, which emit about half the CO_2 – and even better with fish, especially ones (such as herring, mackerel and whiting) that swim close to the surface and – unlike cod and tuna – remain plentiful. Best of all for the planet, Geoff could have had an entirely vegan supper, but it's going to take more than Al Gore and a pretty face to persuade Geoff that this is a good idea.

Geoff was at pains to buy local, organic food. This helped – but only a little. Going organic trims 5 to 15 per cent off the cheeseburger and lamb chop figures. Buying local produce to reduce 'food miles', however, is often a counterproductive exercise. While it's clearly true that freighting food around the world uses

---

*I am using a rule of thumb among policy wonks that methane is about twenty times more potent than carbon dioxide. It's complicated, though. Some scientists – for instance Drew Shindell of the NASA Goddard Institute – believe methane is more damaging than the rule of thumb implies. In any case, methane traps more heat than carbon dioxide, but also breaks down within a few years (into carbon dioxide and water vapour). How much more dangerous a greenhouse gas it is, then, depends on the time horizon over which we make the calculation.

energy, the impact is less than you might think: most of it travels by ship; when it does travel by plane, it doesn't get a big seat with ample legroom and free champagne (the term 'food miles' misleadingly echoes 'air miles', with its connotations of business-class indulgence rather than efficiently packed containers); and it was probably produced in a much more sensible climate.

Geoff's choice of British lamb over New Zealand lamb might well have released *more* carbon dioxide – four times as much, if one team of academic researchers (admittedly, based in New Zealand) is to be believed. The figures are debatable but the basic insight is not: it takes more fossil fuel to produce lamb in the UK than in New Zealand, which has a longer grassy season and more hydroelectric power, and this should be weighed against emissions from transport. Geoff's choice of British over Spanish tomatoes was certainly misguided: the carbon dioxide emitted by road-hauling them from Spain is utterly outweighed by the fact that Spain is sunny, whereas British tomatoes need heated greenhouses. As for avoiding Chilean wine, shipping wine halfway round the world adds only about 5 per cent to the greenhouse gas emissions involved in making it in the first place.

Geoff was pleased he took his own plastic bags to the supermarket, but a plastic bag is responsible for only about one thousandth the carbon emissions of the food you put in it. This didn't come close to compensating for the indulgence he allowed himself of driving to the supermarket, which would have generated over 150 g of carbon dioxide per mile even if he'd already been driving his coveted new Prius. Even that number will be flattering because it assumes an uncongested journey, which is unlikely to be the case in London; and whatever some Prius fans may believe, it turns out that Priuses do have a corporeal form, and a Prius in congested traffic will cause more emissions indirectly by slowing other cars down than it will emit directly.

Still, let's at least give Geoff some credit for taking the bus to work. But not too much credit. The typical London bus has only thirteen people on it, despite the city's size and enthusiasm for public transport. Cars carry, on average, 1.6 people, and at that occupancy rate they actually emit less carbon dioxide, per passenger mile, than a bus at its typical occupancy. Some claim this is irrelevant because the bus was going anyway, and therefore Geoff's contribution to greenhouse gases was close to zero. By the same logic Geoff could enjoy a guilt-free long-distance flight because the plane, too, is going anyway. The point is that Geoff's purchase of the long-distance ticket would contribute to the airline's decision about how many future flights it should run on this route. Unless bus routes are entirely insensitive to passenger demand – which is, one must admit, a possibility – then the same argument applies to catching the bus.

Geoff was, of course, planning to drive alone rather than with 0.6 other people, so by taking the bus he probably saved about 100 g of carbon dioxide per mile – say 300 g on a three-mile round trip commute. Unfortunately, he then wasted about the same amount by boiling his potatoes with the lid off.

Geoff did well to buy the energy-efficient light bulbs, but erred in waiting to install them; the old ones waste electricity so quickly that it's more eco-friendly to chuck them out immediately. He shouldn't have scorned the dishwasher, which is more carbon-efficient than the typical hand-wash – arguably, many times more efficient. The phosphate-free washing powder might be good news for the health of nearby lakes, but when it comes to climate change what matters is that Geoff should have used a low-temperature wash and left enough time to dry his clothes on a line instead of relying on the tumble dryer – thus using 600 g of carbon dioxide rather than 3300 g.

Jude is likely to be unimpressed by all of this. But perhaps Geoff's windmill plan will save his as-yet-imaginary romance? It is unlikely. A small rooftop windmill in an urban environment generates an average of 8 watts, so Geoff would need twelve of them merely to run a standard 100W light bulb; one of these toy windmills will save Geoff just 120 g of carbon dioxide a day. He wasted five times as much as that by thoughtlessly leaving his desktop computer on standby in the office – which is easily done even by the most committed environmentalist, as I can see by looking across our shared office to the computer my wife forgot to turn off this morning. What about the mobile phone charger Geoff unplugged as he was leaving the house? That draws about half a watt, a hundredth of a computer on standby; even the windmill could cope with that. Unplugging it saves a magnificently puny 6 grams of carbon dioxide a day.

To summarise: despite Geoff's good intentions and passing familiarity with the kind of stuff that causes greenhouse gas emissions, he made some decisions that saved much less carbon than he imagined and others that were actively counterproductive. It couldn't be simpler? Not unless you devote your life to studying carbon emissions – and perhaps not even then. Euan Murray can vouch for that.

4 'If I ask my old man "What's the carbon footprint of a sheep?", he looks at me as though I'm mad'

Euan Murray works for The Carbon Trust, an organisation set up by the UK government to help businesses reduce their carbon emissions. He's responsible for 'carbon footprinting' – the study of how much carbon dioxide is released in the course of producing, transporting, consuming and disposing of a product. Murray spends his working life making the kind of calculations on which I relied to assess Geoff's day, and he does it for corporate clients ranging from a bank (200 grams of carbon dioxide per bank account) to PepsiCo (75 grams of carbon dioxide for a packet of potato snacks). A red-haired, blue-eyed, young Scot, Murray is the modern face of climate-change action – dressed in a sharp shirt with cufflinks, he's confident and straight-talking, at home with the technical details of carbon emissions without needing to fortify himself with jargon. He grew up on a sheep farm in southern Scotland, which gives him a suitably down-to-earth perspective on the messy task of calculating carbon footprints. 'If I ask my old man "What's the carbon footprint of a sheep?", he looks at me as though I'm mad,' he explains. 'But he can tell me the stocking density, what he feeds the sheep, and he can answer those questions as part of running his business.' Quite so: carbon footprinting is all about these kinds of specifics.

I chose to ask Euan Murray about Geoff's moment of weakness in buying a fortifying cappuccino before stepping into the office. (Readers of my first book, *The Undercover Economist*, might have noticed a return to a favourite theme.) A cappuccino is easily as complex a product as Thomas Thwaites's toaster: not only does it rely on the espresso machine – an impressive piece of equipment – but it also requires a cow, coffee beans, a cardboard cup, a plastic lid, and so on. Evaluating the carbon footprint of a cappuccino requires an estimate of the carbon footprint of all these different parts of the whole. You can see why I wanted expert help.

But Murray was only able to assist me up to a point. Carbon footprinting is a time-consuming business, and even taking a very broad view of what constitutes a product, there are many thousands of candidates for the footprinting treatment. (Recall Eric Beinhocker's estimate that modern economies offer around 10 billion distinct products. Starbucks alone claims to offer 87,000 different beverages.) The Carbon Trust hasn't been commissioned to calculate the footprint of a cappuccino just yet, so Murray falls back on educated guesswork.

'Transportation is going to be small. Emissions from that are effectively zero, because you can fit a lot of sugar cubes and coffee beans on a boat.' He starts to doodle as he works through the possibilities. 'And sugar and coffee don't require massive inputs of energy or other materials.' After a few minutes blocking out the main possible greenhouse gas emissions from producing a cappuccino, Murray offers a conclusion that will add to Geoff's dairy-related woes. 'My guess is that it's the milk that makes up the lion's share of the carbon footprint.'

Murray's benchmark is a bar of Cadbury's dairy milk chocolate, a product for which the Carbon Trust *has* done a full footprint. The milk is only a third of the mass of the chocolate bar, but even after reckoning the cost of transporting and processing cocoa beans and sugar, melting the chocolate into moulds in the factory, and transporting the final product, the milk is responsible for two-thirds of the carbon footprint of the chocolate. Milk is, of course, almost the sole ingredient of a cappuccino. If Euan were to answer my question as thoroughly as he does for his corporate clients, he would have to crunch through some precise numbers for a whole lot of inputs and even then he'd have some knotty philosophical problems to grapple with: do we give credit to Starbucks because Geoff got there by bus on the way to the office, rather than making a special journey by car? Probably not. But does the barista's commute count? What about the coffee farmer's commute to the fields? Do we figure a lower carbon footprint if the café is double-glazed? The humble cappuccino shows why 'it couldn't be simpler' couldn't be more wrong.

At least Geoff now knows about the milk, but should he be going for a double espresso? Would a black filter coffee be better than the horror of a soya latte? Even if Geoff devotes every waking minute to researching how best he can help the planet – even if he was permanently on the phone to Euan Murray – he'd still make mistakes. It's inevitable: in assessing where his virtuous day went wrong, I had to choose among findings that even the experts disagree about. I have seen figures claiming that driving in typical commuter conditions – even a Prius – emits many times more than I have suggested because of congestion. Mike Berners-Lee, author of *How Bad Are Bananas?*, tells me that bananas are a low-carbon food. Geoff Beattie, author of *Why Aren't We Saving the Planet?*, remarks that bananas are a high-carbon product. I have seen credible research suggesting that meat – if farmed in the right way – might not contribute nearly as much to climate change as it now does. One can think very hard about this subject and sit with a stack of research papers and still not reach a settled conclusion.

What is Geoff to do? When I sought advice from green friends, one opined that the best way to reduce the climate impact of a visit to Starbucks was to abstain altogether. That it not going to impress a caffeine-starved Geoff, and still less people who are less concerned about the planet than Geoff is, which is to say, most people. (A recent opinion poll asked people what was the main thing they, personally, were doing to combat climate change. Thirty-seven per cent said 'nothing', and most of the rest only mentioned light bulbs or recycling.) And while one can abstain from cappuccino it is impossible to abstain from consumption altogether, so the question of *what* to consume quickly resurfaces. The project of simply exhorting people to save the planet by changing their behaviour is inherently limited.

5 The carbon-calculating cloud

We can dream of a high-tech solution to help guide Geoff through the muddle – some sort of smart-phone application that would recognise any of the 10 billion or so products and services in his city and calculate how much carbon dioxide or methane was embodied in their very existence. Geoff could take a snapshot or scan a barcode and within moments receive a report on just how damaging the cookie, or the espresso, or the cheeseburger, would be.

Perhaps this will be possible one day. But imagine the processing job: the phone app would certainly help prevent some of Geoff's sillier mistakes, but for many others the obstacles to getting the number right are formidable. If, as Euan Murray points out, the source of milk matters for the milk's carbon footprint, Starbucks would need to post data online about its milk suppliers – not to mention mileage for its supply trucks, its electricity bills and suppliers, and much else besides. A superficial carbon calculator could be built into any phone, and would help. But an app that calculated the full carbon footprint of any product seems a fantasy.

Even if the colossal database that would be needed could be put together, the problem would be far from solved. Only truly committed environmentalists would take the trouble to scan everything. And only environmentalists would be motivated to pay close attention to the results. For most people – the 37 per cent who say they are doing 'nothing' about climate change, or the much larger proportion who are doing very little – the information that flashed up on the smart-phone screen would be easy and painless to ignore.

But perhaps there is a way to make this fantasy a reality, providing real-time information to anyone who pulled their wallet out to make a purchase – without any need for scanners or a central database of every product on the planet. How might that work?

Imagine that the governments of the world's major fossil fuels producers agreed to the following approach: that each of them would levy a tax of about $50 per tonne of carbon contained in any fossil fuel mined or extracted in its territory – roughly $14 per tonne of carbon dioxide. This would be, roughly, an extra $5 per barrel of oil, and nearly $40 per tonne of coal.*

That decision might appear to have nothing to do with a carbon-calculating phone app, but in fact it has everything to do with it. The carbon tax would piggyback on the system of market prices, which acts as a vast analogue cloud computer, pulling and pushing resources to wherever they have the highest value. A $50 carbon tax would increase the price of gasoline by about 12 cents a gallon, creating a small incentive to drive less, and more efficiently, and to buy more efficient cars. It would

---

*I am not advocating a particular level of carbon tax here, merely explaining the principle. A figure of $50 per tonne of carbon is not wildly out of line with informed estimates of a sensible carbon price, although the range of estimates is large.

increase the price of a kilowatt hour of electricity – by about a cent and a half if the energy came from coal, but only by three quarters of a cent if the energy came from natural gas. That would create a small incentive to use less electricity, to buy home insulation, and for power companies to build natural gas power stations instead of coal-fired power stations – or, indeed, to invest in nuclear capacity or renewable energy sources.

That would just be the start. As the relative price of energy from different sources began to change, and the average price of energy increased, any energy-intensive product would begin to reflect that. Spanish tomatoes would rise in price because of the energy cost of shipping them from Spain; but British tomatoes would rise in price even more because of the cost of heating the greenhouse.

This would not be because of any grand plan. It would just happen: a trucker who ignored the higher price of diesel in setting his shipping charges would simply go out of business; so would a tomato cultivator who tried to absorb the cost of heating a greenhouse, rather than raising his prices. That said, if a tomato farmer came to market with local tomatoes grown under glass without heating, she would find that the carbon tax had given her an edge over her energy-hungry rivals. Geoff, arriving at the supermarket intending to buy tomatoes, wouldn't have to point his smart phone at any barcodes: he could just look at the price. The more carbon-intensive the tomato, the higher the price would creep. And the price would be something Geoff would want to consider, regardless of how he felt about climate change.

What the carbon tax would do, then, is recreate the fantasy carbon calculator app, and give it teeth. No central database would be needed. Every product in the world would change in price according to the carbon content of the energy that produced it, and that would give every decision maker, from the electricity company to Geoff himself, an incentive to reduce their carbon footprint using whatever tactics occurred to them.

Even though a carbon tax has been floating around as a proposal for many years, it's an idea that has yet to make much political headway. There are a few countries with carbon taxes on small sections of the economy. The European Union has a cap-and-trade scheme, with similar effects to a carbon tax, but the scheme has had teething problems and omits large chunks of the economy. India has a tax on coal, but it is small. No large country has introduced a substantial carbon price across the entire economy, and international negotiations continue to struggle.

So let's step back from the carbon tax idea for a moment, and look instead at what governments seem to have embraced as the alternative: regulations designed to reduce carbon dioxide emissions from the top down.

6 The unexpected consequences of the Merton Rule

The 'Merton Rule' was devised in 2003 by Adrian Hewitt, a local planning officer in Merton, southwest London. The rule, which Hewitt created with a couple of colleagues and persuaded the borough council to pass, was that any development beyond a small scale would have to include the capacity to generate 10 per cent of that building's energy requirements, or the developers would be denied permission to build. The rule sounded sensible and quickly caught on, with over a hundred other local councils following suit within a few years. In London, the mayor at the time, Ken Livingstone, introduced 'Merton Plus', which raised the bar to 20 per cent. The national government then introduced the rule more widely. Adrian Hewitt became a celebrity in the small world of local council planning, and Merton council started scooping awards for its environmental leadership.

It is easy to see why the rule became popular. It is a simple and intuitive way to encourage something that most people agree is desirable – the growth of the renewable energy industry. It encourages developers to install highly visible and cool-looking new technology such as solar panels, rather than boring stuff such as insulation. And the costs are invisible. The rule costs the government nothing (one council introduced the rule after agreeing that the financial implications were 'zero' – presumably they had in mind the financial implications for the council, rather than for anyone else). It also costs the developers little, as in a competitive market they will pass on most of the costs to the final buyer of the building. And the final buyer of the building doesn't really notice the rule's extra costs in the middle of the much larger costs of owning or renting a building.

But all is not well with the Merton Rule. The drawback that should have been most obvious is that just because renewable energy capacity is installed doesn't mean it will be used. A simple renewable energy option is often a dual-fuel boiler that can burn both natural gas and biomass such as wood pellets – it can be installed without any great upheaval in a developer's designs, thus satisfying the letter of the Merton Rule. Of course, once such a boiler is installed, it will be simpler and cheaper to burn natural gas and not bother about the wood at all. Installed renewable capacity: 10 per cent. Renewable energy produced: zero. Perversely, the 'Merton Plus' rule of 20 per cent makes such an outcome more likely, because there are fewer on-site alternatives to biomass that can hit the more challenging target.

With a hefty dose of bureaucratic oversight, perhaps the regulations could be adjusted to make it compulsory to use the renewable capacity. That might not be such a wonderful idea either. I spoke to Geoffrey Palmer, who as well as being an ardent environmentalist is the managing director of engineering firm Roger Preston Partners. Palmer ran up against the Merton Rule when refurbishing Elizabeth House, a large office block beside London's Waterloo station: 'We worked on various options,' sighed Palmer, 'but we always knew it was going to end up being biomass.' To meet the rule given the size of the building, Palmer's team designed a biomass boiler with a storage bunker the size of a 25-metre swimming pool – this held just fourteen days' worth of fuel. Palmer calculated that keeping the bunker full of woodchips, pellets and IKEA offcuts would take two 30–40-ton lorries a week to drive right into the heart of London and reverse into Elizabeth House's loading bay. This may not be the kind of thing we'd like to see enforced too rigidly.

Nor will building owners be keen to repair costly renewable energy sources if they break. Even the best machinery will need repairing eventually, and as renewable technologies are still young they can be especially prone to problems. 'If you install PV solar panels on your roof, and they break down just after the five-year warranty,' says Geoffrey Palmer, 'you're not going to pay to reinstall them.'

There are other problems with the Merton Rule. By demanding that the renewable capacity be located on the same site as the building, it closes off opportunities. A huge wind turbine on a nearby hill could be quite efficient, even when pitted against 2 billion years of concentrated energy resources in the form of coal or oil. A small wind turbine on a rooftop that is sheltered on all sides by other buildings isn't ever going to do much more than keep your mobile phone charged. Geoffrey Palmer is working on a biomass system for a redevelopment of London's iconic Battersea Power Station; as it sits on the River Thames, and woodchips can be easily shipped in by barge, this could provide enough renewable power not only for all of its own needs but potentially for other nearby developments, too. But the Merton Rule makes no allowance for such idiosyncratic local experiments.

We've seen again and again that the local context matters: it will often make a nonsense of plans that look good on paper, while suggesting ideas that seem strange but work perfectly on the ground. The Merton Rule takes no account of what is feasible on a particular site. Consider a new out-of-town supermarket, which may be a miniature environmental catastrophe in other ways but offers a big flat roof, perfect for solar panels; a big site that may also allow a decent-sized windmill; and huge potential underneath the car park for ground-source heat pumps. Ten per cent renewable capacity may be a ridiculously small target for such a development. On the flip side, high-rise office developments such as Elizabeth House are naturally energy-efficient because each floor provides heat to the floor above it – and when situated right next to a railway station, as Elizabeth House is, they encourage workers to commute on public transport rather than driving in. Is it reasonable to demand exactly the same on-site renewable energy generation at Elizabeth House that we demand at a big-box supermarket?

There is something perverse about all this. The Merton Rule appears to be every bit as clumsy as Geoff, the amateur environmentalist. In some ways it is clumsier: at least Geoff is likely to learn from his mistakes over time, but government regulations, by their very nature, tend to be somewhat impervious to the possibility of improvement.

And the Merton Rule is far from an isolated case. Look at policy after policy in country after country, and you see environmental regulations making the same mistakes. Sometimes the regulations are worse than useless; sometimes they are merely far less effective than they could be.

A famous example is the set of CAFE standards in the USA. CAFE stands for 'corporate average fuel efficiency', and the standards, introduced in 1975, were designed to improve the fuel efficiency of American cars. Yet the CAFE rules suffered from similar drawbacks to the Merton Rule. They incorporated separate and looser standards for 'light trucks' – at the time, a niche category covering largely commercial vehicles that were intended to carry cargo. But manufacturers realised that it was possible to build a car that looked like a light truck to the regulator, thereby sidestepping onerous rules. The result was that CAFE standards actively encouraged the emergence of a new breed of bigger, heavier car, and the efficiency of new cars sold in the US fell steadily between 1988 and 2003.

CAFE suffered from other Merton-style shortcomings. One was that there is no incentive for manufacturers to go beyond the standard, so once CAFE standards were achieved, improvements in engine technology that could have produced more efficient cars were instead used to make cars larger and faster. An exclusion for ethanol-burning vehicles created a class of cars that burned ethanol in theory but rarely used the capability in practice – very reminiscent of the unused Merton-compliant dual-fuel boilers. And on top of all that, even if the CAFE standards had created a new breed of super-efficient cars, they wouldn't have encouraged their drivers to drive them less.

A third example of such unintended consequences comes from the European Union's Renewable Energy Directive, which mandates that each EU member state will ensure that 10 per cent of the energy for transportation will come from renewable energy sources. In principle, this could refer to electric cars powered by windmills and solar panels. In practice, the cheapest and simplest option is to fill up conventional or slightly modified cars with liquid fuels such as biodiesel and ethanol. The consequences are now well known: arable land used for growing food can be used to grow corn to produce ethanol.

Meanwhile the actual contribution to fighting climate change of ethanol-powered cars is highly variable. Sugarcane ethanol can actually lower emissions by harnessing harmful byproducts such as methane; corn ethanol can actually be worse than gasoline, and palm-oil biodiesel grown on former rainforest land can be responsible for the release of over *twenty times* more carbon dioxide than good old gasoline. The impact of producing biofuels all depends on what crops are grown and how they are processed; the European rules do not yet reflect this, and if they try, they will struggle to do justice to the complexity. Three separate environmental regulations, designed to deal with three separate problems and promulgated by three very different institutions – the United States Congress, the European Commission, and Merton Borough Council – all suffer from similar weaknesses. This suggests that there is some important link which explains why it is hard to get these regulations right. But what?

7 Economic bulldogs

Think back, for a moment, to chapter 1 and the video Karl Sims made of the strange creatures that evolved inside his computer. The evolutionary process was amazingly powerful: 'Grab the red cube', said Sims, and a huge range of different strategies evolved; 'Swim', he decreed, and creatures emerged that could swim, some strikingly familiar and some using techniques that seemed quite unearthly. As the biochemist Leslie Orgel famously remarked, 'Evolution is cleverer than you are', meaning that when an evolutionary process is let loose upon a problem, it will often find solutions that no human designer would have dreamed of.

But there is an unhelpful corollary to Orgel's maxim: if the problem is misstated then evolution is likely to find loopholes few of us could have imagined. In biological evolution, of course, there is no one to misstate the objective. Genes succeed if they are passed down the generations. But with Karl Sims's virtual evolution, it was Sims who set the criteria for reproductive success and the results were sometimes perverse. There is a revealing moment in the video which displays a creature that evolved to move quickly on land. The creature, a crude slab of a body with two blocks loosely attached, simply rolls around and around in a wide circle, its 'head' staying still while its 'legs', crossing and uncrossing, mark out the circle's circumference. The virtual creature looks like one of life's losers, but it isn't: it's a winner, because it is achieving the goal Karl Sims set: move quickly on a flat plane.

In chapter 1, we discovered that the economy is itself an evolutionary environment in which a huge variety of ingenious profit-seeking strategies emerge through a decentralised process of trial and error. As Leslie Orgel's rule suggests, what emerges is far more brilliant than any single planner could have dreamed up. But as the dark side of Orgel's rule predicts, if the rules of the economic game are poorly written, economic evolution will find the loopholes. That is why sensible-seeming environmental rules can produce perverse results: rainforest chopped down to produce palm oil; trucks laden with woodchips braving the congestion of central London; the rise and rise of the SUV. Evolution is smarter than we are, and economic evolution tends to outsmart the rules we erect to guide it.

Perhaps the mascot of these unlovely consequences should be the great British bulldog. This creature's Churchillian jowls have made it one of the most charismatic and beloved of all thoroughbred dogs. The breed has a distinctive short nose, bow legs and folds of skin that make the dog's face resemble a piece of scrunched-up velvet. It did not acquire these characteristics by accident: the bulldog is the product of over a century of careful selective breeding to produce the shortest noses, bowiest legs and scrunchiest, jowliest faces. Alas, the breed suffers from problems that are a direct consequence of its carefully selected physical appearance. Many bulldogs cannot mate without assistance because of sheer anatomical considerations. Artificial insemination is one solution. Recruiting three or four people to hold the dogs is another possibility. Special cradles are also available, and the manufacturers boast that with one of these cradles, bulldog mating becomes a one-person job – if one that still requires two bulldogs. But even when bulldogs do get pregnant, they often require a Caesarean section because bulldogs have big heads and small birth canals. Bulldogs, unlike most dogs, cannot regulate their temperature by panting, so are at risk of heat stroke. The adorable folds of skin around the eyes make them vulnerable to infected tear ducts. Bulldogs often breathe through, and damage, their voice boxes because the usual breathing passages are compressed. Evolution – and its perverse consequences – is smarter than pedigree dog breeders.

Just as Karl Sims and the breeders of bulldogs can cause mal-formed creations to prosper by changing the rules of the game, so can governments. In New Zealand in the 1970s, a bizarre new breed of business evolved: the 'television assembly industry', which approached Japanese manufacturers and commissioned them to gather together the component parts for their televisions and to ship them, neatly sorted and with instructions in English, to New Zealand. (This was disruptive for the Japanese, so the kits were more expensive than finished television sets.) The government had demanded that television sets be produced locally, a prohibitively expensive proposition for such a tiny economy. Local entrepreneurs figured out the cheapest way to do the job. Economic evolution was cleverer than the government of New Zealand – and it produced a spectacular economic bulldog.

The dark side of Leslie Orgel's law means that whenever we leap to conclusions about what a particular solution would look like – buildings with inbuilt renewable energy capacity, or cars that run on biofuels – we are likely to discover unwelcome consequences. The Merton Rule, CAFE standards and other environmental regulations have produced a series of economic bulldogs – buildings and cars that tick all the regulatory boxes, but waste money on technology that will never be used and pass up opportunities to save carbon dioxide emissions in other ways.

8 Tilting the playing field

While all these examples are depressing, they are also perversely inspiring. If the stroke of a legislator's pen can cause Japanese television components to be shipped to New Zealand at greater expense than Japanese televisions, or propel trucks full of wood-chips into the congested streets of central London, or have rainforests chopped down in the name of saving the planet, then all that is a testament to the unexpected ingenuity that can be unleashed when people have to adapt to new sets of rules. Better rules should turn Orgel's law to our advantage, harnessing an ingenious, serendipitous process to produce environmental solutions from the most unexpected sources.

The root cause of the loophole problem is something we also met with the Merton Rule: the crucial difference between the letter and the spirit of the law. This point was hammered home to me over a world-saving coffee (I had an espresso; he had a soya cappuccino) with the environmental economist Prashant Vaze, author of *The Economic Environmentalist*. Vaze was waxing lyrical about the concept of the 'nudge', proposed by the behavioural economist Richard Thaler and polymath legal scholar Cass Sunstein. The idea is that subtle influences could be used to direct thoughtless behaviour, while preserving individual rights consciously to choose. For example, incandescent light bulbs – which are a very wasteful way to produce light, but preferred by people with partial sight and certain light-sensitive skin conditions – could be removed from open shelves, but available from storage on request. Nobody would buy such a light bulb out of carelessness, but someone who really wanted an incandescent bulb could seek one out without too much trouble.

The idea of a nudge itself is very clever. The idea of legislating one is more difficult. Vaze waved airily behind him towards the café counter as he related the classic Thaler–Sunstein nudge: the government could decree that the café's healthy salads should be placed in a prominent position, and the fattening desserts tucked away somewhere less accessible.

The only problem was, the café didn't *sell* any salads.

It's not a coincidence that most of the best examples Thaler and Sunstein suggest are innovations in the private or voluntary sectors, usually from people with the ability to apply the spirit of the law as well as the letter of it. The prominent-salad nudge might work well for a healthy-eating drive in a workplace cafeteria, but if you tried to introduce it through legislation, what effect would it have? Perhaps legislators could mandate that all cafés had to offer salads, though that starts to look silly if we're talking about an espresso bar on a railway station platform. An alternative is to say that if a café does offer salads, then the salads must be displayed prominently. But what if the salads are a minority interest and cakes and pastries make all the money? In that case the nudge might be a real money-loser; faced with a choice of prominently displaying salads or not offering salads at all, cafés might drop the healthy option entirely. It would be yet another economic bulldog.

A clumsy nudge is better than a clumsy shove or a clumsy ban, but it's still clumsy. And since the language of 'nudge' became fashionable, it has itself come to suffer from lax definitions. I recently visited the UK Treasury to discover that officials were waxing lyrical about nudging through 'choice editing'. 'When you say, "choice editing",' I asked, 'does that mean "banning things"?' The sheepish reply was in the affirmative.

Which brings us back to the idea of a carbon tax – or more precisely, a carbon price, since the price of carbon-intensive goods can be raised either through taxes or through a tradable permit system. (The differences between a carbon permit scheme and a carbon tax are insignificant relative to the differences between having some kind of carbon price and not having one.)

Carbon pricing tries to harness Orgel's law by focusing on what we think the ultimate goal is: a reduction of the greenhouse gas emitted into the atmosphere, at the lowest possible cost. To put it another way, carbon pricing hitches a ride on an amazing decentralised cloud computer – the markets that make up the world's economy – to provide feedback to billions of individual experiments, all aimed at cutting carbon emissions, because cutting carbon emissions saves money.

Of course, it's not *that* simple. The carbon price proposal raises many questions. Fortunately, because the idea has been around for a while, an army of policy wonks has had plenty of time to figure out some answers. The most important question

seems to be: 'Who should pay the carbon price?' And the unexpected answer is 'It doesn't matter'. As a rough approximation, if
the carbon price is 5 cents a kilogram of carbon dioxide – and
assuming that methane emissions can be included – then the
carbon price will raise the price of cheeseburgers by 12 cents.
Consumers will pay more and producers will receive less, after
the tax has been paid. But surprisingly, who takes the hit does
not depend on whether the person who physically writes the
cheque to the government is the beef farmer, the fast-food chain
or the individual consumer.

There are more legitimate questions over the details of how a
carbon price would be administered, but by far the most challenging issue is whether international agreement could ever be
reached. Such agreement is needed, because carbon dioxide is a
global pollutant – there is little point in tightening up on carbon
dioxide and methane emissions in one country if other countries
will opt out of the deal. But the agreement doesn't have to be an
all-singing and all-dancing allocation of pollution permits to
every country across the next century. Even an informal agreement that each country will levy and enjoy the revenues of its
own carbon tax, at levels roughly aligned with the taxes of
others, would do much good.

A carbon price – even if it could be expanded beyond fossil
fuels to reflect problems such as methane emissions, or direct
carbon dioxide emissions from farming and cement production –
would not solve the climate problem by itself. We know, from
the experience of the energy crisis in the 1970s, that high energy
prices spur energy-saving patents in every field from heat
exchangers to solar panels. But as we saw in chapter 3, the innovation system could probably use some help, above and beyond
the effect of a carbon price. Innovation prizes for low-carbon
technologies are another essential way to stimulate a vast range
of different experiments, each with the aim of providing a solution to part of the problem.

Nobody knows what an economy with a significant carbon

price might look like – and that is the point. Orgel's law tells us that economic evolution, with the playing field tilted by the new rule, 'Greenhouse gases are expensive', will produce entirely unexpected ways to reduce greenhouse gases. It's probably a safe bet that cars would become more efficient, buildings would be built with more insulation and passive heating and cooling systems, and that we'd see more use of technologies such as nuclear, hydroelectric and even 'carbon capture' – preventing carbon dioxide emerging from a coal-fired power station. But what other changes we might see, who knows? Global supply chains might be reconfigured. Hundreds of millions of people might move to places where the climate or the geography allows a more energy-efficient lifestyle.

Or world-saving ideas could emerge from even more unexpected sources. If there was some way to reduce the methane being belched out by cows and sheep – almost a tenth of the total contribution to greenhouse gas emissions – then that would be a huge achievement. Australian scientists have realised that kangaroos don't emit methane, and are even now trying to figure out how to get kangaroo-gut bacteria into the stomachs of cows. It may be a blind alley. It may not. But a proper price on greenhouse gases would encourage every path to be explored, even if one of the quests is simply to make cows belch like kangaroos.

Carbon pricing will work because it takes a global objective – reduce greenhouse gas emissions – and delegates that objective. Individuals like Geoff know their own circumstances and priorities. Businesses understand their costs. Entrepreneurs and engineers have myriad ideas waiting for the right business environment to make them profitable. Governments know very little of all this – but they do have the long-term perspective and the mandate to do what is best for society. Governments should not be picking and choosing, in our complex economies, specific ways to save the planet. They should be tilting the playing field to encourage us to make all our decisions with the planet in mind.

Six

Preventing financial meltdowns or: Decoupling

'We have involved ourselves in a colossal muddle, having blundered in the control of a delicate machine, the working of which we do not understand.'

– John Maynard Keynes

'Any intelligent fool can make things bigger, more complex, and more violent. It takes a touch of genius – and a lot of courage – to move in the opposite direction.'

– attributed to E.F. Schumacher

1 When failure is unthinkable

On the morning of 6 July 1988, maintenance workers on Piper Alpha, the largest and oldest oil and gas rig in the North Sea, dismantled a backup pump to check a safety valve. The work dragged on all day and the workers stopped work in the early evening, sealing the tube off and filling out a permit noting that the pump was unusable. An engineer left the permit in the control room but it was busy and there were constant interruptions. Later in the evening, the primary pump failed and – pressed for time, not knowing about the maintenance, and unable to find any reason why the backup pump should not be used – the rig's operators started up the half-dismantled pump. Gas leaked out, caught fire and exploded.

The explosion, serious in itself, was compounded by several other failures. Normally, a gas rig such as Piper Alpha would have blast walls to contain explosions, but Piper Alpha had originally been designed to pump oil, which is flammable but rarely explosive. The retrofitted design also placed hazards too close to the rig's control room, which the explosion immediately disabled. Fire-fighting pumps, which were designed to draw in huge volumes of sea water, did not automatically start, because of a safety measure designed to protect divers from being sucked into the pump inlet. The safety system could have been overridden from the control room, but the control room had been destroyed. This also meant no evacuation could be coordinated, so platform workers retreated to the rig's accommodation block.

Two nearby rigs continued to pump oil and gas towards the blazing Piper Alpha, their operators watching the inferno but fretting that they lacked authority to make the expensive decision to shut down production. It might have made little difference anyway, given the presence of so much high-pressure gas in the supply lines. When this gas exploded, a fireball half the height of the Eiffel Tower engulfed the platform. The blast even killed two rescuers in a nearby boat, along with rig crewmen whom they had hauled from the water. Other pipelines ruptured in the heat, feeding the fire and driving away another fire-fighting rescue boat. It was impossible to approach the rig, and less than two hours after the initial explosion, the entire accommodation block slid off the melting platform into the sea. One hundred and sixty-seven men died. Many of the fifty-nine survivors had leapt ten storeys into deathly cold waves. The rig burned for three more weeks, wilting like old flowers in a betrayal of mass, steel and engineering.

Industrial safety experts pored over what had gone wrong with Piper Alpha and learned lessons for preventing future tragedies. But fewer lessons seem to have been learned from a related accident: a meltdown in the financial markets which was triggered by Piper Alpha's destruction. This was the 'LMX spiral', and it nearly destroyed the venerable insurance market Lloyd's.

Insurers often sign contracts in which one insurer agrees to cover another insurer's extraordinary losses on a particular claim. These 'reinsurance' contracts have a sound business logic and a long history. Yet in the Lloyd's market, where different insurance syndicates traded risk with each other, reinsurers had begun to insure the total losses of other insurers, rather than losses on a single claim. The subtle distinction proved important. The reinsurance contracts pulled losses from one syndicate to a second, then a third – and perhaps then from the third back to the first. Insurance syndicates could and did find that, through a circle of intermediaries, they were their own reinsurers.

The spiral was coiled and ready to unwind when Piper Alpha was destroyed. The insurance syndicates who traded on Lloyd's were hit with an initial bill for about a billion dollars, one of the largest single claims in history. But then some reinsurance claims were triggered, and others, and then others in a chain reaction. The eventual total of claims resulting from the billion-dollar loss was $16 billion. Some hapless insurance syndicates discovered that they had insured Piper Alpha many times over. Parts of the spiral are still being unwound over two decades later.

If this sounds familiar, it should. Within the first few days of the credit crunch in 2007, long before most people were aware of the scale of the trouble, the economist John Kay was pointing out the similarities between the crunch and the LMX spiral. As in the credit crunch, financial institutions and regulators told themselves that sophisticated new financial tools were diluting risk by spreading it to those best able to cope. As in the credit crunch, historical data suggested that the packaged reinsurance contracts were very safe. And as in the credit crunch, the participants found the true shape of the risk they were taking almost impossible to discern until after things had gone horribly wrong. In both cases, innovative financial techniques proved to be expensive failures.

So far, this book has argued that failure is both necessary and useful. Progress comes from lots of experiments, many of which will fail, and we must be much more tolerant of failure if we are to learn from it. But the financial crisis showed that a tolerant attitude to failure is a dangerous tactic for the banking system. So what happens when we cannot allow ourselves the luxury of making mistakes, because mistakes have catastrophic consequences?

As I studied the LMX spiral, in the hope of discovering something that would prevent future financial crises, I realised that I was missing a hidden, yet vital, parallel. It was the horror of Piper Alpha's destruction itself, rather than the financial meltdown that followed it, which could tell us more about financial accidents. If we want to learn about dealing with systems that have little room for trial and error, then gas rigs, chemical refineries, and nuclear plants are the place to start.

2 'Banking exceeds the complexity of any nuclear plant I ever studied'

The connection between banks and nuclear reactors is not clear to most bankers, or to banking regulators. But to the men and women who study industrial accidents such as Three Mile Island, Piper Alpha, Bhopal or the Challenger shuttle – engineers, psychologists and even sociologists – the connection is obvious. James Reason, a psychologist who has spent a lifetime studying human error in aviation, medicine, shipping and industry, uses the downfall of Barings Bank as a favourite case study. Barings was London's oldest merchant bank when, in 1995, it collapsed after more than 300 years' trading. One of its employees, Nick Leeson, had lost vast sums making unauthorised bets with the bank's capital. He destroyed the bank single-handedly, assisted only by the gaps in Barings Bank's supervision of him.

'I used to speak to bankers about risk and accidents and they thought I was talking about people banging their shins,' James Reason told me. 'Then they discovered what a risk is. It came with the name of Nick Leeson.'

Another catastrophe expert who has no doubt about the parallel is Charles Perrow, emeritus professor of sociology at Yale. He is convinced that bankers and banking regulators could and should have been paying attention to ideas in safety engineering and safety psychology. Perrow made his name by publishing a book, *Normal Accidents*, after Three Mile Island and before Chernobyl. The book explored the dynamics of disasters and argued that in a certain kind of system, accidents were inevitable – or 'normal'.

For Perrow, the dangerous combination is a system that is both complex and 'tightly coupled'. The defining characteristic of a tightly coupled process is that once it starts, it's difficult or impossible to stop: a domino-toppling display is not especially complex, but it is tightly coupled. So is a loaf of bread rising in the oven. Harvard University, on the other hand, is not especially tightly coupled, but is complex. A change in US student visa policy; or a new government scheme to fund research; or the appearance of a fashionable book in economics, or physics, or anthropology; or an internecine academic row – all could have unpredictable consequences for Harvard and trigger a range of unexpected responses, but none will spiral out of control quickly enough to destroy the university altogether.

So far, this book has looked at complex but loosely coupled systems, like Harvard. The sheer complexity of such systems means that failures are part of life, and the art of success is to fail productively.

But what if a system is both complex and tightly coupled? Complexity means there are many different ways for things to go wrong. Tight coupling means the unintended consequences proliferate so quickly that it is impossible to adapt to the failure or to try something different. On Piper Alpha, the initial explosion need not have destroyed the rig, but it took out the control room, making an evacuation difficult, and also making it impossible to override the diver-safety catch that was preventing the seawater pumps from starting automatically. Although the rig's crew had, in principle, shut down the flow of oil and gas to the platform, so much pipework had been damaged that gas and oil continued to leak out and feed the inferno. Each interaction was unexpected. Many happened within minutes of the initial mistake. There was no time to react.

For men like James Reason and Charles Perrow, such disasters need to be studied not just for their own sakes, but because they offer us vital lessons about the unexpected traps that lie in wait in complex and tightly coupled systems – and the psychological and organisational factors that can help to prevent us from falling into them. Few human inventions are more complex and tightly coupled than the banking system; Charles Perrow says it 'exceeds the complexity of any nuclear plant I ever studied'. So if the bankers and their regulators did start paying attention to the unglamorous insights of industrial safety experts, what might they learn?

3 Why safety systems bite back

Among the bitter recriminations over the financial crisis of 2008, if there's consensus about anything it's that the financial system needs to be made safer. Rules must be introduced, one way or another, to prevent banks from collapsing in future.

It might seem obvious that the way to make a complex system safer is to install some safety measures. James Reason is celebrated in safety-engineering circles for the 'Swiss cheese model' of accidents. Imagine a series of safety systems as a stack of Emmental slices. Just as each piece of cheese has holes, each safety device has flaws. But add enough pieces of cheese and you can be fairly sure that the holes will never line up with each other. The natural temptation is thus to layer more and more Emmental onto the financial system – but unfortunately, it's not quite so straightforward. As safety experts like Reason are only too well aware, every additional safety measure also has the potential to introduce an unexpected new way for something to go wrong.

Galileo described an early example of this principle in 1638. Masons at the time would store stone columns horizontally, raised above the soil by two piles of stone. The columns often cracked in the middle under their own weight. The 'solution' was to reinforce the support with a third pile of stone in the centre. But that didn't help. The two end supports would often settle a little, and the column, balanced like a see-saw on the central pile, would then snap as the ends sagged.

The Piper Alpha disaster is another example: it began because a maintenance operation crashed into rules designed to prevent engineers working long tiring shifts, and it was aggravated by the safety device designed to prevent divers being sucked into the seawater pumps. At the Fermi nuclear reactor near Detroit in 1966, a partial meltdown put the lives of 65,000 people at risk. Several weeks after the plant was shut down, the reactor vessel had cooled enough to identify the culprit: a zirconium filter the size of a crushed beer can, which had been dislodged by a surge of coolant in the reactor core and then blocked the circulation of the coolant. The filter had been installed at the last moment for safety reasons, at the express request of the Nuclear Regulatory Commission.

The problem in all of these cases is that the safety system introduced what an engineer would call a new 'failure mode' – a new way for things to go wrong. And that was precisely the problem in the financial crisis: not that it had no safety systems, but that the safety systems it did have made the problems worse.

Consider the credit default swap, or CDS – a three-letter

acronym with a starring role in the crisis. Credit default swaps are a kind of insurance against a loan not being repaid. The first CDS was agreed between JP Morgan and a government-sponsored development bank, the European Bank for Reconstruction and Development, in 1994. JP Morgan paid fees to the EBRD, and in exchange the EBRD agreed to make good any losses in the almost unimaginable event that the oil giant Exxon defaulted on a possible $4.8 billion loan. In a narrow sense, it was a sensible deal: the EBRD had idle cash and was seeking some low-risk income, while JP Morgan had plenty of useful things it could do with its own funds, but banking regulations dictated that it must set aside nearly half a billion dollars just in case there was a problem with the Exxon loan. The CDS deal offloaded the risk to the EBRD, liberating JP Morgan's cash. It did so with the explicit permission of the regulators, who felt that this was a safe way of managing risk.

There were two ways in which these credit default swaps led to trouble. The first is simply that having insured some of their gambles, the banks felt confident in raising the stakes. Regulators approved; so did the credit-rating agencies responsible for evaluating these risks; so did most bank shareholders. John Lanchester, a chronicler of the crisis, quips, 'It's as if people used the invention of seatbelts as an opportunity to take up drunk-driving.' Quite so – and in fact there is evidence that seatbelts and airbags do indeed encourage drivers to behave more dangerously. Psychologists call this 'risk compensation'. The entire point of the CDS was to create a margin of safety that would let banks take more risks. As with safety belts and dangerous drivers, innocent bystanders were among the casualties.

The subtler way in which credit default swaps helped cause the crisis was by introducing new and unexpected ways for things to go wrong – just as with Galileo's columns or the zirconium filter at the Fermi reactor. The CDS contracts increased both the complexity and the tight coupling of the financial system. Institutions that hadn't previously been connected turned out to be bound together, and new chains of cause and effect emerged that nobody had anticipated.

The bond insurance business is a case in point.* As the banks cranked out complex new mortgage-related bonds, they turned to insurance companies called 'monolines', and huge general insurers such as AIG, to provide insurance using credit default swaps. This seemed to make sense for both sides: for the insurers, it was profitable and seemed extremely safe, while investors enjoyed the security of being backed by rock-solid insurance companies.

But as we saw with the LMX spiral, even insurance, the quintessential safety system, can create unexpected risks. The hidden danger came through 'credit ratings', which are a measure of a bond's risk devised by companies called rating agencies. If a bond was insured, it simply inherited the credit rating of the insurer. Insurance companies such as AIG, of course, had very high credit ratings, so even a risky bond could acquire an excellent credit rating if it was insured by AIG.

Unfortunately, this process also works in reverse. If an insurance company has mistakenly insured too many risky bonds, it will find itself flirting with bankruptcy, and so it will lose its high credit rating – precisely what happened to AIG and the monoline insurers. And as its rating is downgraded, so is the rating of all the bonds it has insured. As large numbers of bonds were downgraded in unison, banks were legally forced to sell them in unison by sensible-seeming regulations forbidding banks to hold too many risky bonds. It doesn't take a financial wizard to see that the combination of safety system and safety regulation produced a recipe for a price collapse.

The consequence of all that is that a bank could avoid all the major sources of financial trouble – such as the subprime mortgage market – and still be pushed into bankruptcy. The bank

*A bond is a kind of tradable loan: if you buy the bond, you're getting the right to receive the loan repayments, perhaps from a company, perhaps from a government, or perhaps from some more complex financial process.

would be quietly holding a sensible portfolio of medium-risk bonds, insured by an insurance company. The insurance company itself would get into trouble because it had insured subprime mortgage products, and the bank's portfolio would have its credit rating downgraded not because the quality of the portfolio changed, but because its insurer was in trouble. The bank would be legally obliged to sell its assets at the same time as other banks were doing the same. It was like a mountaineer, cautiously scaling a cliff while roped to a reckless team, and suddenly finding himself pulled into the abyss by his own safety harness. The insurance companies and their web of credit default swaps acted as the rope.

Rather than reducing risk, credit default swaps instead contrived to magnify it and make it pop up in an unexpected place. The same thing was true of other financial safety systems – for instance the infamous collateralised debt obligations, or CDOs, which repackaged financial flows from risky 'subprime' mortgages. The aim was to parcel out the risk into well-understood slices, some extremely risky and some extremely safe. The result, instead, was to magnify certain risks almost beyond imagination – twice the losses on the underlying mortgages would be squared by the repackaging process once, twice, or more, to turn into losses that were 4, 16, 256 or even 65,000 times greater than expected. (These numbers are illustrative rather than precise, but the illustration is a fair portrait of the CDOs.) In both cases, the safety systems made investors and banks careless – and more fundamentally, they transformed small problems into catastrophes. Industrial safety experts – if anyone had asked – could have warned that such unexpected consequences are common.

Better designed safety measures might work differently, of course, but experience from industrial disasters suggests that it's harder than it looks to develop safety measures that don't bite back. So if a Rube Goldbergesque accretion of one safety system after another is not the solution either to industrial or financial catastrophes, what is?

4 'The people who were operating the plant were absolutely, completely, lost'

The 1979 crisis at Three Mile Island remains the closest the American nuclear industry has come to a major disaster. It started when engineers trying to clear a blocked filter acciden- tally let a cupful of water leak into the wrong system. The leak – harmless in its own right – triggered an automatic safety device that shut down the main pumps which circulated water through the heat exchanger, steam turbines and cooling towers. The reactor now needed to be cooled in some other way. What fol- lowed was a classic example of one of Charles Perrow's system accidents, with individually recoverable errors snowballing.

Two backup pumps should have started to inject cold water into the reactor vessel, but valves in both pipes had been mistak- enly left closed after maintenance. Warning lights should have alerted operators to the closed valves, but they were obscured by a paper repair tag hanging from a switch. As the reactor began to overheat, a relief valve – like on a pressure cooker – automatically popped open. When the pressure fell back to optimal level, it should have popped shut again. But it jammed open, causing the reactor to depressurise to dangerous levels.

If operators had realised the valve was jammed open, they could have shut another valve further down the pipe. But the control panel seemed to show that the valve had closed as normal. In fact, the panel merely showed that a signal had been sent to close the valve as normal, not that the valve had responded. As they struggled to make sense of what was going on, the supervisor figured out that there was a chance that the relief valve might be open. So he asked one of the engineers to check the temperature reading. The engineer reported all was normal – because he had looked at the wrong gauge.

This was a serious error, but understandable in its context. A cacophony of over a hundred alarms provided the backdrop to these confused discussions. The control panels were baffling: they displayed almost 750 lights, each with a letter code, some near the relevant flip switch and some far. Some were above and some below. Red lights indicated open valves or active equipment; green indicated closed valves or inactive equipment. But since some of the lights were typically green and others were normally red, it was impossible even for highly trained operators to scan the winking mass of lights and quickly spot trouble.

At 6.20 in the morning, the arrival of a new shift finally brought fresh eyes and the realisation that superheated coolant had been gushing out of the depressurised reactor for over two hours. The new shift successfully brought the situation under control – not before 32,000 gallons of highly contaminated coolant had escaped, but in time to avert complete meltdown. With better indicators of what was happening, the accident could have been much more swiftly contained.

I asked the head of nuclear installation safety at the International Atomic Energy Agency, Philippe Jamet, what we had learned from Three Mile Island. 'When you look at the way the accident happened, the people who were operating the plant were absolutely, completely, lost,' he replied.

Jamet says that since Three Mile Island, much attention has been lavished on the problem of telling the operators what they need to know in a format they can understand. The aim is to ensure that never again will operators have to try to control a misfiring reactor core against the sound of a hundred alarms and in the face of a thousand tiny winking indicator lights.

The lesson is apparent at Hinkley Point B, an ageing power plant overlooking the Bristol Channel in southwest England. The site was once designed to welcome visiting school children, but is now defended against terrorists by a maze of checkpoints and perimeter fencing. At the heart of the site, which I visited on a mizzling unseasonable day in late July, looms a vast grey slab of a building containing a pair of nuclear reactors. A short distance away is a low-rise office that would have looked at home in any

suburban business park. At the heart of that office is the simulator: a near perfect replica of Hinkley Point B's control room.
The simulator has a 1970s feel, with large sturdy metal consoles
and chunky bakelite switches. Modern flat-screen monitors have
been added, just as in the real control room, to provide additional computer-moderated information about the reactor.
Behind the scenes, a powerful computer simulates the nuclear
reactor itself and can be programmed to behave in any number
of inconvenient ways.

'There have been vast improvements over the years,'
explained Steve Mitchelhill, the simulator instructor who
showed me around. 'Some of it looks cosmetic, but it isn't. It's
about reducing human factors.' 'Human factors', of course,
means mistakes by the nuclear plant's operators. And Mitchelhill
goes out of his way to indicate a deceptively simple innovation
introduced in the mid-1990s: coloured overlays designed to help
operators understand, in a moment of panic or of inattention,
which switches and indicators are related to each other. That
humble idea alone would probably have allowed operators to
stop the Three Mile Island accident within minutes.

The lesson for financial regulators might seem obscure. Yet
the same baffled, exhausted mistakes that characterised Three
Mile Island also bedevilled decision making during the financial
crisis. There was a Three Mile Island moment in the second
week of September 2008. All eyes were focused on Lehman
Brothers, which by then was sliding into deep trouble. Among
the eyes focusing on Lehman were those of Tim Geithner, then
President of the Federal Reserve Bank of New York, which
supervised the banks. Geithner had just completed a transatlantic flight when the Chief Executive of the American
International Group, AIG, Robert Willumstad, requested a
meeting. According to the journalist Andrew Ross Sorkin,
Geithner kept Willumstad waiting for half an hour because he
was on the phone to Lehman Brothers. And when the two men
did meet, Willumstad asked if AIG could have access to the same

borrowing facilities at the Federal Reserve that were available to the investment banks.

Willumstad handed Geithner a briefing note confessing that AIG was exposed to $2,700 billion ($2,700,000,000,000) worth of perilous-looking financial contracts – more than a third of which were credit default swaps and similar deals agreed with twelve top financial institutions. The implication was that if AIG collapsed, it would bring the global financial system to its knees. AIG was both a bigger threat than Lehman Brothers, and a far more surprising one. Yet alarm bells cannot have sounded in Geithner's head as loudly as perhaps they should have. AIG was, after all, an insurance company, regulated by the Treasury rather than Geithner's New York Fed. For some reason – possibly fatigue, perhaps because he had no time to study Willumstad's note, or maybe the note had been too indirect – Tim Geithner set the AIG question to one side and turned back to concentrate on the Lehman Brothers problem.

Frantic negotiations to save Lehman went on between government officials and top investment bankers throughout the weekend. It was only on Sunday evening that the penny dropped, when one of those investment bankers received a call from a Treasury official to ask if she could put together a team and start working on similar rescue discussions for AIG instead. The surprising news was greeted with an unsurprising response: 'Hold on, hold on . . . You're calling me on a Sunday night saying that we just spent the entire weekend on Lehman and now we have this? How the fuck did we spend the past forty-eight hours on the wrong thing?' Just as in Three Mile Island, those in charge of a complex system had apparently been unable to pick out the essential information from a blizzard of financial noise.

'We always blame the operator – "pilot error",' says Charles Perrow, the Yale sociologist. But like a power-plant operator staring at the wrong winking light, Tim Geithner had the wrong focus not because he was a fool, but because he was being supplied with information that was confusing and inadequate. It may be satisfying to castigate the likes of Geithner and the heads of Lehman Brothers and AIG, but safety experts like Perrow know it is far more productive to design better systems than to hope for better people.

Air-traffic control is one celebrated example of how a very reliable system was created despite the inherent difficulty of the task. So could we design the equivalent of an air-traffic control system for financial regulators, showing them when institutions are on a collision course? Regulators currently have little idea about whether there is another AIG out there, and no systematic method for finding out. They need more information – and more important, they need information in a format that's as easy to understand as moving dots on a radar screen.

Andrew Haldane, director for financial stability at the Bank of England, looks forward to the day when regulators will have a 'heat map' of stresses in the financial system, harnessing the technologies now used to check the health of an electricity grid. With the right data and the right software to interpret it, regulators could look at a financial network map, highlighting critical connections, overstressed nodes, and unexpected inter-actions. Rather than poring over disconnected spreadsheets or puzzling PowerPoint slides, they would be looking at clear, intu-itive presentations of risks emerging in the system. Ideally the map would be updatable daily, hourly – perhaps even in real time.

'We're a million miles away from that at the moment,' Haldane readily admits. The Dodd–Frank reform act, signed by President Obama in July 2010, establishes a new Office for Financial Research which seems likely to try to draw up a map. The technology should, in principle, reveal which companies are systemically important – 'too big to fail' – and how systemic importance is changing over time. (The new 'Basel III' regula-tions discuss what rules should apply to systemically important institutions, but at present the definition of systemic importance is no clearer than the definition of art, literature or pornography.) A future Tim Geithner should never again be surprised to discover the unexpected importance of an institution such as AIG.

For all the attractions of a systemic heat map, it is unlikely to solve the problem by itself, any more than Donald Rumsfeld's 'information dominance' solved the problem of waging war. Keeping the financial system safe will require proper systemic information for regulators, but it will also require much more. As on a battlefield, what goes on at the front line of finance can be impossible for any computer to summarise.

5 'We had no time'

One Saturday evening in September 2008, while Tim Geithner and a slew of top investment bankers in New York were busily spending forty-eight hours on the wrong thing, Tony Lomas was enjoying a meal at a Chinese restaurant with his family when his phone rang. At the other end of the line was the senior lawyer for the British operations of Lehman Brothers. The lawyer asked Lomas to come along the next day to the firm's offices at Canary Wharf in London with a small team of insolvency experts. Lomas already knew that Lehman Brothers was in trouble. The shares had lost more than three quarters of their value in the past week. Some kind of rescue deal was being brokered in New York, but Lehman's European directors wanted a Plan B – wisely, as Lehman Brothers fell apart shortly after the New York deal evaporated, leaving each national subsidiary to fend for itself. Plan B meant sending for the boss of the biggest insolvency practice in the UK. And that man was Tony Lomas.

The speed of Lehman's collapse took even Lomas and his seasoned colleagues at PwC by surprise. Insolvency is typically a less sudden process – potential administrators tend to be lined up, just in case, weeks before a company declares that it is bankrupt. Yet suddenness is in the nature of a financial-services bankruptcy. Nobody wants to do business with a bank that seems like a credit risk, so there is no such thing as an investment bank that slowly slides towards bankruptcy. It happens fast, or it does not happen at all. The effect of such a sudden end to Lehman's was chaos, most immediately for the personal lives of the accountants. One PwC partner said goodbye to his family at Sunday lunchtime and didn't leave Canary Wharf for a week. His car ticked up an enormous bill in the short-stay car park – just one modest contribution to the cost of the administration process. PwC earned £120 million in the first year of working on the European arm of the Lehman bankruptcy, while the first year's fees paid to administrators in the US and Europe totalled about half a billion dollars.

Lomas quickly took over the 31st floor of the Lehman offices in Canary Wharf, previously the executive dining suite; ostentatiously expensive works of art found themselves sharing wall space with hand-scrawled signs of guidance for the mushrooming team of PwC number-crunchers. The situation was an instant crisis. On Sunday afternoon, the administrators learned that the New York office had swept up all of the cash in Lehman's European accounts on Friday evening – standard practice every day, but on this occasion there was little chance that the money would come back. That would make it impossible, and illegal, to trade on Monday morning. And Lehman had countless unresolved transactions open with many thousands of companies. On Monday morning – after a 5 a.m. board meeting – a judge signed over control of Lehman Europe to the PwC team, making the bankruptcy official. This happened at 7.56 a.m.; the ink wasn't even dry by the time the London markets opened four minutes later.

The PwC team scrambled to figure out how Lehman's operations worked. They were shown a baffling diagram of the bank's Byzantine but tax-avoiding legal structure, with hundreds of subsidiary legal entities, only to be told that what looked like the Gordian knot was in fact just the simplified summary. It wasn't that the team lacked experience: they'd overseen the restructuring of the European arm of Enron, the disgraced energy trading company famous for its financial wizardry. But Enron's contracts were nowhere near as complex. Lomas was forced to assign staff to 'mark' senior Lehman officials, following them around all day in a desperate attempt to figure out what they actually did.

The scale of the chaos was mind-boggling. As a broker, Lehman Europe held over $40 billion in cash, shares and other assets on behalf of its clients. That money was frozen, so some clients found they were, as a result, at risk of bankruptcy themselves. Lehman was responsible for fully one in eight trades on the London Stock Exchange, but the last three days' worth of trades had not been fully settled. Remarkably, this was typical. These unsettled trades were swinging in the winds of an unprecedentedly volatile market. Lehman had also hedged many of the risks it faced, using derivatives deals to protect it from volatility. But as the cancellation emails started to arrive on Monday, it became apparent that the bankruptcy made some of these deals void. When Lehman Brothers failed, it had one million derivatives contracts open.

It was only Lehman's traders who understood how to untangle these deals, so only if some of them could be persuaded to stay on temporarily could the open positions be closed without the loss of still vaster sums of money. Infuriatingly for Lehman's creditors – the cleaners, the cooks, the providers of telephone service and electricity – Lomas had to conjure up a $100 million loan to hand the traders generous bonuses. Even then, they couldn't do it alone: any trader from another firm who became aware that Lehman was on the other end of the phone trying to offload an asset would be able to exploit the knowledge that the sale was forced. So Tony Lomas recruited teams at other banks, operating under hush-hush conditions, to do the job instead. To make matters worse, as it was itself a rather large bank Lehman didn't have its own bank account. It couldn't open one with another bank because they were all Lehman creditors and so would be legally able to grab any money Lehman deposited.

Lomas had to enlist the help of the Bank of England, opening dozens of accounts in different currencies directly with the Old Lady of Threadneedle Street.

And that was just the immediate firefighting. Tidying up the charred remains would take a long, long time. It was over a year after Lehman Brothers collapsed before a British court started to hear testimony from Lehman's clients, the financial regulator and PwC about what might be the correct way to treat a particular multi-billion dollar pool of money that Lehman held on behalf of clients. Who should get paid, how much and when? As PwC's lawyer explained to the court, there were no fewer than four schools of thought as to the correct legal approach. The court case took weeks. Another series of court rulings governed whether Tony Lomas was able to execute a plan to speed up the bankruptcy process by dividing Lehman creditors into three broad classes and treating them accordingly, rather than as individuals. The courts refused.

It slowly emerged that the bank had systematically hidden the extent of its financial distress using a legal accounting trick called Repo 105, which made both Lehman's tower of debt and its pile of risky assets look smaller and thus safer than they really were. Whether Repo 105 was legitimate in this context is the subject of legal action: in December 2010, New York State prosecutors sued Lehman's auditors, Ernst and Young, accusing them of helping Lehman in a 'massive accounting fraud'. But if that case remains unproven, it is quite possible that Lehman's financial indicators were technically accurate despite being highly misleading, like the indicator light at Three Mile Island which showed only that the valve had been told to close, and not that it actually had.

Interviewed by the *Financial Times* on the first anniversary of Lehman Brothers' collapse, Tony Lomas was hopeful of having resolved the big issues some time in 2011, about three years after the bankruptcy process began.

Lomas explained what would have made a difference: 'If we

had walked in here on that Sunday, and there had been a manual there that said, "Contingency plan: If this company ever needs to seek protection in court, this is what will happen" – wouldn't that have been easier? At Enron, we had two weeks to write that plan. That wasn't long enough, but it did give us an opportunity to hit the ground running. Here, we had no time to do that.'

Tony Lomas found an operation of bewildering complexity, and he was dealing only with the European office of Lehman Brothers – just a subsidiary of the entire bank, itself just a component of the global financial machine. But as we have seen, complexity is a problem only in tightly coupled systems. The reason we should care about how long it took to untangle Lehman Brothers is not because bankers and bank shareholders deserve any special protection – it is that tens of billions of dollars of other companies' money were entombed with the dead bank for all that time. If that problem could be solved, the next Lehman Brothers could be allowed to fail – safely. That means turning a tightly coupled system into one where the interconnections are looser and more flexible.

6 Dominoes and zombie banks

The rather quirky sport of domino toppling is perhaps the ultimate example of a tightly coupled system. You've seen domino stunts as the last item on the evening news: record attempts in which someone has painstakingly stacked up thousands upon thousands of dominoes, ready to topple them all with a single gentle push. Dominoes, unlike banks, are supposed to fall over – but not too soon. One of the first domino toppling record attempts – 8000 dominoes – was ruined when a pen dropped out of the pocket of the television cameraman who had come to film the happy occasion. Other record attempts have been disrupted by moths and grasshoppers.

It might be possible to topple dominoes in a strictly

controlled environment, free of insects and television crews. This would reduce the complexity of the domino system, meaning that being tightly coupled wouldn't be so much of a problem. But it is clearly far more practical to loosen the coupling of the system instead. Professional domino topplers now use safety gates, removed at the last moment, to ensure that when accidents happen they are contained. In 2005, a hundred volunteers had spent two months setting up 4,155,476 stones in a Dutch exhibition hall when a sparrow flew in and knocked one over. Because of safety gates, only 23,000 dominoes fell. It could have been much worse. (Though not for the hapless sparrow, which a domino enthusiast shot with an air rifle – incurring the wrath of animal rights protesters, who tried to break into the exhibition centre and finish the job the poor bird had started.)

The financial system will never eliminate its sparrows (perhaps black swans would be a more appropriate bird), so it needs the equivalent of those safety gates. If the system's coupling could be loosened – so that one bank could run into distress without dragging down others – then the financial system could be made safer even if errors were as common as ever.

Banks can act like dominoes – toppling many other firms when they fall over – in two ways. Most obviously, they can go infectiously bankrupt, meaning that they can collapse while holding their customers' money. The nightmare scenario is that depositors from ordinary consumers to large companies find their cheques bouncing, not because they have run out of money but because the bank has.

Then there are zombie banks. They avoid going bankrupt, but only by stumbling around in a corporate half-life, terrorising other businesses. Here's what happens. All banks have assets (a mortgage is an asset because the homeowner owes money to the bank) and liabilities (a savings account is a liability because the bank has to give the saver her money back if she asks for it). If the assets are smaller than the liabilities, the bank is legally bankrupt. Banks have a buffer against bankruptcy, called 'capital'. This is money that the bank holds on behalf of its shareholders, who are at the back of any queue for repayment if the bank gets into trouble.

If the assets are barely larger than the liabilities, the bank is on the brink of bankruptcy – and to avoid that fate, it is likely to resort to the undeath of zombiehood. We'd ideally want the bank to avoid bankruptcy by seeking fresh capital from shareholders, inflating the capital cushion and letting the bank continue doing business with confidence. Yet most shareholders would be unwilling to inject capital, because much of the benefit would be enjoyed by the bank's creditors instead. Remember: the creditors get paid first, then the shareholders. If the bank is near bankruptcy, the capital injection's biggest effect is to ensure that creditors are paid in full; shareholders benefit only if there's money left over.

So zombie banks do something else. Instead of inflating their capital cushion, they try to shrink in size so that a smaller cushion is big enough. They call in loans and use the proceeds to pay off their own creditors, and become reluctant to lend cash to any new businesses or homebuyers. This process sucks cash out of the economy.

Both zombie banks and infectiously bankrupt banks can topple many dominoes. No wonder governments responded to the financial crisis by guaranteeing bank debts and forcibly injecting big chunks of capital into banks. This prevented the crash from having more serious effects on the economy, but it had a cost – not only the vast expenditure (and even bigger risks) that taxpayers were forced to take, but also the dangerously reassuring message to bank creditors: 'Lend as much as you like to whomever you like, because the taxpayer will always make sure you get paid.' Instead of a capital cushion, it was the taxpayer who was pushed into the middle of the crash to soften the impact on the financial system. Decoupling the financial system means setting up the financial equivalent of those safety gates, so that when a bank such as Lehman Brothers gets into distress in future, it can be allowed to topple.

7 Decoupling

The first and most obvious way we can insert a safety gate between banks and the dominoes they could topple is making sure banks hold more capital. This not only reduces the chance that an individual bank will fail, but also reduces the chance that the failure will spread. Banks will not voluntarily carry thick cushions of capital, so regulators have to force them, and there is a cost to this. Capital is expensive, so higher capital requirements are likely to make loans and insurance more costly. It is possible to have too much of a good thing, even capital. But the credit crunch made it clear that the banks were carrying too little.

The second possible safety gate involves the curiously named 'CoCo' bonds – short for contingent convertible bonds. CoCos are debt, so under normal circumstances CoCo holders are paid interest and take priority over shareholders just as ordinary bank creditors do. But a CoCo is a bit like an airbag: if the bank crashes, it suddenly turns into a cushion, converting from bond to capital. Effectively, given certain triggers, the creditors who held CoCos find that, instead, they are now holding newly minted bank shares. This means they take the same risks as other shareholders.

Nobody is going to rejoice about this. Existing shareholders find they own a smaller slice of the firm, along with any profits. CoCo holders find they're taking more risk than they wanted to. But the point about CoCo bonds is that they're a pre-agreed piece of contingency planning: *if* the bank is on the verge of turning into a zombie, *then* the CoCo clause is triggered. Ordinary bondholders are safer because they get priority over CoCo bondholders; ordinary shareholders enjoy a higher return than they would have if the bank had simply to have ordinary capital rather than contingent capital. And in normal times the CoCo holders, because they are acting as insurers, will be paid a higher return than other bondholders.

It all sounds great. But remember that airbags can cause injuries as well as prevent them. CoCo bonds – like other insurance-style schemes – can move risk around the financial system, and we've seen what that can lead to. In Japan in the 1990s, CoCos acquired the charming name of 'death spiral bonds', which many people will find less than reassuring. One bank's distress would trigger the CoCo clause, and other banks holding bonds that had suddenly been converted into equity were forced to sell them at a loss, possibly facing distress themselves. The answer is to ban banks from holding each other's CoCo bonds: instead, those bonds should be held by private individuals or by pension funds, which are more robust in the face of short-term problems.

The third way to loosen the system is to have a much better way of handling bankruptcy if a bank does fail. Recall Tony Lomas's lament that Lehman Brothers had no contingency plan for bankruptcy. Regulators could and should insist that major financial companies prepare such contingency plans and file them every quarter for inspection. The plans should include estimates of the time it would take to dismantle the company – information that the regulator would take into account when setting minimum capital requirements. If an investment bank's operations are hellishly complex – often to avoid tax – and bankruptcy would take years, fine: let the capital cushion be luxuriously plump. A simpler operation with clearly defined contingency plans would cause less disruption if it went bankrupt and can be allowed a slimmer cushion. Since capital is expensive, this would encourage banks to simplify their operations and perhaps even to spin off subsidiaries. Currently, the playing field is tilted the other way, in favour of sprawling megabanks – complexity often brings tax advantages, while larger banks seem to be better credit risks.

It's also absurd that a year after Lehman Brothers went bankrupt, the courts were exploring four different possible legal treatments of money in Lehman accounts. Regulators should have the authority to rule on ambiguities quickly. Of course, fairness is important when billions of dollars are at stake – but when a bank goes bankrupt, the worst possible decision is indecision. The physical economy can be paralysed by the tangle of claims against the banks – like some modern-day equivalent of Jarndyce and Jarndyce, the inheritance dispute in Charles Dickens's *Bleak House*, which dragged on for so long that legal fees consumed the entire estate and none of the relatives got a penny.

Regulators also need the authority to take over banks or other financial institutions and quickly restructure them. As Tony Lomas discovered, international banks splinter into national banks as they die, so this kind of authority would need international agreement. But technically, it is simpler than it might seem.

One simple way to restructure even a complex bank has been invented by two game theorists, Jeremy Bulow and Paul Klemperer,* and endorsed by Willem Buiter, who subsequently became chief economist of perhaps the world's most complex bank, Citigroup. It's such an elegant approach that at first it seems like a logical sleight of hand: Bulow and Klemperer propose that regulators could forcibly split a struggling bank into a good 'bridge' bank and a bad 'rump' bank. The bridge bank gets all the assets, and only the most sacred liabilities – such as the deposits ordinary people have left in savings accounts, or in the case of an investment bank, the cash deposited by other businesses. The rump bank gets no assets, just the rest of the debts. At a stroke, the bridge bank is fully-functioning, has a good capital cushion and can keep lending, borrowing and trading. The rump bank is, of course, a basket case.

Haven't the rump bank's creditors been robbed? Not so fast. Here comes the conjuring trick: the rump bank owns the bridge

*Readers of *The Undercover Economist* may recall Klemperer as one of the designers of the 3G spectrum auctions.

bank. So when the rump bank goes bust, and its creditors see what they can salvage, part of what they can salvage will include shares in the still-functioning bridge bank. That ought to leave them better off than trying to salvage only from the wreckage of the original bank. And meanwhile the bridge bank continues to support the smooth running of the economy, too.

If you are blinking at the idea that one can produce a healthy bridge bank like a rabbit from a troubled-bank top hat, without injecting new funds and without resorting to expropriation, you should be. But it seems to be true.

An even more radical – and probably safer – idea comes from the economist John Kay and is known as 'narrow banking'. Kay suggests splitting the 'casino' and the 'utility' functions of modern banking. Utility banking is what ensures that ATMs give out cash, credit cards work, and ordinary people can deposit money in bank accounts without fearing for their savings. Casino banking incorporates the more speculative side of banking – financing corporate buyouts, investing in mortgage-backed bonds, or using credit derivatives in the hope of making money. A narrow bank is one that supplies all the utility functions of the banking system without dabbling in the casino side, and the idea of narrow banking is to make sure that banks that provide utilities cannot also play in the casino.

The truth is, naturally, messier. It is not quite fair to liken all risky banking to playing in a casino. As we saw in chapter 3, new ideas need rather speculative sources of funding, and many good ideas fail. There is always something of a gamble about the process of moving money to where it may achieve astonishing things, so without the presence of 'casino' activities such as venture capital, the world would be a poorer and less innovative place than it is. Nor is it quite so easy to differentiate between utilities and casinos: some casino-style activities are in fact simply sensible, even conservative pieces of risk hedging. If I bet that my neighbour's house will burn down, that should raise some eyebrows, but if I bet that my own house will burn down, that's insurance – it's not only sensible but compulsory in many countries. Similarly, whether a bank's particular financial transaction counts as a gamble or a piece of sensible risk management very much depends on what else the bank may be doing.

Nevertheless, the idea of narrow banking may be workable. Kay suggests that narrow banks would require a licence, and to get that licence they would have to satisfy regulators that their deposits were backed solidly with plenty of capital, and their 'casino' activities strictly limited to supporting the utility side, rather than designed to make money in their own right. Narrow banks would be the only institutions legally allowed to call themselves 'banks', the only ones allowed to take deposits from small businesses and consumers, the only ones allowed to use the basic inter-bank payments systems which transfer money from one bank account to another and which underpin the ATM network, and the only ones qualifying for deposit protection provided by the taxpayer.

This might sound like excessive regulatory meddling, but John Kay points out that in some ways it is less meddlesome. Rather than supervising the entire financial system in a vague and – we now know – inadequate way, dedicated regulators would focus on the simpler task of working out whether a particular bank deserved a narrow banking licence or not. Other financial firms could take the usual risks with their shareholders' money. They could even own narrow banks: if the parent casino bank got into trouble, the narrow bank could be lifted wholesale out of difficulty and placed somewhere safer, without disruption to depositors or cost to the taxpayers – in the same way that if an electricity company went bankrupt, its power stations would keep running under new ownership.

All this harks back to Peter Palchinsky's second principle: make failures survivable. Normally, carrying out lots of small experiments – variation and selection – means that survivability is all part of the package. But in tightly coupled systems, failure in one experiment can endanger all. That is the importance of successfully decoupling.

'We cannot contemplate keeping aircraft circling over London while the liquidator of Heathrow Airport Ltd finds the way to his office,' says John Kay. That is pretty much what happened to the dealings of Lehman Brothers while Tony Lomas's team tried to resolve the mess, and Kay is right to seek a more sensible resolution system in future. His approach is in sharp contrast to the prevailing regulatory philosophy, which unwittingly encouraged banks to become larger and more complicated, and actively encouraged off-balance-sheet financial juggling. I do not know for sure whether Kay has the right answer, but normal accident theory suggests he is certainly asking the right question.

8 Slips, mistakes and violations

James Reason, the scholar of catastrophe who uses Nick Leeson and Barings Bank as a case study to help engineers prevent accidents, is careful to distinguish between three different types of error. The most straightforward are *slips*, when through clumsiness or lack of attention you do something you simply didn't mean to do. In 2005, a young Japanese trader tried to sell one share at a price of ¥600,000 and instead sold 600,000 shares at the bargain price of ¥1. Traders call these slips 'fat finger errors' and this one cost £200 million.

Then there are *violations*, which involve someone deliberately doing the wrong thing. Bewildering accounting tricks like those employed at Enron, or the cruder fraud of Bernard Madoff, are violations, and the incentives for them are much greater in finance than in industry.

Most insidious are *mistakes*. Mistakes are things you do on purpose, but with unintended consequences, because your mental model of the world is wrong. When the supervisors at Piper

Alpha switched on a dismantled pump, they made a mistake in this sense. Switching on the pump was what they intended, and they followed all the correct procedures. The problem was that their assumption about the pump, which was that it was all in one piece, was mistaken. The mathematical assumptions behind CDOs were also a mistake – the whiz-kids who designed them were wrong about the underlying distribution of risks, and the CDO structure dramatically magnified that mistake.

In the aftermath of disaster, we typically devote lots of attention to distinguishing violations from mistakes. Violations mean people should be fined, or sacked, or sent to jail. Mistakes are far less of an outrage. But what mistakes and violations have in common is at least as important as what separates them: they are generally much harder to spot than slips are, and so they lead to more of what Professor Reason calls 'latent errors'.

Latent errors lurk unnoticed until the worst possible moment – like maintenance workers accidentally leaving valves closed on backup cooler pumps, and paper repair tags obscuring the view of warning lights. By their nature, such safety devices are used only in emergencies – and the more safety systems there are, the less likely latent errors are to be noticed until the very instant we can least afford them. Very often latent errors are tiny, almost impossible to pick up without being right at the business coal face. In James Reason's Swiss cheese metaphor, the holes in one slice after another begin to line up, and stay lined up, without anyone noticing that the risk of disaster is rising.

The financial system is particularly vulnerable to latent error, partly because of its inherent complexity, and also because the incentive for violations is so much stronger in finance. Airline pilots, surgeons and nuclear plant operators are human – they will make mistakes, and they may sometimes cut corners. But we can usually hope that they will try in good faith to avoid accidents. We can have no such hope in finance, where the systemic consequences of bending the rules can pop up far away from the perpetrators and long after the profits have been banked.

Yet even in finance, latent errors can be spotted and fixed before any damage is done. The question is how. The assumption underpinning financial regulation is that if a bank is creating latent errors – whether through deliberate violations or innocent mistakes – then the people who will spot the risks are auditors and financial regulators. It is, after all, their job to do so. But do they? That is the question three economists tried to answer with an exhaustive study of corporate fraud. Not all potential problems involve fraud, of course, but the ability to uncover fraud is a good indicator of the ability to spot other latent errors. Alexander Dyck, Adair Morse and Luigi Zingales examined 216 serious allegations of fraud in US companies between 1996 and 2004. The sample excludes frivolous cases and includes all the famous scandals such as WorldCom and Enron.

What Dyck, Morse and Zingales found completely undermines the conventional wisdom. Out of the frauds that were discovered, auditors and financial regulators discovered only one in six. So who *did* spot corporate fraud? In some larger cases it was journalists. But non-financial regulators such as the Federal Aviation Administration spotted twice as many frauds as did the Securities and Exchange Commission. Evidently the contacts a non-financial regulator has with the everyday operations of a business are more likely to reveal wrongdoing than the auditors' reviews of accounts.

That suggests that the best-placed people of all to spot fraud – or indeed any kind of hidden danger in an organisation – are employees, who are at the front line of the organisation and know most about its problems. Sure enough, Dyck, Morse and Zingales found that employees did indeed lift the lid on more frauds than anyone else.

Yet it is a brave employee who does this. Frauds and other latent errors are often uncovered only when the situation is desperate, because the whistleblowers who speak out often suffer for their actions.

9 'There was nothing in it for me to tell them the truth'

When Paul Moore interviewed 140 front-line staff at Britain's largest mortgage lender, HBOS, he says 'it was like taking the lid off a pressure cooker – *fpow!* – it was amazing.' Moore was the head of group regulatory risk at HBOS between 2002 and 2005, and his job was to make sure that the banking group didn't take too many gambles. He found that staff at HBOS's major subsidiary, Halifax, were worried that they faced pressure to sell mortgages and hit targets, no matter what the risks were. One person complained to Moore that a manager had introduced a 'cash and cabbages' scheme, where staff would be given cash bonuses for hitting weekly sales targets, but publicly handed a cabbage if they failed. Another said, 'We'll never hit our sales targets and sell ethically.' The risk, of course, was the same that brought down the subprime mortgage market: that given the pressure to hit their targets, HBOS staff would lend money to people who couldn't afford to repay it. Moore mustered his evidence and presented a hard-hitting summary to the board of HBOS.

He says that he was thanked by the Chairman of HBOS and by the head of the HBOS audit committee for bringing to light such serious problems. Soon afterwards he was called in to meet Sir James Crosby, then the Chief Executive of HBOS. As Moore describes it, Moore's concerns about the risks HBOS was running were dismissed 'like swatting a fly' and he was sacked. Moore walked out on to the street in front of the HBOS offices and burst into tears. Crosby's account is different: he says that Paul Moore's concerns were fully investigated and were without merit

If Paul Moore's fate seems extreme, it pales beside that of the stock market analyst Ray Dirks. Dirks was an unconventional man, at least by the standards of New York financiers in 1973. A tubby, bespectacled and dishevelled figure, he eschewed the well-trimmed Wall Street conformity of the day, in favour of a duplex flat in Greenwich Village that was adorned by little more than a spiral staircase, two telephones and the occasional girl-friend. Dirks was a nonconformist in another way: in an era when many analysts were simply cheerleaders, he had a reputation as a ruthlessly candid analyst who wasn't afraid to dig up bad news about the companies he was analysing. But the bad news he received about the Equity Funding Corporation beggared belief.

A senior employee of Equity Funding had just quit, and decided that Dirks was the man to whom to tell his incredible story: Equity Funding had for years been running a massive fraud with its own dedicated computer system, specifically designed to create non-existent life insurance policies and sell them to other insurance companies. Over the course of a decade, over half of Equity Funding's life insurance policies were ficti-tious. The company was selling the future income stream from these fake policies – cash today in exchange for promises of cash tomorrow. When the bills came due, it would simply manufac-ture more fakes and sell them to raise the money.

Dirks was astonished, and as he began to make enquiries, he became alarmed: he began to hear rumours that Equity Funding had mafia connections; at one stage, when visiting the company in Los Angeles, he received a call from his boss telling him that by discussing the possibility of fraud he was laying himself open to being sued for libel; two days later, a former auditor of Equity told Dirks he'd better go into hiding for his own safety. As his suspicions grew, Dirks had told the *Wall Street Journal*, Equity's auditors, and the Securities and Exchange Commission (SEC) – but not before warning his clients of his fears.

Shortly after the Equity Funding Corporation collapsed, Ray Dirks was rewarded for his efforts: the SEC prosecuted him for insider trading, a charge that would at the very least have ended his career. Dirks fought his case for ten years before eventually being cleared by the US Supreme Court.

The SEC seems to have learned few lessons: when a former fund manager, Harry Markopolos, handed them a dossier of evidence that Bernard Madoff was running a gigantic fraud, he was ignored. (At least he was not prosecuted.) It is true that some whistleblowers have an axe to grind. Some are disgruntled former employees looking to make trouble. Mr Markopolos was Mr Madoff's rival; Paul Moore had plenty of reasons to complain about HBOS, whether or not his complaints had merit. It is hard to know who to take seriously. But when billions are at stake, it is unwise to dismiss whistleblowers too casually.

Many whistleblowers later say they regret speaking out – more than four fifths of those who uncovered fraud in the Dyck–Morse–Zingales study say they had to quit, or were fired or demoted. If we rely on the pure public-spiritedness of employees to blow the whistle on fraud, reckless selling, incompetent mathematical modelling, poor maintenance, or any other risky latent condition, then we are relying on individuals to take a big personal risk for the benefit of society as a whole. Most, it seems, prefer to live and let live, and it is easy to understand why.

Only the exceptionally motivated follow through, and the very qualities that make them determined to persist may also make them hard to take seriously. Ray Dirks was a stubborn contrarian by nature, which helped him speak up but also isolated him. Paul Moore seems to have been driven by religious conviction: he speaks of having 'sinned', 'examined my conscience very very closely' and doing 'a lot of praying'. But this religiosity, unusual for a British risk manager, may have chipped away at his credibility at the same time as it toughened his resolve against intimidation. And there was intimidation: Moore recounts how one colleague leaned across the table towards him and warned, 'Don't you make a fucking enemy of me.' Moore persisted, despite the fact that – his voice wavers as he says this – 'There was nothing in it for me to tell them the truth.'

But it is not impossible to encourage whistleblowers to speak out when they see evidence of a financial accident in the making – or an industrial accident. One piece of evidence for this comes from the Dyck–Morse–Zingales research. They looked at the healthcare sector, which relies on the taxpayer for much of its revenue. Because of this, whistleblowers can receive bonuses for saving tax dollars. The sums of money are breath-taking: such whistleblowers collected an average of almost $50 million in the study's sample of alleged frauds. Not surprisingly, the prospect of a lottery-win reward coaxes more employees to blow the whistle. This happens three times more often in the healthcare business than elsewhere.

Another example: the Inland Revenue Service recently increased the rewards people could earn by reporting suspected tax evaders, and the number of tip-offs increased sixfold. The sums of money at stake are much larger now, too, often involv-ing tens or hundreds of millions of dollars.

It would be harder to reward whistleblowers who spot more subtle latent errors. But the problem is worth thinking about, because it's quite clear that during the financial crisis many people saw signs of trouble inside individual banks and financial institutions, but did not see the percentage in speaking out.

Less than four years after Moore stood sobbing on the street outside HBOS, the company – including the proud, three-centuries-old Bank of Scotland – tottered on the verge of bankruptcy. It had to be bailed out twice in quick succession – first it was forced to sell itself to its rival, Lloyds TSB, and then the merging group accepted a total of £17 billion from the British government. It was all very unexpected, not least to the UK's financial regulator, the FSA. The deputy chair-man of the FSA at the time? None other than the man who'd sacked Paul Moore, Sir James Crosby.

10 Making experiments survivable

The financial crisis was so traumatic that it is tempting simply to conclude that all banking risks should be legislated out of exis-tence, with fancy financial instruments outlawed, and banks compelled to hold gigantic capital cushions. But that would take for granted – and threaten – the benefits we now enjoy from banking. The end of error in finance would also be the end of new ideas, and indeed of most banking as we know it.

We'd miss it. In the 1960s, my father-in-law tried to get a mortgage. He couldn't. He was a dentist, so self-employed – too risky. Property was concentrated in the hands of a narrow class of wealthy landlords, who were able to buy it cheap, without much competition, and rent it out to the masses. Immigrants or those with the wrong colour of skin were often the last to be able to get hold of a loan to buy their own home. Let's not forget that, although we ended up taking several steps too far in making mortgages easy to come by, those steps started off as being in the right direction. As in any other sector, some innovations in finance will inevitably fail. And as in any other sector, those inevitable failures are a price well worth paying for innovations that succeed – but only if the failures are survivable. John Kay's 'narrow banking' proposal aims to structure banks in such a way that the financial system can continue to take risks and develop valuable new products, but without endangering the system as a whole.

That is the key lesson that emerges from industrial safety. We can make a priority of getting more reliable indicators of what is going on, in a format that might enable a regulator both to anticipate systemic problems and to understand crises as they are occurring. We can get better at spotting latent errors more quickly by finding ways to reward – or at least to protect – those who speak up. We can be more systematic about publicising latent errors, too: the nuclear industry now has a system for recording near-misses and disseminating the information to other power plants that might be on the verge of making the same mistake. But above all, we should look at decoupling connections in the financial system to make sure that failures remain isolated.

After those fateful few days in 2008 when the US government

let Lehman Brothers fail and then propped up AIG, many people drew one of two contradictory conclusions: either AIG should have been treated like Lehman, or Lehman should have been treated like AIG. But the real lesson is that it should have been possible to let both Lehman and AIG collapse without systemic damage. Preventing banks from being 'too big to fail' is the right kind of sentiment but the wrong way of phrasing it, as the domino analogy shows: it would be absurd to describe a single domino as being too big to fail. What we need are safety gates in the system that ensure any falling domino cannot topple too many others.

Above all, when we look at how future financial crises could be prevented, we need to bear in mind the two ingredients of a system that make inevitable failures more likely to be cataclysmic: complexity and tight coupling. Industrial safety experts regard the decoupling of different processes and the reduction of complexity as valuable ends in themselves. Financial regulators should, too.

11 Deepwater Horizon

After nightfall on 20 April 2010, Mike Williams was in his workshop on a floating drilling rig in the Gulf of Mexico. The rig was a colossal engineering achievement, with a deck 400 feet by 250 feet, and the world record for deep-water drilling to its credit: over 35,000 feet – deeper than Mount Everest is high. The rig's team had just completed the drilling and sealing of the Macondo oil well, and that very day had hosted executives from the rig's operator, Transocean, and the well's owner, BP, to celebrate seven years without a notable accident. But the accident that was about to occur would be far more than merely notable: it was to be the worst environmental disaster in American history. The name of the rig was Deepwater Horizon.

Williams first realised something was amiss when the rig's

engines began revving wildly. He did not realise that explosive methane gas had bubbled up from the seabed, a mile below the surface of the water. It was being sucked into the rig's engines, forcing them to excessive speeds. Alarms sounded; lights glowed so brightly that they shattered; Williams pushed back from his desk just as his own computer monitor exploded. He was then hurled across the room by a far larger explosion – pinned under a three-inch steel fire door that had been ripped off its hinges by the force of the blast. He crawled towards the exit and was again flung across the room by a second flying blast door. Bleeding profusely from a head wound, he finally reached the deck of the rig to see that the crew were already evacuating, not realising that he and a few other crew had survived and remained behind on the rig. With a last thought of his wife and young daughter, and a prayer, Williams leapt from the deck of Deepwater Horizon. Like the few survivors of the Piper Alpha disaster, he faced a ten-storey drop. Mike Williams survived; eleven others died.

The exact distribution of blame for the Deepwater Horizon explosion and the gigantic oil spill that followed will be left to the courts – along with a bill of many billions of dollars. Almost five million barrels of oil surged into the Gulf of Mexico just 40 miles from the coast of Louisiana. How did it happen?

Blame could possibly be attached to the rig's operator, Transocean; to the contractor responsible for sealing the well with cement, Halliburton; to the regulator responsible for signing off on the drilling plans; and of course to BP, which owned the Macondo well and was in overall charge of the project. Each party has a strong financial incentive to blame the others. Still, amidst the confusion, the details that have emerged at the time of writing suggest a pattern that will now be familiar.

The first lesson is that safety systems often fail. When the boat that picked Mike Williams up circled back to tow a life raft away from the burning rig, it found the life raft tied to the rig by a safety line. Transocean, the rig's operator, banned crew from carrying knives – so the boat, and the life raft, found themselves attached to a blazing oil rig by an interacting pair of safety precautions. (The safety line was eventually severed and the crew rescued.) Or consider a safety device called the mud-gas separator: when the well started to leak, blowing mud and gas onto the deck of the rig, the crew directed the flow into the separator, which was quickly overwhelmed, enveloping much of the rig in explosive gas. Without this device, the crew would simply have directed the flow over the side of the rig, and the worst of the accident might have been prevented.

The second lesson is that latent errors can be deadly. BP's own review of the accident concluded that eight separate lines of defence had been breached – in James Reason's language, eight holes in the Swiss cheese had managed to align. But that is no great surprise; in such disasters, multiple lines of defence are almost always breached. The most noticeable failure was that of the blowout preventer, a massive seabed array of valves and hydraulic rams designed to seal the well in the event of disaster. A congressional hearing has heard that the preventer appeared to be in a shocking state: one of the automatic triggers had no battery power, while another had a faulty component. The preventer was leaking hydraulic fluid, meaning that when it was eventually triggered by a robot submersible, it lacked the power to seal the well. All this sounds shocking, but failsafe systems such as the blowout preventer are often in a poor state of repair because in an ideal world they would never be used: Deepwater Horizon's blowout preventer, which operated in extreme conditions a mile under the sea, had last been inspected five years before the accident.

The third lesson is that had whistleblowers felt able to speak up, the accident might have been prevented. The well had been unstable for weeks, and for months BP engineers had been expressing concern that the specific design of the well might not be up to the job. The Macondo well's manager reported problems with the blowout preventer three months before the accident.

Meanwhile, Transocean's safety record had been deteriorating for the few years prior to the accident: the company was showing signs of stress after a merger. On paper, BP has a clear policy of protecting people who blow the whistle with safety concerns. But in practice, the tight-knit community of an offshore drilling rig can encourage the kind of conformist thinking we encountered in chapter 2, regardless of the official policy. Oil companies, like banks, need to find ways to encourage whistleblowers.

Fourth, the rig system was too tightly coupled. One failure tended to compound another. The rig was designed as the key defence against minor and major spills: the rig contained the mud-gas separator to prevent small spills, and also controlled the blowout preventer. But at the very moment when the rig's capabilities were most needed to plug the leak, the rig itself was being torn apart by a series of explosions. In an awful echo of Piper Alpha, the blowout preventer could not be triggered from the rig's deck because power lines had been severed in the initial explosion. A safer design would have decoupled the blowout preventer from the rig's control room.

Fifth, as Tony Lomas could have attested, contingency plans would have helped. BP – along with other oil majors – was humiliated when it was discovered that their contingency plans for a major spill included measures to protect the local walrus population. This was not actually necessary: walruses typically look after themselves when oil is spilled in the Gulf of Mexico by staying exactly where they are, in the Arctic Circle. The implication was clear: BP and others seem to have grabbed a contingency plan off the shelf, one that was originally designed for drilling in Alaska or the North Sea.

The final lesson is that of 'normal accident' theory: accidents will happen, and we must be prepared for the consequences. The US government signed off on the Macondo drilling project because the risk of trouble was thought to be small. Perhaps it was small – but the chance of accidents is never zero.

As the economy we have created becomes ever more complex, both the engineering that underpins it and the finance that connects it all together will tend to become more complex, too. Deepwater Horizon was pushing the limits of deep sea engineering; Three Mile Island came at a time of constant innovation in nuclear technology; the burgeoning market in credit derivatives also tested the boundaries of what was possible in finance. The usual response to complexity, that of trial and error, is not enough when faced with systems which are not only complex, but also tightly coupled. The costs of error are simply too high.

The instinctive answer is to eliminate the errors. This is an impossible dream. The alternative is to try to simplify and to decouple these high-risk systems as much as is feasible, to encourage whistleblowers to identify latent errors waiting to strike, and – sadly – to stand prepared for the worst. These are lessons that some engineers – both petroleum engineers and financial engineers – seem to have to learn again and again.

Seven

The adaptive organisation

'One doesn't have to be a Marxist to be awed by the scale and success of early-20th-century efforts to transform strong-willed human beings into docile employees.'

– Gary Hamel

'Your first try will be wrong. Budget and design for it.'

– Aza Raskin, designer at Firefox

1 Adapting as we go along

When John Endler first studied guppies in the streams of Venezuela and Trinidad in the 1970s, he noticed an intriguing pattern: guppies in the pools at the bottom of waterfalls tended to be rather drab, while those in pools further upstream were eye-catchingly gaudy. Endler suspected the likely cause of the difference: while guppies were able to swim upstream past the waterfalls, the voracious guppy-eating pike cichlid could not, so the upper pools were cichlid-free. The drab guppies were camouflaged because they had evolved in a dangerous environment. The brightly-coloured ones lived in Guppy Eden, safely separated from the cichlids by a waterfall, and their colours were simply useful for attracting the attentions of other amorous guppies.

Endler decided to test his hypothesis in a more controlled environment, and filled a large greenhouse with ten guppy pools. Some pools had pebbles on the bottom, other pools were lined with finer gravel. Endler released the dangerous pike cichlids into some of each type of pool, and other pools were stocked either with gentler predators or no predators at all. Within fourteen months, ten generations, the guppy population adapted. In the dangerous pools, only the most boring guppies survived to breed; what is more, the guppy camouflage fitted the lining of the pool, with larger patterning in the pebble-floored pool and smaller patterning in the gravel-floored pool. In the safer pools, it was the brightly-spotted guppies that bred more – female guppies, it seems, have a taste for colourful polka dot males.

Professor Endler's guppy experiments are a modern classic in evolutionary biology, and a striking example of how a population adapts to a new problem, such as the appearance of a pike cichlid. Not only was the adaptation fast, it was sensitive to context: the right response to a pike cichlid depends on what sort of material the pool is lined with. It was a decentralised process, because no guppy planned the response. And it was driven by failure: some guppies were eaten, while others went on to produce future generations of well-adapted baby guppies.

If this was a straightforward guide to business success and personal growth, this would be the point at which the author would urge you to use the principles of adapting to gain wealth and success working just one hour a day, or to create the next Apple or Google. If only it was that easy.

Adapting is not necessarily something we do. It may well be something that is *done to us*. We may think of ourselves as Professor Endler, but we're actually the guppies. No individual guppy adapted, but some guppies avoided being eaten and some did not. This book has so far taken John Endler's view of things. We've seen how policymakers and the leaders of organisations can set up systems that either unleash or suppress adaptive behaviour: carbon taxes promote eco-efficiency; innovation prizes encourage new ideas; Donald Rumsfeld's thought-policing of the US Army held back the process of adapting in Iraq; 'too big to fail' bailouts encouraged banks that were, well, too big. But this closing pair of chapters takes the guppy-eye view, asking how the principles of adapting can be applied in two areas: corporate strategy and personal life.

As the pike cichlid closes in for a meal, it's little consolation to the polka-dotted guppy that its failure is helping clear space for a thriving population of pebble-coloured nieces and nephews. A struggling entrepreneur is just as unlikely to be comforted by the thought that the failure of her start-up is part of a wealth-generating process of creative destruction.

So let's first acknowledge a crucial difference: individuals, unlike populations, can succeed without adapting. The guppy *population* evolved pebble-camouflage through trial and error, but no *individual* guppy did: each was born either with good-enough camouflage, or not. Similarly, many of the heroes of this book – Reginald Mitchell, Mario Capecchi, H.R. McMaster – are admirable not because they themselves adapted, but because they had the courage to experiment with new ideas in the face of overwhelming pressure to stick with the crowd. In business, if you're in the right place at the right time and happen to hit the right strategy, you'll thrive without much need for adapting. The basic story of, say, Amazon, is not of a business that self-consciously experimented its way to success, but of a business with founders who had the luck or vision to spot the new oppor-tunity of internet retailing and grasp it.

But unlike Amazon, or geniuses like Mitchell or Capecchi, or a pebble-coloured guppy, we don't all get it right first time. Fortunately we have something that guppies do not: the ability to adapt as we go along. Guppies only get one shot at what colour they are: get it wrong, and they die in the jaws of a pike cichlid, or are unable to attract a mate. Few of our own failures are fatal. Within limits, we can experiment either sequentially or concurrently: we can try being pebble-coloured first and switch to polka-dot if it doesn't work out, or we can split our time between them.

There are three essential steps to using the principles of adapting in business and everyday life, and they are in essence the Palchinsky principles. First, try new things, expecting that some will fail. Second, make failure survivable: create safe spaces for failure or move forward in small steps. As we saw with banks and cities, the trick here is finding the right scale in which to experiment: significant enough to make a difference, but not such a gamble that you're ruined if it fails. And third, make sure you know when you've failed, or you will never learn. As we shall see in the next chapter, this last one is especially difficult when it comes to adapting in our own lives.

First, this chapter looks at how corporations can become less like an individual guppy and more like a population of guppies: trying things out, running with what works. We've already seen one example of how to do this in corporate life: the 'skunk works' idea of a Galapagan island of innovation. But there are other approaches, and organisations which have actively adopted Palchinsky-style principles of pluralism, gradual experimentation, and learning from mistakes, with great success. They do not offer the only path to business success, but they suggest what might be possible.

2 'I don't want the people at head office to run the business'

Let me describe a fast-growing company that embodies some of the key principles of adapting – we can call it 'Difference Machine' for now. The company operates on several different sites but it is more decentralised than that fact alone would suggest, being organised around small teams of which there are over half a dozen on each site. Within these specialised groups, staff have a lot of autonomy to decide what product features to offer to customers, at what price and with what sort of marketing push. These decisions are taken at a very local level rather than being passed to head office or even the senior managers on site – this allows new ideas to be tried out on a small scale and in response to a particular situation.

More radical still, the teams are self-selecting: a new recruit is placed with a team for four weeks for a trial period, at which point they can stay only if they win the vote of two thirds of their team members. (The mark of a good team is said to be its willingness to defy the advice of the team leader and kick out a new member who isn't pulling his weight.) The team selection method is used not just for the site offices but for senior managers at head office, too.

Difference Machine has a suitably progressive philosophy of ethical business which helps provide guidance to this decentralised, experimental organisation. Coupled with the radical employee empowerment programme, that mission might make it sound soft-headed about the basic business of making money. Not at all: the company's CEO explained some years ago in a blog post that 'we can't fulfil [our] mission unless we are highly profitable'. Employees are acutely aware of the bottom line. Many employees have stock options, but the profit focus is more local and immediate than that: every four weeks, each team receives a bonus if its profitability over the past month has exceeded a certain threshold. Healthy competition is promoted by a 'no secrets' policy of strict transparency: many of the company's financial statistics are available to employees, and every team knows how every other team is performing – a mechanism that also allows bad ideas to be noticed and nipped in the bud, and good ideas to spread horizontally through the company.

This radical devolution of power and responsibility to frontline employees is working: the company has been a permanent feature on *Fortune* Magazine's Top 100 'best companies to work for'; sales were $8 billion in 2009 and have been doubling every three years since the company floated on the stock market. The company's market value is comparable to that of large competitors with ten times as many staff.

What industry might this paragon of corporate innovation inhabit? We might assume it's one of the brash young software houses, or perhaps a green technology company, something big in genetics, or possibly some hyper-global outsourcing operation. In fact, 'Difference Machine' is an alias not for the next Google, but for one of the world's most boring lines of business: a supermarket, an industry synonymous with dead-end jobs and disempowered staff, where every decision is taken at central office and mediated by a computer and a loyalty card. Difference Machine is actually Whole Foods Market, the high-end, organically-minded and lushly-stocked grocery chain. (The description of many of the management practices comes from Gary Hamel's recent book, *The Future of Management*.)

Of course, this kind of business model is not the only way to succeed in the supermarket trade. Far more centralised supermarkets such as Wal-Mart in the US and Tesco in the UK are clearly very profitable – they still experiment but have managed to centralise and automate that experimentation. Yet Whole Foods demonstrates that even in this most regimented of industries it is possible to succeed with a radical, employee-led management model that would not seem out of place in a utopian Silicon Valley start-up.

Whole Foods isn't unique, either. Almost every management innovation described above applies equally to one of the UK's least glamorous brands, Timpson. Timpson has several hundred small branches which adorn many British high streets, offering a bric-a-brac of services such as key-cutting, shoe and watch repairs, and engraving. Like Whole Foods Market, Timpson has a 'no secrets' policy, sending round a frequent newsletter to all staff explaining how the business is doing and how much money there is in the bank. Like Whole Foods, the staff in an individual shop are in charge of deciding what exactly goes on the shelves and whether to offer deals or promotions – the company's chairman, John Timpson, calls it 'upside-down management'. If a boy comes in trying to engrave something for his grandmother, and doesn't have enough money to pay the usual price, it's up to the local staff to decide whether to offer him a price he can afford; if a customer has a complaint, the lowliest shop assistant has the authority to spend up to £500 putting it right. Timpson doesn't have a large complaints department at head office: it doesn't need one. And the small team of staff at each shop is paid a performance bonus every week based on the performance of that particular team. No wonder they know exactly how the shop is doing when Mr Timpson drops in – and he drops in frequently, because he spends four days a week on the road doing nothing but visiting his shops to talk to staff.

The first thing Timpson does when it buys another business is to rip out the electronic point-of-sale machines (there are always EPOS machines) and replace them with old-fashioned cash registers. 'EPOS lets people at head office run the business', explains John Timpson. 'I don't *want* them to run the business.' EPOS machines empower head office but they make it harder to be flexible and give customers what they need. John Timpson describes one instance where he couldn't buy half-price happy-hour drinks at a hotel bar, because midway through giving his order, the hour ended and the bar's computerised sales system refused to allow the half-price offer to be applied. He fumes at the idea of powerless staff telling irritated customers that 'I can't put that through the till.'

John Timpson, and John Mackey of Whole Foods, have learned the same lessons as H.R. McMaster in Iraq: the best computer systems in the world cannot substitute for being there, talking about what's going on and responding at once to subtle situational clues – or in Hayek's now familiar words, 'knowledge of the particular circumstance of time and place'. The correct balance between centralised control and decentralised experimentation depends on circumstance: at a nuclear power station, we want engineers to keep an eye on each other but we don't want them improvising with new ways to run the reactor. Nor do we want to allow a situation where a company such as AIG, with 120,000 employees, can be devastated by a unit employing barely a hundred.

Overall, though, as we saw in chapter 2, more and more companies are decentralising, flattening their hierarchies and paying performance bonuses to more junior staff, and they are doing this because the world is increasingly rewarding those who can quickly adapt to local circumstances. H.R. McMaster criticised the idea that 'situational understanding could be delivered on a computer screen'; John Timpson might put it more bluntly, but these two very different men with very different responsibilities have reached very similar conclusions.

3 'If you tell anybody what to do here, they'll never work for you again'

'We only have two rules,' explains John Timpson. 'One: look the part. Wear your tie, turn up on time, be nice to the customers. Two: put the money in the till.' The second rule is an intriguing one: with so much autonomy, it is not hard for employees to steal money from the company. It is part of a broader problem: if an organisation grants radical autonomy to its members, how does it guarantee that the members will respect the organisation's interests rather than simply pursuing their own?

Partly this is a matter of trust. Timpson's company training manual describes the twenty easiest ways to defraud the company, making it clear that the company understands the risks it is running and trusts its employees anyway – and many people respond to being trusted by becoming more trustworthy. Partly it's the strong focus on performance: both Timpson and Whole Foods Market monitor performance closely and reward it frequently. But in large part, these systems work because staff keep an eye on each other and have a strong incentive not to tolerate slackers and crooks.

'It made us pay more attention to the people themselves because our way of running a business only works if you've got the right people,' says John Timpson. And he emphasises that poor performers don't just damage the company, they damage their colleagues. 'If somebody is just not interested, just turns up for work, we don't want them. Nor does anyone else working with them.' Half of Timpson employees join through a 'refer a friend' scheme – in other words, Timpson uses its own employees to recruit the 'right people'. At Whole Foods Market, remember, new team members have a four-week tryout, after which they need to have won the confidence of two thirds of their colleagues.

Whole Foods and Timpson both use a system of peer-monitoring. This makes sense: if power is delegated to the front line of the organisation, then that is where good ideas need to be separated out from bad – and good people, too. It's the 'worm's-eye view' we saw advocated by Muhammad Yunus. And there's also a parallel with the whistleblowers of the last chapter: it is the people who work regularly on a particular site or in a particular division who notice that something is amiss. The problem is persuading them to speak up, so it's not hard to see why both Timpson and Whole Foods Market place such a premium on team performance and measure it, publicise it and reward it every month or even every week. Peer monitoring does not always work, of course; peer groups can turn into self-serving or even corrupt cliques. (It is no wonder that John Timpson spends most of his working life visiting Timpson stores.) But it offers a subtlety and sensitivity that monitoring from corporate HQ simply cannot match.

Peer monitoring can take many forms. At Timpson and Whole Foods it's about making sure everyone does their bit. But the same approach prevails at Google, where peer monitoring is all about maintaining an atmosphere of intellectual challenge.

Eric Schmidt, Google's chairman and, until recently, its CEO, views his role at Google as mediating a debate and forcing other people to reach decisions, rather than making the decisions himself. (The company, in any case, gave him few of the trappings of authority: on his first day at Google he discovered that his assigned two-desk office had been spotted and colonised by an engineer; Schmidt took the second desk without protest.)

At W.L. Gore, the company that developed Gore-Tex, the CEO was effectively elected by her peers: the board of directors polled Gore 'associates' about who in the company – anyone – they were willing to follow. The name that came up was Terri Kelly, and she was duly appointed. Gore associates find their own colleagues and their own projects to pursue, and they must rely on the power of their case rather than the authority of the org chart. One Gore associate comments, 'If you tell anybody what to do here, they'll never work for you again.' John Timpson speaks of 'upside-down management', but the practice obviously has its uses well beyond the high street.

Peer monitoring is closely associated with the virtual world: it's the fundamental building block of Google's search algorithm (giving weight to how popular a site is with other sites), phenomena like eBay (which relies on buyers and sellers rating each other's reliability) and Wikipedia (in which anyone can edit anyone else's articles), and the open-source software movement which has delivered such successes as Firefox and Apache. But as Timpson shows, it's applicable far behind the cutting edge of crowd-sourced technology.

I witnessed a striking example of peer monitoring on my visit to the Hinkley B nuclear power station. I'd just received a briefing on Hinkley's safety culture from Peter Higginson, an avuncular physicist from Shropshire who was responsible for the safety of Hinkley's two massive advanced gas-cooled reactors. The safety culture sounded impressive, and depended heavily on peer monitoring. All significant actions, such as flipping a switch in the reactor control room, were double-checked by a colleague.

Every employee – receptionists, security guards and press officers included – took a course on nuclear safety; everyone was responsible for taking care of everyone else. It all sounded great – but also a bit too good to be true.

Then we changed into overalls and toecapped boots to prepare for a visit to the turbine hall. Just as we were about to leave the meeting room, a portly middle-aged lady in a hard hat walked in pushing a trolley laden with sandwiches. She took one look at us and politely but firmly admonished our host that we'd left our shoes in a place where they constituted a tripping hazard, and asked us to move them. Perhaps the incident was unusual, and of course a tripping hazard is a far cry from a failure in the reactor core. Yet it was hard to forget seeing peer monitoring in action: the instant correction of a problem, no matter how small and no matter what the hierarchical relationship might be between head of safety and tea lady.

4 Google's corporate strategy: have no corporate strategy

At Hinkley Point, the key priority is ensuring that the power station operates exactly as planned, without deviation. But at other companies, the challenge is to do something new every day, and nowhere is this truer than at Google.

The company's CEO Eric Schmidt had a surprise when he walked into Larry Page's office in 2002. Page is the co-creator of Google and the man who gave his name to the idea at the company's foundation: its PageRank search algorithm. But Page had something rather different to show Schmidt: a machine he'd built himself which cut off the bindings of books and then scanned their pages into a digital format. Page had been trying to figure out whether it might be possible for Google to scan the world's books into searchable form. Rather than instructing an intern to rig something up, or commissioning analysis from a consulting firm, he teamed up with Marissa Mayer, a Google vice-president, to see how fast two people could produce an image of a 300-page book. Armed with a plywood frame, a pair of clamps, a metronome and a digital camera, two of Google's most senior staff tried out the project themselves. (The book went from paper to pixels in forty minutes.)

Larry Page regarded the time he devoted to the project not as something he could do because he was Google's founder and could do whatever he wanted, but as something to which he was entitled because *every* engineer at Google had the same deal. Famously, Google has a '20 per cent time' policy: any engineer (and some other employees) is allowed to spend one fifth of his or her time on any project that seems worthwhile. Google News, Google Suggest, Adsense and the social networking site Orkut are all projects that emerged from these personal projects, along with half of all Google's successful products – and an astonishing portfolio of failures.

Whole Foods Market would have little to gain from letting its employees noodle around on whatever project took their fancy, but Google's 20 per cent time is a practice made successful by the same basic mechanism that Whole Foods relies on: peer approval. Managers stay out of the way of personal staff projects. It is other engineers who determine which projects gain momentum and which languish: if you can't persuade your peers to help you with your idea, it will go nowhere. Managers can provide the space for innovation, but it is peers who provide most of the time and energy. More recently, Google has grown so big that Eric Schmidt, Larry Page and Sergey Brin have formalised a process of supporting promising innovations. Even so, the aim is not to stifle more projects but to give extra funding and resources to projects that might otherwise be lost in the noise of 20,000 employees.

It's hard to imagine two more different companies than the shoe-repair chain Timpson and the internet search giant Google, but look at the similarities in the language: Google wants to maintain a 'bozo-free zone', Timpson is insistent about keeping 'drongos' out of the business. Bozos are less-than-brilliant engineers; drongos are shop assistants who don't care about the business and don't pull their weight. The basic idea is the same: in a company where the selection mechanism is your teammates rather than top-down rules, there is no room for people who don't play their part.

The 20 per cent time policy isn't unique to Google: not only is it being widely emulated across Silicon Valley, but it long predates the creation of the Googleplex. A similar deal has been standard practice for half a century at W.L. Gore, where all employees get a half-day each week of 'dabble time'. Again, we see that while the experimental approach may be perfectly exemplified by the denizens of Silicon Valley, and even more by the online communities they make possible, the basic ideas have been around and successful much longer than the World Wide Web.

A serial innovator such as Google or W.L. Gore knows that if you give smart people some space, you may get a Spitfire, the solution to the longitude problem, the technique for knocking out genes in mice – or Gmail. A few such successes justify a lot of slack time. One example is W.L. Gore's 'Elixir' range of acoustic guitar strings, which now dominate the market. They emerged via a long period of experimentation when a W.L. Gore engineer, Dave Myers, applied the Gore-Tex polymer first to cables on his mountain bike and then to guitar-strings. Gore had no experience in the music industry and Myers had no management approval for what he was doing. He didn't need it.

The management guru Gary Hamel argues that Google in particular is actively pursuing a Darwinian strategy of pushing out the largest possible range of products – not a single guppy but a greenhouse full of different guppy strategies. Google is quite simply an evolutionary organisation: it began with a search engine, then turned site hits into revenue when it teamed up with AOL and Yahoo, then developed a system of displaying adverts alongside search results. Google then stumbled upon the idea of Adsense, the ability to make adverts relevant to any web page. This discovery was made serendipitously while developing Gmail, and trying to deliver context-sensitive adverts alongside the Gmail inbox, and then expanded into Google apps and other projects. Hamel comments that 'like an organism favored by genetic good fortune, Google's success owes much to serendipity'. That is true of many successful companies – John Mackey, the CEO of Whole Foods, calls himself 'the accidental grocer' – but Google have elevated it to a guiding principle.

If any company can be said to embrace trying new things in the expectation that many will fail, it is Google. Marissa Mayer, the vice-president who helped Larry Page bodge together the first book scanner, says that 80 per cent of Google's products will fail – but that doesn't matter, because people will remember the ones that stick. Fair enough: Google's image seems to be untarnished by the indifferent performances of Knol, a Google service vaguely similar to Wikipedia which didn't seem to catch on; or SearchMash, a testbed for alternative Google search products which was labelled 'Google's Worst Ever Product' by one search expert and has now been discontinued. According to the influential TechRepublic website, two of the five worst technology products of 2009 came from Google – and they were major Google products at that, Google Wave and the Android 1.0 operating system for mobile phones. Yet most internet users know and rely on Google's search, Google Maps and Image search, while many others swear by Gmail, Google Reader and Blogger. As long as the company doesn't pour too much money into failing products, the few big successes seem to justify the many experiments.

This is fundamental to the way Google does business. Google has established its own equivalent of John Endler's guppy ponds and is seeing what emerges. The company's corporate strategy is to have no corporate strategy.

5 'Success is the number of experiments that can be crowded into twenty-four hours'

Some years ago, a craft and fabric chain called Jo-Ann Fabrics offered its customers a surprising deal. It wasn't surprisingly creative or surprisingly generous. In fact, it was surprisingly lame: buy one sewing machine, get a second one at 20 per cent off. Who on earth wants to buy two sewing machines? But the deal was also surprisingly successful. Customers found that the prospect of saving 10 per cent per sewing machine was tempting enough to make it worth having, so they went hunting for friends who might also want to buy a sewing machine. In short, the quirky offer turned out to be an unexpected way to recruit amateur sales staff.

More interesting than the special offer was how it was discovered: Jo-Ann Fabrics was using its website, JoAnn.com, as a laboratory. Different customers would automatically be shown different website designs and different offers, the particular combination chosen at random by a computer. In line with the first two Palchinsky principles, Jo-Ann Fabrics was prepared for many such offers to fail, and could afford for them to do so. The deal for bulk-buyers of sewing machines was one of the unlikely successes that this random process discovered, and the use of randomised experiments on the website more than tripled revenue per visitor.

As Ian Ayres explains in his book *Supercrunchers*, stories like that of Jo-Ann Fabrics are becoming more and more commonplace. Credit-card providers have long used combinatorial experiments in their junk mail – these experiments turbocharge the randomised trial method we've already encountered by layering multiple randomisations on top of each other to generate a very rich set of data. The results are all used to refine the mailshot and to hook more customers. But whereas these experiments once required statistical experts and cutting-edge computer technology, they are now very easy to run online. Anyone can buy two or more advertisements on Google AdWords and see which one works best. (Ian Ayres did just that, which is why his book is called *Supercrunchers* and not his own favourite, *The End of Intuition*.) Or for bigger projects, professional help is available to unleash the full power of combinatorial experiments.

Such experiments aren't limited to the web. Supermarkets can and do randomise their price offerings, their shelf placement, the vouchers they send to customers with loyalty cards, or the design of the advertisements they place in local newspapers. Fast-moving consumer goods companies play with the packaging of key brands. Publishers sometimes offer several different covers to a magazine or a book and see what sells.

Experiments have been going on in corporations behind the scenes for over a century. Thomas Edison may have been known as the Wizard of Menlo Park, but his experimentation hit a systematic, industrial scale in 1887 after he built large laboratories a few miles north in West Orange, New Jersey. He employed thousands of people in an 'invention factory' and made sure the storerooms were well stocked and that the physical layout of the laboratories allowed the largest number of experiments in the shortest possible time. He was the father of industrial research. Famous for saying, 'If I find 10,000 ways something won't work, I haven't failed. I am not discouraged, because every wrong attempt discarded is just one more step forward,' he also commented more directly on the industrialisation of the trial-and-error process: 'The real measure of success is the number of experiments that can be crowded into twenty-four hours.'

That number can now be dozens, hundreds or even tens of thousands thanks to the introduction of cheap supercomputers and other techniques for systematising experiments. Pharmaceutical companies use 'combinatorial chemistry' to search through a colossal range of possible drugs: thousands of different chemical compounds can now be synthesised on the surface of a single silicon chip, or bonded to the surface of poly-mer beads to allow easy mixing and further synthesis, or synthesised in larger quantities in robot labs without human intervention. The resulting compounds can then be tested in parallel to answer simple but vital questions: Are they toxic? Can the body absorb them? Silicon chip manufacturers design bespoke chips in a virtual environment before testing and refin-ing them experimentally. The faster computers become, the faster new computer chips can be designed and tested. The same process is applied to the aerodynamics of a car, or its safety during a crash. And the fundamental point of all these massively parallel experiments is the same: when a problem reaches a cer-tain level of complexity, formal theory won't get you nearly as far as an incredibly rapid, systematic process of trial and error.

We saw in chapter 4 that randomised trials make some people queasy in medicine and in foreign aid, and the same is true in business. Some years ago, a consumer-goods company approached Dan Ariely, a marketing professor at Duke and MIT, for advice in running some experiments on its own customers. It was a sharp move: Ariely has since become one of the most cel-ebrated behavioural economists after the success of his book *Predictably Irrational*. Ariely uses experiments all the time to develop and test ideas in psychology and behavioural economics, such as the hypothesis that 'free' isn't just a price of zero; 'Buy one get one free!' feels different to 'Buy two get both at half price!', even though the offers are identical. Real-world applica-tions of this insight were something the company might be able to use, and Ariely could use the collaboration to harvest data for his academic research.

All went well at first. An experiment, with multiple websites and various combinations of offers, was due to go live when sud-denly some higher-ups at the company began to raise concerns. Their objection was much the same as the long-standing com-plaint about randomised trials elsewhere: that some customers would miss out on the good stuff. 'Because we were extending differing offers,' explains Ariely, 'some customers might buy a product that was not ideal for them, spend too much money, or get a worse deal overall than others.' In some ways, the executives' worries were more valid than those we dismissed in chapter 5. The two key counterarguments – that subjects of trials can be approached for their informed consent, and that trials bring wider social benefits – don't apply in business. You can't inform a customer that they're being charged full price to see how much difference it makes to offer another set of customers a discount. And customers are not necessarily the ones who will benefit from research that is designed to make the business more profitable.

But these concerns could have been addressed very easily. If a retailer is simply testing out whether a discount will pay for itself in increased sales, then there's a simple way of compensating customers in the full-price arm of the trial: after they have made their purchase decision, give them the discount anyway, either immediately or as a cash refund when the trial is complete.

In the end, the executives decided to revert to a way of doing business they were more comfortable with: they asked Dan Ariely simply to tell them the best marketing technique. This was Archie Cochrane's 'God complex', with Dan Ariely cast in the role of God. But Ariely didn't think his expert opinion was worth much compared with the insight that would emerge from a proper experiment: 'Companies pay amazing amounts of money to get answers from consultants with overdeveloped confidence in their own intuition,' he marvels. The project was canned.

Despite such setbacks, the routine experimentation advocated by Edison is now widely practised. It feels much safer than 20 per cent time or upside-down management; it's less anarchic, less of a threat to the existing power structure in a company, and less of a threat to the status quo. When experiments become routine, a company such as Wal-Mart or Capital One can crunch the numbers from head office without upsetting the corporate hierarchy. By contrast, creating the space for employees in your medical products division to get together and create the market-leading brand of guitar string is exhilarating in retrospect but profoundly disquieting to most corporations at the time. There is surely a reason why so few companies have actually emulated W.L. Gore over the past half-century. And yet some business scholars wonder if even the approach of a W.L. Gore or a Google is really radical enough to cope with truly disruptive business ideas.

6 When companies become dinosaurs

Guppies breed so quickly that John Endler was able to produce guppy evolution within months. When Clayton Christensen of Harvard Business School wanted to understand why some apparently capable companies find themselves wiped out by a sudden shift in the competitive landscape, he looked for the economic equivalent of a greenhouse full of guppies. The disk-drive industry was his first port of call: a market in which upstarts frequently seem to usurp the market leaders. As with John Endler's guppies, what Christensen discovered points to a much wider truth.

Christensen's initial explanation for the brief life-span of a disk-drive manufacturer was the 'technology mudslide': the pace of technological change is so frenetic that companies frantically scramble to reach the technological summit as the ground keeps slipping away beneath their feet. No wonder one decade's dominant manufacturer is the next decade's corporate basket case. But this plausible-sounding theory makes little sense on close inspection. Top disk-drive manufacturers have the cash flow to fund further innovation, and are constantly refining their procedures and responding to a constant stream of feedback from customers. They are farther up the mudslide than new entrants, and win purely technological races against upstarts again and again, whether this is disk-drive manufacturers coming first to market with faster drive speeds and denser storage, or camera makers with the latest, sharpest lenses, or sports-shoe companies with new styles and better-designed soles.

Christensen found that it isn't cutting-edge technology that tends to undo the market leaders. It is the totally new approach, often with quite primitive technology and invariably of little value to the best customers of the leading industry players. In the late 1970s, leading disk-drive manufacturers were making their products better and better for their main customer base of large corporations and banks with room-sized mainframe computers. To these customers, a new generation of physically smaller drives – with much less storage – was of no interest. But these new drives tapped into a new market for the desk-side computers then being pioneered by the likes of Wang and Hewlett-Packard. Eventually the smaller drives became more technologically advanced and even the mainframe customers began to buy them, and by that stage the traditional manufacturers were hopelessly far behind.

The more familiar example of digital photography offers much the same lessons. The first digital cameras were expensive, performed poorly and offered little storage. They were of little use to either the amateur snapper, who wanted something cheap, or the professional photographer who wanted a sharpness of image that such cameras could not provide. Leading manufacturers of film cameras, which had been the only game in town since the invention of photography, might have worried but would have seen little cause for concern from the market itself.

But early digital cameras appealed to some niche users who wouldn't otherwise have bothered with a film camera at all: in the late 1990s, for example, I used one to photograph flip charts at corporate meetings so they could be stored on a floppy disk and transcribed later. Neither the price tag nor the poor image quality was a problem: what mattered was that it was easy to get the pictures onto a computer and emailed to an assistant back at head office. These niche markets gave the technology a foothold to improve – and very quickly – until only a few nostalgic hold-outs were sticking with film. By then, the photocopier company Canon had a powerful position in the market, and many established names such as Fuji, Kodak, Olympus and Leica were scrambling to catch up in a landscape that had dramatically changed.

The battle between desktop email software and webmail is in some ways even more telling. Back in the 1990s, the desktop program Microsoft Outlook was clearly the superior product: webmail services had limited storage, were cumbersome, and were extremely slow over a dial-up connection. Outlook handled most corporate email and Outlook Express served the still-small home market in a way that most users found far superior to web-mail. But webmail did have a niche as a backup account for the web-savvy, or for students who had free internet access and wanted the ability to hop from computer to computer across campus. Only later did connection speeds, storage costs and the sophistication of browsers improve sufficiently to demonstrate the true potential of webmail: it could be used to archive and store every email you ever received; used as a document backup; used as a primary email account, packed with features; and used offline. What is striking is the difficulty Microsoft had with this transition, even though it had bought the leading webmail service, Hotmail, quite early in the game, and even though webmail wasn't a complicated technology for Microsoft software engineers to master. Yet Hotmail's features were eclipsed by those of Google's Gmail.

Disruptive innovations are disruptive precisely because the new technology doesn't appeal to the traditional customers: it is different and for their purposes, it's inferior. But for a small niche of new customers the new disruptive product is exactly what is needed. They want smaller, cheaper hard drives, or cameras that produce digital files, or email that you can access on any computer – and they are willing to tolerate the fact that the new product is inferior to the old one along all the traditional dimensions. That foothold in the niche market gives the new technology an opportunity to develop into a true threat to the old way of doing things.

The problem for a market leader in the old technology is not necessarily that it lacks the capacity to innovate, but that it lacks the will. When a disruptive technology appears, it may confound an existing player because the technology itself is so radically different (that was true of digital cameras, but not of webmail or smaller disk drives, which were assembled using off-the-shelf technology). More often, Christensen found, the problem was not technological but psychological and organisational: it is hard for a major organisation to pay much attention to a piddling new idea that makes little money and invites a yawn or a blank stare from important customers. Microsoft bought Hotmail, yes – but it was always going to be hard for Microsoft to pay more attention to Hotmail than to Outlook. Microsoft's core corporate customers regarded webmail as an irrelevance. Google's users did not. Google only made web applications, and Gmail was a natural fit.

We already know one possible solution for corporations faced with a potentially disruptive innovation: a skunk works, a sort of corporate version of Lübeck, in which the regular culture and priorities and politics of the old corporation do not apply. Lockheed's Skunk Works got its name (originally 'skonk works') because it began life inside a circus tent pitched next to a foul-smelling plastics factory. Its engineers – who dressed down even in the 1950s – let off steam from their high-pressure, top-secret projects by playing pranks on each other. Lockheed's basic corporate culture, whatever its strengths and weaknesses, had little influence on how the skunks behaved.

The skunk works can be a quasi-independent division, or even an entirely new organisation. It can focus on core business in a new way, as the original skunk works did, or it can branch into totally new lines of business.

This idea can work far beyond the arms industry. Target, the discount retailer, was a largely separate entity within the more traditional department store chain Dayton Hudson. It adapted more naturally to the big-box, out-of-town format and grew to overshadow its parent – an outcome far preferable to the obvious alternative of Dayton Hudson letting some other upstart overshadow it. Charles Schwab, the stockbroker, decided to get into the internet brokerage business by setting up a completely independent organisation to run a discount share-trading service online. The online organisation grew so quickly that it swallowed up the parent within eighteen months. If Schwab had taken a more cautious approach, the online service might well have been smothered by vested interests, and Schwab itself would likely have been marginalised by some other online player within a couple of years.

Another example is Richard Branson's Virgin Group. Branson started in music distribution before setting up a record label, Virgin Records. His other projects have included transatlantic airlines, no-frills airlines, mobile phone services, passenger trains, bridal wear, cola, vodka, high-end tourism (including space tourism), radio stations and financial services. Each of these enterprises has been attempted within a separate, stand-alone company – sometimes several stand-alone companies in different countries. Some of the ideas flopped: Virgin Cola's main achievement was in provoking a crushing response from Coca-Cola. Others, such as the Virgin Megastore music shops, had years of success before the business model eventually waned and Branson moved on. But the whole structure of the Virgin Group has always been to maintain a high degree of separation between different lines of business: this allows different organisations to focus on their own priorities, and it also allows the failures to fail in isolation.

When the US Army faced the 'disruptive innovation' of guerrilla warfare in Vietnam, there was great reluctance to accept that it had changed the nature of the game, making obsolete the

Army's hard-won expertise in industrial warfare. As one senior officer said, 'I'll be damned if I permit the United States army, its institutions, its doctrine, and its traditions to be destroyed just to win this lousy war.' That is exactly how senior executives must feel when their cutting-edge, market-leading business finds itself being disrupted by a foolish-looking new technology. A sufficiently disruptive innovation bypasses almost everybody who matters at a company: the Rolodex full of key customers becomes useless; the old skills are no longer called for; decades of industry experience count for nothing. In short, everyone who counts in a company will lose status if the disruptive innovation catches on inside that company – and whether consciously or unconsciously, they will often make sure that it doesn't. As a result, the company may find itself in serious trouble. It may even die. And remembering the 'Who's excellent now?' experience of Tom Peters we discovered in chapter 1, such a fate is highly likely to befall many companies – even those praised in this chapter.

But when companies die, does that matter?

7 Built to fail

Corporations have become such a fixture of life that they seem more permanent to us than they were ever intended to be. A central point of the corporation, as a legal structure, is that it's supposed to be a safe space in which to fail. Limited liability companies were developed to encourage people to experiment, to innovate, to adapt – safe in the knowledge that if their venture collapsed, it would merely be the abstract legal entity that was ruined, not them personally.

I spent a few years working for an oil company, Shell, which – with an eye on keeping up with potentially disruptive innovations in its field – made various sallies into solar energy, wind farms and other renewable energy technology. Nothing much seems to have come of this yet. Conspiracy theorists may believe that this is because Shell has an evil plan to dominate and disrupt the threat from renewable technologies. I doubt this. If there really is a cost-effective renewable alternative to the eons of energy concentrated into crude oil, it would be very much in Shell's interests to commercialise it. The explanation is simpler: following Clayton Christensen's logic, there is simply no reason to expect an oil company to be particularly good at inventing, manufacturing or distributing photovoltaic solar panels. Oil companies are good at very different things: negotiating with African and Middle Eastern governments, complex drilling operations, building and operating refineries and chemical engineering plants, and selling liquid fuels in roadside forecourts. When renewable energy takes off, there is no more reason to expect Shell, Exxon and BP to prosper from it than there is to be surprised that the leading internet company is Google rather than some giant of former technologies such as Texas Instruments or Univac.

Even a skunk works operation is no guarantee of success in the face of disruptive innovations. Skunk works are, by their nature, isolated from the parent company. That gives them latitude to innovate and freedom to fail without bringing down the parent. But that may not be enough. Good ideas may simply stay trapped in the skunk works because the parent company does not understand them. If so, the company may well be doomed.

Fine. There is nothing that says a business must live for ever – and, as we saw in chapter 1, the entire success of the market system is predicated on the fact that they don't. Suppose that in some start-up, right now, a breakthrough renewable form of energy far cheaper than oil or gas has been discovered and it is about to hit the market. The likes of Shell, Exxon and BP could then, quite plausibly, quickly die. They would not be much missed. It would be inconvenient for their employees and costly for their shareholders, but the employees would in most cases find other uses for their talents. Shareholders accept risks and, if they are wise, put their eggs in more than one basket. Former employees and shareholders alike would, meanwhile, feel the benefits of cheaper and cleaner power just like everyone else.

Corporations exist precisely because we don't – and shouldn't – care when abstract legal entities fail. We care about individuals. And it is to individuals, struggling to adapt and learn and grow, that we finally turn.

Eight

Adapting and you

'He was not a very careful person as a mathematician. He made a lot of mistakes but he made mistakes in a good direction ... I tried to imitate him but I found out that it is very difficult to make good mistakes.'

– mathematician Goro Shimura, on his friend Yutaka Taniyama

'Let us try for once not to be right.'

– Tristan Tzara

1 'How did this happen?'

On Friday, 19 July 2002, *Movin' Out* premiered at the Shubert Theater in Chicago. It was a ballet and a musical at the same time, an ambitious and unlikely collaboration between Twyla Tharp, a cerebral and challenging choreographer, and Billy Joel, the writer of some of the most popular and likeable songs ever created. It was due to transfer to Broadway three months later. And it stank.

'Stupefyingly clichéd and almost embarrassingly naïve,' concluded the *Chicago Sun-Times*. The *Chicago Tribune* called it 'crazily uneven', 'pile-driving and ill-conceived' and noted that while one scene was 'at least as silly as anything in "Reefer Madness",' another 'leaves half the audience asking the other half: So what just happened? Who died? Huh?'

To add injury to the insult, the New York paper *Newsday* broke with tradition to republish a particularly vigorous review from the Chicago press. Usually the understanding is that Broadway-bound shows will iron out their kinks with a brief run in Boston, Chicago or Philadelphia, and the New York press will hold back until they see the polished show appear on Broadway itself. Not this time: perhaps the reviews were so ferocious, and the name of Billy Joel such a draw, that it was impossible for *Newsday* to resist the temptation.

The mess landed in Twyla Tharp's lap. She was the person who had persuaded Billy Joel to hand over his life's work to her. She had conceived, directed and choreographed the show while Joel took a deliberate back seat. ('If you stand in Twyla's way, you die!' was his light-hearted explanation.) Eight million dollars had been invested in the show. The morale of the cast had evaporated under the heat of the critical scrutiny in Chicago, and the New York press were waiting for the theatrical car crash to arrive on Broadway.

There is an honourable history of rewrites in musicals. *A Funny Thing Happened on the Way to the Forum* was originally (and unsuccessfully) staged without its brilliant opening number, 'Comedy Tonight'. *Oklahoma!* started as the flop *Away We Go*. But the scale of the task facing Tharp was monumental, and one does not fix a Broadway-bound musical in the way that one can edit an essay on a word processor – it's too late for that. *Movin' Out* had become not only a very public failure, but one that had dragged in scores of other human beings, with careers to worry about and egos to nurture. As she changed lines and cut characters, Tharp had to minister to wounded souls and keep spirits high – all at a time when her credibility with her team had been severely strained by her failure. Moreover, these bruised and frightened dancers had to perform the old show every night to dwindling audiences while turning up at the studio every morning to practise the new choreography. One of the stars, Elizabeth Parkinson, simply froze on stage at the Shubert Theater one evening, trapped between what she had learned that morning and what she needed to dance that night. 'I was completely lost,' she said.

Three months later, the new *Movin' Out* hit Broadway. It was a triumph. A *New York Times* reviewer called it a 'shimmering portrait of an American generation', while another commented, 'to understand why two separate and equal casts of major ballet dancers and rock musicians have propelled Billy Joel fans into delirious ovations ... is to measure Ms. Tharp's achievement.' Other reviewers said that the show was 'in a different league' and 'a blast'. And the show is indeed sensational: look at the dancing to 'Keeping the Faith' and you'll see men and women moving with a speed, originality and graceful power that makes you rub your eyes in disbelief.

Before long the show had scooped two Tony awards, one for Twyla Tharp and the other for Billy Joel himself and the arranger, Stuart Malina. It was widely acknowledged to be the most rapid and total transformation of a Broadway show in many years. Michael Phillips, the *Chicago Tribune* reviewer whose stern review had been so controversially picked up by *Newsday*, also applauded, but added a question whose answer should interest us all: 'How did this happen?'

2 'Challenge a status quo of your own making'

Part of the answer lies is the very institution of the out-of-town tryout, the show business equivalent of the corporate 'skunk works' idea: creating a space to experiment in which failures can be instructive and recoverable. As Tharp writes in her book *The Creative Habit*, 'The best failures are the private ones you commit in the confines of your room, alone, with no strangers watching. Private failures are great.' Quite so: you can learn from them without embarrassing yourself. But the next-best kind is in front of a limited audience. If your new show is going to fail, better that it does so away from Broadway, giving you a shot at recovering before it hits the big stage.

Being willing to fail is the essential first step to applying the ideas of Adapt in everyday life. Twyla Tharp makes a point of failing in private every day. She rises at 5.30 am to work out, improvising alone or – increasingly, as she danced on into her fifties and sixties – with a younger dancer, 'scratching', looking for ideas. She films three hours of improvisation and is pleased enough if she can find thirty seconds that she can use. 'Like a jazz musician jamming for an hour to find a few interesting notes, a choreographer looks for interesting movement … inspiration comes in molecules of movement, sometimes in nanoseconds.' The next step is finding, whenever possible, relatively safe spaces in which to fail: when the time came to unveil her new creative work to the public, she did so not directly on Broadway – from where an initial panning would have been even harder to recover – but in a way that allowed for the possibility that the show might not be as good as she must have thought it was.

In a radically different context, Tharp's approach follows Peter Palchinsky's principles: First, try new things; second, try them in a context where failure is survivable. But the third and final essential step is how to react to failure, and Tharp avoided several oddities of the human brain that often prevent us from learning from our failures and becoming more successful.

The first of those quirks leads to denial. It's why Sir James Crosby sacked Paul Moore rather than accept his valid critique of the bank, why Joseph Stalin ordered Peter Palchinsky to be killed for his correct analysis of the great Soviet engineering projects, and why Donald Rumsfeld forbade his senior general to use the accurate word 'insurgency'. It seems to be the hardest thing in the world to admit that we have made a mistake and to try to put it right. Twyla Tharp herself has the perfect explanation of why:

because 'it requires you to challenge a status quo of your own making.'

Tharp, who was sixty-one at the time *Movin' Out* flopped in Chicago, had an unimpeachable reputation and had worked with everyone: Philip Glass, David Byrne, Milos Forman, Mikhail Baryshnikov. It would have been easy for someone of her stature to reject outright the critics' views, refuse to change the show, lose her investors' money, set back the careers of her young dancers, and go to the grave convinced that the world had misunderstood her masterpiece.

Why is denial such a natural tendency? Psychologists have a name for the root cause which has become famous enough that many non-psychologists will recognise the term: cognitive dissonance. Cognitive dissonance describes the mind's difficulty in holding two apparently contradictory thoughts simultaneously: in Tharp's case, 'I am a capable, experienced and respected choreographer' and 'My latest creation is stupefyingly clichéd.' This odd phenomenon was first pinned down in an ingenious laboratory experiment half a century ago. Leon Festinger and James Carlsmith asked their experimental subjects to perform a tedious task – emptying and refilling a tray with spools, using one hand – for half an hour. On some plausible-sounding pretext they then offered a third of their subjects $1 – a small sum even in 1959, about an hour's wage – to tell the next experimental subject (actually an actress) what a great time they'd had stacking spools onto trays for half an hour. They offered another third of their subjects a much more substantial sum, $20, half a week's typical wages, to do the same thing. The remaining third went straight to the questionnaire which all the subjects finally filled in, asking if they had enjoyed themselves.

Unsurprisingly, most people said they hadn't. Yet there was a very odd exception: the students who'd been asked to reassure this stranger about what fun they'd been having, *and* who'd been paid only one dollar to do so, were much more likely to tell the experimenters that they'd enjoyed themselves. The unconscious cognitive process seems to be: 'With very little incentive, I told this girl I enjoyed myself. That's a contradiction to the idea that I didn't enjoy myself. So, I guess I must have enjoyed myself, right?' By contrast the ones who'd been paid $20 seemed more able to separate the events in their minds: 'Hey, if the pay is good, who wouldn't tell a white lie?'

The remarkable power of denial is nowhere better illustrated than by the reactions of some lawyers when DNA evidence became admissible in courts and many apparently sound convictions were overturned. Consider the response of Michael McDougal, a prosecutor in Texas, when faced with the evidence that Roy Criner, a man convicted of raping and murdering a young woman, was not the man whose semen was found in the victim's body. McDougal accepted the evidence but, incredibly, rejected the implication. 'It means that the sperm found in her body was not his. It doesn't mean he didn't rape her, doesn't mean he didn't kill her.' The chief judge of the Texas Court of Appeals, Sharon Keller, pointed out that Criner might have committed the murderous rape while wearing a condom.

Such denial is far from unique. What if the DNA of the semen on the victim doesn't match the convicted man's, and the victim is *eight years old*? Easy. Perhaps she was a sexually active eight-year-old. Or perhaps her eleven-year-old sister was sexually active while wearing the eight-year-old's underpants. Or perhaps the girls' father had masturbated over their underwear. Or perhaps the convicted man was a biological chimera with two different DNA structures (there are just thirty recorded cases of this in medical history). Every single one of these hypotheses – and more – was advanced by Michael McGrath, then Montana's Attorney General, after a man called Jimmy Ray Bromgard had had his conviction for raping a young girl overturned after DNA evidence showed he was innocent. Bromgard had spent fifteen years in prison.

For a prosecutor, the idea that you convicted the wrong man is upsetting. As Richard Ofshe, a social psychologist, comments, it's 'one of the worst professional errors you can make – like a physician amputating the wrong arm'. Of course the correct way to resolve the apparent contradiction is to believe, 'I am a good person and an experienced prosecutor but nevertheless I made a mistake.' For a human mind that is apparently unable to grasp 'I was fibbing when I said I enjoyed stacking spools', this may be too much to ask. For Tharp, who said of her debut, 'I didn't promote myself as a star. I had always seen myself as a star: I wanted to be a galaxy', the tension between 'I am a star' and 'My new work is risible' must have been particularly tempting to repress.

The second trap our minds set for us is that we chase our losses in an attempt to make them go away. Recall Frank, the luckless contestant on *Deal or no Deal*: having discarded the box containing half a million euros, he proceeded to reject ever more reasonable offers from the Banker until he ended up with next to nothing. All because, to quote the psychologists Kahneman and Tversky, he had not 'made peace with his losses'.

Making peace with our losses can be unbearably difficult to do – even for Twyla Tharp. In 1965, she was in a relationship with the artist Bob Huot. He wanted marriage and babies, she wanted to concentrate on her dancing. When she became pregnant anyway, she endured a horrific backstreet abortion without anaesthetic before being abandoned by the abortionists, bleeding heavily, at an ice-cream parlour in New Jersey. As she wrote in her autobiography, 'That experience remains intensely painful, one of the few that make me wonder whether my professional and artistic aspirations were really worth the price.'

Now comes the moment of chasing the loss: Tharp went on to marry Bob Huot. Only with hindsight did she identify her motivation at the time: 'Bob and I had lost a baby; marriage would prove our love and confirm us once again.'

The marriage lasted just four years.

Three decades later, Tharp did not chase her losses. It must have been tempting to stick to her original vision for *Movin' Out*, deluding herself that the New York critics might prove more discerning, or that New York audiences would like it more. Instead, she made peace with her losses and immediately set about the hard work of winning back both the critics and the audiences.

The final danger Tharp avoided is one we might call 'hedonic editing', borrowing a term coined by Richard Thaler, the behavioural economist behind the book *Nudge*. While denial is the process of refusing to acknowledge a mistake, and loss-chasing is the process of causing more damage while trying to hastily erase the mistake, hedonic editing is a subtler process of convincing ourselves that the mistake doesn't matter.

One way we do this is by bundling together losses with gains, like a child trying to eat some disliked healthy foodstuff by mashing it up with something tasty until the whole mess is palatable but unrecognisable. Think of that reliable tool of office life – indeed, of life in general – the 'praise sandwich'. The praise sandwich is a criticism sandwiched between two delicious slices of praise: 'I think this is excellent work. It would be great if you could [*important feedback here*]. But overall, as I say, it's excellent work.' It's a good way to avoid alienating everyone who works with you, but the criticism sandwiched between praise may be lost in the larger whole. You say, 'It's excellent, but you need to fix . . . ' I hear, 'It is broadly excellent.' I feel better, but I will not become better.

A different psychological process, but with a similar effect on our ability to learn from our mistakes, is simply to reinterpret our failures as successes. We persuade ourselves that what we did was not that bad; in fact, everything worked out for the best. Twyla Tharp could have decided that what she'd actually set out to achieve was something artistically radical rather than commercially mass-market, so the incomprehension of the critics was, in a way, validation; she could have found a few audience members who liked it, and convinced herself that the views of this discerning clientele should be given greater weight.

How profoundly this tendency runs in the human brain was demonstrated by a team of researchers including the psychologist Daniel Gilbert. The researchers showed their experimental subjects an array of six prints of paintings by Claude Monet – the lilies, the Houses of Parliament at sunset, the haystacks, and others – and asked them to rank the images in order from the one they liked most to the one they liked the least. The researchers then offered the experimental subjects a choice of two spare prints they 'just happened' to have, and the spares were always the pair ranked in the middle – number three and number four. Naturally the subject usually chose number three, having just declared it to be preferable to number four.

The researchers came back on a later occasion with the same set of six prints and asked their subjects to re-rank them from one to six. The ranking changed: the print that the subjects had chosen earlier was now ranked one or two; more surprisingly, the print that the subject had previously rejected was demoted to rank five or six. As Gilbert jokes, this is 'Happiness being synthesised ... "The one I got is really better than I thought! That other one I didn't get, suuuucks!"' We systematically reinterpret our past decision as being better than it really was.

That might sound surprising enough, but psychologists have in fact been observing and measuring this tendency for the last half-century. What is truly astonishing is that the experimental subjects in this case were severe anterograde amnesiacs, people completely unable to form new memories. Gilbert and his colleagues didn't return weeks or months later, but after just thirty minutes, by which time their unfortunate subjects had forgotten everything. They had absolutely no recollection of having ever seen any Monet prints, and yet they strongly preferred the print they had previously chosen *even though they had no conscious knowledge that they had chosen it*. Our capacity to reinterpret our past decisions as having worked out brilliantly is a very deep one.

These, then, are the three obstacles to heeding that old advice, 'learn from your mistakes': denial, because we cannot separate our error from sense of self-worth; self-destructive behaviour, because like the game-show contestant Frank, or Twyla Tharp when marrying Bob Huot, we compound our losses by trying to compensate for them; and the rose-tinted processes outlined by Daniel Gilbert and Richard Thaler, whereby we remember past mistakes as though they were triumphs, or mash together our failures with our successes. How can we overcome them?

3 'You know they're right'

Doing foolish things in an attempt 'to correct the past', like marrying the man whose baby you just aborted, isn't unusual at all. It's part of being human. What is unusual is the unblinking ability revealed by Tharp in her autobiography to analyse her motives, learn from them and become a stronger person.

Some people seem naturally better at this than others. Archie Cochrane never seems to have done anything without asking himself what might happen if he was mistaken, and whether there was any way to test his course of action. Others have to learn to question themselves. David Petraeus was notorious as a young officer for being unable ever to admit that he was wrong. His mentor, Jack Galvin, taught Petraeus that everyone is fallible.

If, like Tharp or Petraeus, we find that self-doubt is a skill we must acquire, how should we do it? Jack Galvin ordered Petraeus to act as Galvin's own private critic – useful in its own right, but also a lesson for the young soldier. Petraeus later sought out dissenting voices as he prepared his counterinsurgency manual. Not everyone finds this so easy: Donald Rumsfeld and Sir James Crosby suppressed dissent, but they suffered for it in the end. We need whistleblowers in our own lives to warn us about the 'latent errors' that we have made and which are just waiting to catch us out. In short, we all need a critic, and for most of us the inner critic is not nearly frank enough. We need someone who can help us hold those two jostling thoughts at the same time: *I am not a failure – but I have made a mistake.*

We need what Twyla Tharp calls 'a validation squad': friends and acquaintances who will back you but also tell it like it is. Good friends will cheer you on – and that is something we all need from time to time, some more than others – but not every friend will tell you when you've made a mistake. The morning after *Movin' Out* opened in Chicago, Tharp had breakfast with her old collaborator, the lighting designer Jennifer Tipton. Tipton had challenged Tharp while they worked together on Tharp's very first ballet, *Tank Dive*, in 1965, and Tharp knew she wasn't going to be handled with kid gloves by her old friend and colleague. They sat together and read the searing reviews. Breakfast did not consist of a praise sandwich: 'She didn't try to console me. She said, "You know they're right."'

Tharp's 'validation squad' included her son Jesse, who methodically sifted through the negative reviews, noting similarities and assessing for her where he felt the criticism was accurate. Tharp explained that Jesse 'took out the venom, concentrating on the substance of the critiques', but that is a revealing comment, because if you read the early Chicago reviews of *Movin' Out*, there is no venom. The reviews are harsh but fair. There's no sneering or personal criticism of Tharp, no sense of an axe to grind. Some of the reviews are very specific about what needs fixing. When Jesse stepped in to protect his mother from the critics, it wasn't because they were bitchy or mean. They weren't. They told the truth. But for a human being the truth can be venomous enough.

Tharp's qualifications for being in the squad are easily stated, if somewhat less easily fulfilled: 'All you need are people with good judgement in other parts of their lives who care about you and will give you their honest opinion with no strings attached.'

One of the underappreciated merits of the marketplace is that it supplies most of the elements of the validation squad. An entrepreneur's customers have good judgement about their own best interest and, by buying what he has to sell – or refusing to buy – they are giving an honest opinion with no strings attached. It's true that the market does not 'care about you', but there is something very significant nonetheless about making a sale – in other words, receiving a thumbs-up from a complete stranger. Perhaps this is one reason why researchers find that self-employed people tend to be happier than the employed: they receive implicit approval of what they do every time somebody pays their invoice, whereas people with regular jobs tend to receive feedback that is both less frequent and less meaningful.

As we have seen throughout this book, when a market test is not available or not appropriate, we need to find other ways to test our ideas: Andrew Haldane's 'heat maps' of financial stress; H.R. McMaster's elaborate role-playing exercises in a virtual Baghdad in Fort Carson, Colorado; the ingenious experiments of the poverty-fighting randomistas. For our own personal projects, there are no heat maps and no double-blind trials. There is sometimes the possibility of being your own validation squad: as a writer, I find the simple process of putting a chapter to one side for a few weeks helps me to let go of it; I read it with fresh eyes and spot flaws far more easily. Performers often find that filming their performance and watching it later gives them the necessary sense of distance, a distance which has two facets: distance in time lets you apply a third-person perspective to yourself, and the film or the document provides an objective record of past achievements; memory alone is not enough. But this has its limits. Honest advice from others is better.

Any evolutionary biologist knows how success emerges from failure in nature: ceaselessly generate random mutations in delicate organisms, toss out the vast majority that make those organisms worse, and preserve the tiny few that make them better. Do this enough, and apparent miracles emerge. When you have three months to conjure up the apparent miracle of evolving a Chicago flop into a Broadway triumph, you need a less extraordinarily wasteful selection process, and this is why Twyla Tharp's 'validation squad' was vital. It wasn't about cheering her from the sidelines; it was about helping her decide what needed to stay and what needed to change. She had already carried out her own ruthless winnowing of her private improvisations, but more was needed. So many new ideas don't work that a good selection mechanism is indispensable, and a good validation squad is a far better editor of our own experience than we will ever be.

4 Creating our own safe spaces to experiment

John Kay, whose book *The Truth about Markets* was a profound influence on this one, uses the term 'disciplined pluralism' to describe how markets work: exploring many new ideas but ruthlessly cutting down the ones that fail, whether they are brand-new or hundreds of years old. But although Kay does not make this claim, 'disciplined pluralism' could also be a credo for a successful and fulfilling life.

Pluralism matters because life is not worth living without new experiences – new people, new places, new challenges. But discipline matters too: we cannot simply treat life as a psychedelic trip through a random series of novel sensations. We must sometimes commit to what is working: to decide that the hobby we are pursuing is worth mastering; that it's time to write that novel, or strive for that night-school degree; or maybe to get married. Equally important: sometimes we need to make the opposite kind of commitment, and decide that the toxic job and the toxic boyfriend are simply not worth the amount of life they cost.

Recall chapter 1's metaphor of the fitness landscape, a vast and ever-changing geography consisting of troughs of failure and peaks of success. Evolution explores this landscape with a serendipitous mixture of wild leaps and small steps. The wild leaps usually end up at the bottom of some chasm, but sometimes they land in the foothills of some totally new range of mountains. The small steps lead uphill rather than down, but perhaps only to the top of a molehill.

In life we tend to notice and idolise those who make the wild leaps: the retired nurse who volunteers with Médecins Sans Frontières and is posted to the Congo; the cubicle colleague who packs it all in to buy a small olive farm in rural Sardinia. In the creative arts, likewise, we celebrate the decisive moment after which nothing is the same again – Joyce's *Ulysses*, Picasso's *Guernica*, Eliot's *The Love Song of J. Alfred Prufrock*, or indeed, *Sgt. Pepper's Lonely Hearts Club Band* by the Beatles. The economist David Galenson provides a different perspective. Galenson studies the creative life cycle, gathering data on when artists, architects, poets, songwriters and others produced their definitive works. He has discovered many examples that confirm our natural tendency to conflate the precocious young talent and the creative genius, but offers equally many counter-examples. For every artist who makes dramatic conceptual leaps – a Picasso, a T.S. Eliot – there is a tentative experimentalist such as Piet Mondrian or Robert Frost. Many of Frost's most anthologised poems were written after the age of fifty; Mondrian's greatest work was painted when he was seventy-one. Galenson argues convincingly that this is because they were slowly but surely perfecting their craft, climbing a single mountain of achievement while Picasso (or Orson Welles, or Jasper Johns, or Bob Dylan) vaulted from one vantage point to another.

Whatever our personal endeavours, for most of us it's worth trying to combine both approaches. We all know someone who wanders around the lower reaches of various mountain ranges, fascinated by the newness of it all but always distracted or discouraged before she has climbed beyond the foothills; and someone else who spends years plodding to reach the summit of the first dull hill he came across. It is a difficult balance to strike.

For many people university is about wild leaps, a relatively safe space and an appropriate time to experiment: with sex, with ideas, with your own identity. Can there be a more exciting world of limitless opportunity than the clubs and societies day, where new students can sign up for the Industrial Society, the Libertarian Society, the Live-Roleplaying club, the Baha'i association or even the Poohsticks Society? And all the while they know that as long as they don't push the sex or the student politics or the Poohsticks too far, they'll graduate having learned a lot and acquired a valuable qualification. Experimentation doesn't get much safer than that.

Our first job, by contrast, involves sitting next to a specific group of colleagues, learning a particular set of skills, and embarking on a particular career path. Rather than opening up new options, the first weeks of a new job are all about shutting them down and focusing. Despite all the apparent similarities to starting at university – new friends, new town, new skills – the situation is fundamentally different. Perhaps it is no coincidence that Google, that most admired and envied of companies, consciously models itself on the freewheeling experimentation of life at Stanford's graduate school.

But most companies are not Google. The excitement that so many students feel as they arrive at university – a world of possibilities, of safe experiments – is one we tend to lose. But we need not: the new possibilities are always out there. It's one thing to be committed; it's another to trap ourselves unnecessarily. Perhaps we become more shy of experimenting as we get older because we become more aware of the truth that has defined this book: that in a complex world, we're unlikely to get it right first time. To embrace the idea of adapting in everyday life seems to be to accept blundering into a process of unremitting failure. So it's worth remembering once again *why* it is worth experimenting, even though so many experiments will, indeed, end in failure. It's because the process of correcting the mistakes can be more liberating than the mistakes themselves are crushing, even though at the time we so often feel that the reverse is true. It's because a single successful experiment can become Reginald Mitchell's Spitfire or H.R. McMaster's counterinsurgency strategy for Iraq. A single experiment that succeeds can transform our lives for the better in a way that a failed experiment will not transform them for the worse – as long as we don't engage in denial or chase our losses. Twyla Tharp's Tony award is testament to the importance of risking something new and adapting until it pays off.

Experimenting can be a frightening process. We are constantly making mistakes, not knowing whether we are on the right lines. Kathryn Schulz, in her elegant book *Being Wrong*, describes the state of profound uncertainty that comes with feeling wrong about some fundamental belief. She compares it to being a toddler lost in the heart of Manhattan. But experimenting doesn't have to be like that. On the very same day on which I read Schulz's words, my three-year-old daughter was lost in the centre of London – on the South Bank, a car-free space that is otherwise just as bewildering as Times Square. And it didn't bother her in the slightest: she bolted out of the door of a café and began to play hide and seek. Witnesses told her increasingly frantic family that she had sauntered along the bank of the Thames, playing on the street furniture, ducking behind benches, dancing around and exploring a space she found delightful. For the ten minutes during which she was lost, it seems that she felt absolutely secure that she would find her family or that her family would find her.

The ability to adapt requires this sense of security, an inner confidence that the cost of failure is a cost we will be able to bear. Sometimes that takes real courage; at other times all that is needed is the happy self-delusion of a lost three-year-old. Whatever its source, we need that willingness to risk failure. Without it, we will never truly succeed.

Acknowledgements

'Write drunk. Edit sober.'

– attributed to Ernest Hemingway

'Ever tried. Ever failed. No matter. Try again. Fail again. Fail better.'

– Samuel Beckett

My own most successful experiment was writing a book called *The Undercover Economist.* One friend, David Bodanis, told me I should take some time off to write it instead of spending five days a week working for an oil company – in other words, pluralism. When the project had stalled and I was planning to do something totally different, a second friend, Paul Domjan, talked me out of that and told me to finish what I had started – that's discipline. A third friend, Andrew Wright, read every page again and again, telling me what was working and what wasn't. I didn't think of them as 'the validation squad', but they were and are. My entire second career as a writer would have been impossible without them. Thank you.

The book you now have in your hands took many years to write, much trial and error, and a great deal of help. I am particularly grateful to those who read parts of this book in draft and offered comments: David Bodanis, Duncan Cromarty, Mark

Henstridge, Diana Jackson, Sandie Kanthal, John Kay, David Klemperer, Paul Klemperer, Richard Knight, Andrew Mackay, Fran Monks, Dave Morris, Roz Morris, Martin Sandbu and Tim Savin.

I am also hugely grateful to my colleagues at the *Financial Times* and the BBC *More or Less* team, in particular: Lionel Barber, Dan Bogler and Lisa MacLeod for their patience while I worked on the book; my colleagues on the leader-writing team; Sue Norris, Sue Matthias, Andy Davis and Caroline Daniel at *FT Magazine*; Peter Cheek and Bhavna Patel of the FT library; the 'economics faculty' of the FT, Chris Cook, Chris Giles, Robin Harding, Martin Sandbu and Martin Wolf; and at the BBC Richard Knight and Richard Vadon.

A large number of people were kind enough to agree to be interviewed or simply to provide suggestions or brief comments. I have also relied on the reporting of other writers, whom I hope I have properly acknowledged in the notes, but whom I wish to thank here where the debt is particularly great. Without in any way implicating them in the book that resulted, I am grateful to:

Chapter One: Thomas Thwaites, Eric Beinhocker, Philip Tetlock, John Kay, Paul Ormerod, Donald Green, Michele Belot, Richard Thaler, David Halpern, Matthew Taylor and Jonah Lehrer.

Chapter Two: H.R. McMaster, Andrew Mackay, John Nagl, George Feese, Dennis DuTray, Jacob Shapiro, Steve Fidler, Toby Dodge, and Adrian Harford.

Chapter Three: Will Whitehorn, Paul Shawcross, Richard Branson, Suzanne Scotchmer, David Rooney, Steven B. Johnson, Alex Tabarrok, Bob Weiss, Owen Barder, Robin Hanson, Jani Niipola and Ruth Levine.

Chapter Four: William Easterly, Owen Barder, Jeffrey Sachs, Michael Clemens, Edward Miguel, Sandra Sequeira, Esther Duflo, John McArthur, Ben Goldacre, Sir Iain Chalmers, Gabriel Demombynes, Michael Klein, Macartan Humphreys,

Daron Acemoglu, Dean Karlan, Chris Blattman, Joshua Angrist, Jonathan Zinman, Clare Lockhart, Mark Henstridge, César Hidalgo, Bailey Klinger, Ricardo Hausmann and Paul Romer.

Chapter Five: Gabrielle Walker, David King, James Cameron, Cameron Hepburn, Mark Williamson, Euan Murray, Justin Rowlatt, David MacKay, Tim Crozier-Cole, Geoffrey Palmer and Prashant Vaze.

Chapter Six: Sophy Harford, James Reason, Charles Perrow, Gillian Tett, Philippe Jamet, Ed Crooks, Steve Mitchelhill, Peter Higginson, Andrew Haldane, Martin Wolf, Raghuram Rajan, Jeremy Bulow and Paul Klemperer.

Chapter Seven: Sandie Kanthal and Peter Higginson.

Chapter Eight: Richard Wiseman.

Although I did not interview them for this book, at certain points I drew heavily on the writing or broadcasting of the following people: Loren Graham, Thomas Ricks, David Cloud, Greg Jaffe, George Packer, Leo McKinstry, Dava Sobel, Ian Parker, Sebastian Mallaby, Andrew Ross Sorkin, Jennifer Hughes, Gary Hamel, Peter Day, Michael Buerk, Twyla Tharp and Kathryn Schulz. I am indebted.

I am also indebted for excellent research assistance to Elizabeth Baldwin, Kelly Chen, Bob Denham and Cosmina Dorobanţu.

My editors, Eric Chinski, Iain Hunt, Tim Rostron and Tim Whiting, have been very supportive. So have my agents, Sally Holloway and Zoe Pagnamenta. And as always I am in awe of Andrew Wright's uncanny ability to provide unconditional support with penetrating criticism.

Above all, thank you to Fran, Stella and Africa for tolerating an absent husband and father for so long. I love you all.

London, January 2011

Notes

1 Adapting

1   Von Hayek quote: Friedrich von Hayek, *The Fatal Conceit* (Chicago: University of Chicago Press, 1991).
1   The electric toaster seems a humble thing: http://www.toaster.org/1900.php
2   'It warms bread when I plug it into a battery': telephone interview with Thomas Thwaites, 30 June 2009.
3   The range of products: Eric Beinhocker, *The Origin of Wealth* (London: Random House, 2007), p. 9.
5   We're proud of the change we've brought: Barack Obama, 'Speech at the White House Correspondents' Dinner, 2009'. Available at: http://politicalhumor.about.com/od/barackobama/a/obama-white-house-correspondents-transcript_2.htm
6   Perhaps we have this instinct: Beinhocker, *The Origin of Wealth*, p. 9.
6   Perhaps the best illustration of this: Philip E. Tetlock, *Expert Political Judgement* (New York: Princeton University Press, 2005).
7   'The best lesson of Tetlock's book': Louis Menand, 'Everybody's an Expert', *New Yorker*, 5 December 2005.
8   Just two years later: *Business Week*: 'Oops! Who's Excellent Now?', 5 November 1984; Christopher Lorenz, '"Excellence" Takes a Knock', *Financial Times*, 1 November 1984.
8   The 'who's excellent now?' experience is reinforced: Leslie Hannah, 'Marshall's "Trees" and the Global "Forest": Were "Giant Redwoods" Different?', in N. Lamoreaux, D. Raff and P. Temin (eds), *Learning by Doing in Markets, Firms and Countries* (London: University of Chicago Press, 1999).

9   At the time of writing, it was not even in the top five hundred: FT
        Global 500, 2008. Available at: http://media.ft.com/cms/8aa8acb8-
        4142-11dd-9661-0000779fd2ac.pdf

9   Ten of Hannah's top hundred: Paul Ormerod, *Why Most Things Fail*
        (London: Faber and Faber, 2005), p. 12.

10   Consider the early printing industry: Ormerod, *Why Most Things
        Fail*, p. 15.

10   It eventually found one: Tom Scocca, 'The First Printed Books
        Came with a Question: What Do You Do with These Things?',
        Boston Globe, 29 August 2010. Available at: http://www.boston.com/
        bostonglobe/ideas/articles/2010/08/29/cover_story/?page=full

10   At the dawn of the automobile industry: Ormerod, *Why Most Things
        Fail*, p. ix.

11   The modern computer industry is a striking example: Beinhocker,
        The Origin of Wealth, p. 333.

11   Meanwhile, Xerox, struggling to survive: John Kay, *The Truth about
        Markets* (London: Penguin Allen Lane, 2003), pp. 101–103.

12   It took several decades: http://www.toaster.org/museum.html

12   Biologists have a word for the way: there is no shortage of popular
        accounts of evolution. I have relied here on Eric Beinhocker's excel-
        lent summary in *The Origin of Wealth*.

14   Yet the blind evolutionary process produced: see Karl Sims,
        'Evolving Virtual Creatures' Computer Graphics', *Siggraph '94
        Proceedings*, July 1994, pp. 15–22. Available at: http://www.karl
        sims.com/papers/siggraph94.pdf. Videos available at: http://
        www.karlsims.com/evolved-virtual-creatures.html

16   Given the likely shape: Beinhocker, *The Origin of Wealth*, ch. 9.

18   He discovered the same thing: Ormerod, *Why Most Things Fail*,
        chapters 9 and 10.

19   If companies really could plan successfully: Ormerod, *Why Most
        Things Fail*, ch. 11; and Paul Ormerod and Bridget Rosewell, 'How
        Much Can Firms Know?', Working Paper, February 2004. Available
        at: http://www.paulormerod.com/pdf/intent6mar03.pdf

21   A railroad foreman named Phineas Gage: Malcolm McMillan of
        Deakin University maintains a trove of information about Gage.
        Available at: http://www.deakin.edu.au/hmnbs/psychology/gage
        page/

22   When Palchinsky sent back his findings: Loren Graham, *The Ghost
        of the Executed Engineer: Technology and the Fall of the Soviet Union*
        (Cambridge, MA: Harvard University Press, 1993), pp. 51–5.

25   'For a day and a half': quoted in Graham, *The Ghost of the Executed
        Engineer*, p. 69.

25 When the US historian Stephen Kotkin: Stephen Kotkin, *Steeltown USSR* (Berkeley: University of California Press, 1991), p. 254.

26 In Magnitogorsk, there were two types: Graham, *The Ghost of the Executed Engineer*, p. 75.

26 There had been no trial: Graham, *The Ghost of the Executed Engineer*, p. 46.

28 'You can be watching TV': Andy Warhol, *The Philosophy of Andy Warhol* (New York: Harcourt, 1975), p. 100.

30 He had been in power for eight years at the time: Tim Harford, 'How a Celebrity Chef Turned into a Social Scientist', *Financial Times*, 7 November 2009. Available at: http://timharford.com/2009/11/how-a-celebrity-chef-turned-into-a-social-scientist/; and Michele Belot and Jonathan James, 'Healthy School Meals and Educational Achievements', Nuffield College Working Paper. Available at: http://cess-wb.nuff.ox.ac.uk/downloads/schoolmeals.pdf

30 There is some evidence that the more ambitious: see James Surowiecki, *The Wisdom of Crowds* (London: Abacus, 2005), pp. 253–4. Surowiecki refers to two studies that reach this commonsense conclusion, but I have not been able to discover a precise citation.

30 Even when leaders and managers: Mancur Olson, *Power and Prosperity* (New York: Basic Books, 2000), pp. 138–9.

31 I spent the summer of 2005 studying poker: Tim Harford, 'The Poker Machine', *Financial Times*, 6 May 2006. Available at: http://timharford.com/2006/05/the-poker-machine/; and Tim Harford, *The Logic of Life* (New York: Random House, 2008).

32 The brain refuses to register: Gary Smith, Michael Levere and Robert Kurtzman, 'Poker Player Behavior after Big Wins and Big Losses', *Management Science*, Vol. 55, No. 9 (September 2009), pp. 1547–55.

32 The great economic psychologists Daniel Kahneman and Amos Tversky: Daniel Kahneman and Amos Tversky, 'Prospect Theory: An Analysis of Decision under Risk', *Econometrica*, Vol. 47, No. 2 (1979), p. 287.

33 Found the perfect setting to analyse the way we respond to losses: Thierry Post, Martijn J. Van den Assem, Guido Baltussen and Richard H. Thaler, 'Deal or No Deal? Decision Making under Risk in a Large-Payoff Game Show', *American Economic Review*, Vol. 98, No. 1 (March 2008). Available at: http://ssrn.com/abstract=636508. Having written about Thaler's research before, and even presented a radio documentary on the show, I am indebted to Jonah Lehrer and his book *How We Decide* (Boston, MA: Houghton Mifflin Harcourt, 2009) for emphasising how striking this result really is.

35   Unfortunately, selling winners and holding on to losers: Terrance Odean, 'Are Investors Reluctant to Realize Their Losses?', *Journal of Finance*, Vol. 53, No. 5 (October 1998), pp. 1775–98. Available at: http://faculty.haas.berkeley.edu/odean/Papers%20current%20versions/AreInvestorsReluctant.pdf.

2 Conflict or: How organisations learn

37   'It's so damn complex': quoted by George Packer, 'The Lesson of Tal Afar', *The New Yorker*, 10 April 2006.

37   'In the absence of guidance': David Petraeus, interview with *The Washington Post*, 9 February 2010, http://views.washingtonpost.com/leadership/panelists/2010/02/transcript-gen-petraeus.html

37   'Saw that children were in the room': Thomas Ricks, *The Gamble* (New York: The Penguin Press, 2009), pp. 3–6.

38   What happened after the bomb exploded: 'A hard look at Haditha', *New York Times*, 4 June 2006, http://www.nytimes.com/2006/06/04/opinion/04sun1.html

38   One marine sergeant admitted: Mark Oliver, 'Haditha marine "watched superior kill surrendering civilians"', *Guardian*, 10 May 2007.

38   'I watched them shoot': 'Collateral damage or civilian massacre in Haditha?', *Time Magazine*, 19 March 2006, http://www.time.com/time/magazine/article/0,9171,1174682,00.html

38   The battalion commander thought: Ricks, *The Gamble*, pp. 3–6.

39   Vast numbers of people fled the country: Ricks, *The Gamble*, chapter 2, and George Packer, 'The Lesson of Tal Afar'.

43   The facts about Haditha: news briefing transcript, Secretary of Defense Donald H. Rumsfeld and Chairman, Joint Chiefs of Staff, Gen. Peter Pace, 29 November 2005, http://www.defense.gov/transcripts/transcript.aspx?transcriptid=1492

43   The fear of the 'i-word': Packer, 'The Lesson of Tal Afar'.

43   General Eric Shinseki had warned: Eric Schmitt, 'Pentagon contradicts General on Iraq occupation force's size', *New York Times*, 28 February 2003, http://www.nytimes.com/2003/02/28/politics/28COST.html?th; and Thom Shanker, 'New strategy vindicates ex-Army Chief Shinseki', *New York Times*, 12 January 2007, http://www.nytimes.com/2007/01/12/washington/12shinseki.html?_r=1

44   He had moved with his pregnant wife: Cloud & Jaffe, *The Fourth Star*, pp. 27–34 & 84–7.

45   Feith had responded with: Cloud & Jaffe, *The Fourth Star*, pp. 113–14.

45 There was the case of Andy Krepinevich: Ricks, *The Gamble*, pp. 16–17.

47 Johnson had sacked three military aides: H.R. McMaster, *Dereliction of Duty* (Harper, 1997), p. 52.

47 Johnson and his advisers saw: McMaster, *Dereliction of Duty*, pp. 88–9.

47 McNamara himself looked for 'team players': McMaster, *Dereliction of Duty*, pp. 60, 109.

47 A famous set of experiments: S. E. Asch, 'Effects of group pressure upon the modification and distortion of judgment', in H. Guetzkow (ed.), *Groups, Leadership and Men* (Pittsburgh, PA: Carnegie Press, 1951).

48 Less famous but just as important: S. E. Asch, 'Opinions and social pressure', *Scientific American*, 193 (1955), pp. 31–5.

48 In a surreal variant: Vernon L. Allen & John M. Levine, 'Social support and conformity: the role of independent assessment of reality', *Journal of Experimental Social Psychology*, vol. 7(1) (Jan. 1971), pp. 48–58.

49 Their decision-makers are simple automatons: Lu Hong & Scott E. Page, 'Groups of diverse problem solvers can outperform groups of high-ability problem solvers', *Proceedings of the National Academy of Sciences*, vol. 101, no. 46, 16 November 2004, pp. 16385–9, http://www.cscs.umich.edu/~spage/pnas.pdf

50 H.R. McMaster's book gives a telling example: McMaster, *Dereliction of Duty*, pp. 89–91.

50 Johnson 'made the critical decisions': McMaster, *Dereliction of Duty*, p. 324.

51 The first glimmerings of success came in a place called Tal Afar: for this section I draw heavily on George Packer's comprehensive 'The Lesson of Tal Afar'. Other sources include Ricks, *The Gamble*; Cloud & Jaffe, *The Fourth Star*; and my own interviews with H.R. McMaster in March and August 2009.

51 Some of the FOBs were enormous: see Packer, 'The Lesson of Tal Afar'; also Jim Garamone, '"Head Fobbit" works for quality of life at forward operating base', *Armed Forces Press Service*, http://www.defense.gov/news/newsarticle.aspx?id=18520

52 On his first day in Iraq, Major Nagl: author interview with John Nagl, 4 February 2010.

52 It was why Iraqi teachers made excuses: Packer, 'The Lesson of Tal Afar'.

53 'Every time you treat an Iraqi disrespectfully': Ricks, *The Gamble*, p. 60.

54 'In one case,' recalls Col. H.: H.R. McMaster interview with *Sunday Times*, 'Leaving now not the way out of Iraq', 29 July 2007.

55   He apparently had little time for: Cloud & Jaffe, *The Fourth Star*, pp. 199–200, 207.

55   When I first spoke to him: author interview with H.R. McMaster, 18 March 2009.

55   Col. H. was twice passed over: Cloud & Jaffe, *The Fourth Star*, p. 291.

56   As early retirement beckoned: http://smallwarsjournal.com/blog/ 2007/07/contrary-peter-principle/ and http://www.outsidethe beltway.com/archives/hr_mcmaster_passed_over_-_reverse_peter_ principle/

56   MacFarland's men started in Tal Afar: Niel Smith & Sean MacFarland, 'Anbar awakens: the tipping point', *Military Review*, 1 March 2008.

57   MacFarland learned from McMaster's approach: Ricks, *The Gamble*, pp. 60–72.

57   David Kilcullen's '28 Articles: George Packer, 'Knowing the enemy', *The New Yorker*, 18 December 2006.

57   Kilcullen said he wrote with the aid of: Kilcullen interview with *Men's Journal*: http://www.mensjournal.com/is-this-any-way-to-fight-a-war/3

58   'We willingly implement lessons': Correspondence with Brig. Gen. Andrew Mackay, February 2010.

58   Another famous piece of bottom-up advice: Travis Patriquin, 'How to win the war in Al Anbar by Cpt. Trav', available in various locations online including http://abcnews.go.com/images/us/how_to_ win_in_anbar_v4.pdf

58   At his memorial service: Andrew Lubin, 'Ramadi from the Caliphate to capitalism', *Proceedings Magazine*, April 2008, http://www.usni. org/magazines/proceedings/story.asp?STORY_ID=1420

59   It's not that David Petraeus was an empty vessel: Cloud & Jaffe, *The Fourth Star*, chapter 7.

60   Petraeus's predecessor at Leavenworth: Cloud & Jaffe, *The Fourth Star*, p. 217.

61   'What is startling is the severity of his comments': Richard Norton-Taylor & Jamie Wilson, 'US army in Iraq institutionally racist, claims British officer', *Guardian*, 12 January 2006.

61   Petraeus didn't just seek out: Ricks, *The Gamble*, pp. 23–5.

61   One of the journalists at the conference: James Fallows of *The Atlantic*, as described by John Nagl in the *Counterinsurgency Manual* foreword: http://www.press.uchicago.edu/Misc/Chicago/841519 foreword.html

61   'H.R. was conducting counterinsurgency': Author interview with John Nagl, 4 February 2010.

61 'David Petracus is the best general': Ricks, *The Gamble*, p. 22.

62 Galvin was a man who understood: Cloud & Jaffe, *The Fourth Star*, p. 42.

62 Can quickly fall into the habit of reinforcing: Irving Janis, *Victims of GroupThink* (Boston: Houghton Mifflin Company, 1972).

63 Passing through Dublin Airport: Cloud & Jaffe, *The Fourth Star*, p. 172.

63 The diversity of opinions: Cloud & Jaffe, *The Fourth Star*, p. 220; and Ricks, *The Gamble*, pp. 24–31.

64 Petraeus had recommended that he be appointed: Ricks, *The Gamble*, p. 96, and more generally on the entire process by which Jack Keane, David Petraeus and Ray Odierno changed the strategy in Iraq.

66 If he tried to respond to a tip-off: author interview with John Nagl, 4 February 2010, and Peter Maass, 'Professor Nagl's war', *New York Times*, 11 January 2004, http://www.nytimes.com/2004/01/11/magazine/professor-nagl-s-war.html?pagewanted=all

67 Explain what the images had been supposed to advertise: author interview with Andrew Mackay, May 2009.

68 His efforts did lead to a more efficient: Michael Ellman, 'Economic calculation in socialist countries', *The New Palgrave Dictionary of Economics*, ed. Steven N. Durlauf & Lawrence E. Blume (Palgrave Macmillan, 2008).

69 McNamara's centralised analytical approach did not bring victory: Raymond Fisman & Edward Miguel, *Economic Gangsters* (Princeton:Princeton University Press, 2008), pp. 160–7.

70 'We are and always shall be in favour': Eden Medina, 'Designing freedom, regulating a nation: socialist cybernetics in Allende's Chile', *J. Lat. Amer. Stud.* 38 (2006), pp. 571–606, http://www.informatics.indiana.edu/edenm/EdenMedinaJLASAugust2006.pdf

70 Moved to a cottage in rural Wales: Andy Beckett, 'Santiago dreaming', *Guardian*, 8 September 2003, http://www.guardian.co.uk/technology/2003/sep/08/sciencenews.chile

71 Yet the control room itself never became operational: Stafford Beer, *The Brain of the Firm* (Chichester: Wiley, 2nd edition, 1981), chapters 16–20.

71 Donald Rumsfeld had better computers: James Kitfield, 'The counter-revolution in military affairs', *National Journal*, 5 December 2009; and Cloud & Jaffe, *The Fourth Star*, p. 171.

71 An air-conditioned tent inside a metal shell: Cloud & Jaffe, *The Fourth Star*, p. 111.

71 It was hard to persuade them to telex: Medina, 'Designing freedom,

regulating a nation', pp. 571–606, http://www.informatics.indiana .edu/edenm/EdenMedinaJLASAugust2006.pdf

72 Hayek's essay pre-dated modern computers: Friedrich A. Hayek, 'The use of knowledge in society', *American Economic Review*, XXXV, no. 4 (September 1945), pp. 519–30, http://www.econlib.org/ library/Essays/hykKnw1.html

72 Similar problems plagued coalition forces: H.R. McMaster, 'On war: lessons to be learned', *Survival* 50:1 (2008), 19–30.

72 'We had been moving through what was': H.R. McMaster inter- viewed for a documentary posted on YouTube by 'ColdWarWarriors', http://www.youtube.com/watch?v=aBG_G678Trg&feature=related

73 Eagle Troop 'dramatically illustrates': Robert Scales, *Certain Victory: The U.S. Army in the Gulf War* (Office of the Chief of Staff, U.S. Army, 1993), chapter 1, and Tom Clancy, *Armoured Cav* (Berkeley Trade, 1994).

75 Examined large US firms from the mid-1980s throughout the 1990s: Raghuram Rajan & Julie Wulf (2003), 'The flattening of the firm', NBER Working Paper 9633.

76 To get the most out of that flexibility: Daron Acemoglu, Philippe Aghion, Claire Lelarge, John van Reenen & Fabrizio Zilibotti, 'Technology, information and the decentralization of the firm', *Quarterly Journal of Economics*, November 2007, and Erik Brynjolfsson & Lorin M. Hitt, 'Beyond computation: informa- tion technology, organizational transformation and business performance', *Journal of Economic Perspectives*, vol. 14, No. 4 (Fall 2000).

76 Didn't have the authority to print his own propaganda: John Nagl, lecture at King's College London, 2 February 2010.

76 He couldn't tap into the massive USAID budget: Cloud & Jaffe, *The Fourth Star*, pp. 146–7.

76 Sean MacFarland's men broadcast news from loudspeakers: Ricks, *The Gamble*, p. 70.

77 A careful statistical analysis later found: Eli Berman, Jacob N. Shapiro & Joseph H. Felter, 'Can hearts and minds be bought? The economics of counterinsurgency in Iraq', NBER Working Paper no. 14606, December 2008.

77 'Every officer I spoke with knew about it': Fred Kaplan, 'Challenging the generals', *New York Times*, 26 August 2007, http://www.nytimes.com/2007/08/26/magazine/26military-t .html?_r=2&ref=magazine&pagewanted=all&oref=slogin

78 David Petraeus took the unprecedented step of flying: Cloud & Jaffe, *The Fourth Star*, p. 291, and Ricks, *The Gamble*, p. 276. Ricks

says that the flight to the Pentagon was made in November 2007, Cloud & Jaffe date it 2008. The decision was announced in the summer of 2008.

78 Army doctrine declared that 'unmanned systems': 2001 capstone concept quoted in H.R. McMaster, 'Centralization vs. decentralization: preparing for and practicing mission command in counterinsurgency operations', in *Lessons for a Long War: How America Can Win on New Battlefields.* 2009 concept is available at: http://www.tradoc.army.mil/tpubs/pams/tp525-3-0.pdf

79 His first assignment as a general redeveloping Army doctrine: Video promotion for the 2009 Army Capstone Concept: http://www.vimeo.com/7066453

3 Creating new ideas that matter or: Variation

80 'Nothing we design': David Pye, *The Nature of Design*, quoted in Daniel Roth, 'Time your attack', *Wired*, January 2010.

80 'The end of surprise': Robert Friedel, 'Serendipity is no accident', *The Kenyon Review*, vol. 23, no. 2 (Spring 2001).

81 The Air Ministry briefly went so far as: Leo McKinstry, *Spitfire: Portrait of a Legend* (London: John Murray, 2007), p. 37.

81 When Supermarine approached the ministry with a radical new design: McKinstry, *Spitfire*, p. 47.

82 'The bastards can make such infernally': all quotes collected in McKinstry, *Spitfire*, pp. 3–6.

82 Hitler had been single-mindedly: Andrew Roberts, 'Hitler's England: what if Germany had invaded Britain in May 1940?', in Niall Ferguson (ed.), *Virtual History: Alternatives and Counterfactuals* (New York: Basic Books, 1997), p. 284.

82 The RAF boasted fewer than 300 Spitfires: McKinstry, *Spitfire*, pp. 188–9.

82 Predicted that the Luftwaffe's first week: Roberts, 'Hitler's England', pp. 285–6.

82 It might even have given Germany the lead: Roberts, 'Hitler's England', pp. 310, 320.

82 The prototype cost the government: McKinstry, *Spitfire*, p. 51, and Lawrence H. Officer, 'Purchasing power of British pounds from 1264 to present', MeasuringWorth, 2009, http://www.measuringworth.com/ppoweruk/

83 'Positive black swans': Nassim Nicholas Taleb, *The Black Swan* (New York: Random House, 2007).

85   We should now build: McKinstry, *Spitfire*, p. 12.

86   He soon discovered some remarkable examples: Richard Dawkins,
      The Greatest Show on Earth (London: Bantam, 2009), pp. 254–73.

87   Bright ideas emerge from the swirling mix of other ideas: See also
      Richard Florida, 'The world is spiky', *The Atlantic Monthly*, October
      2005, my *The Logic of Life* (2008), Matt Ridley's *The Rational Optimist*
      (2010) and Steven Johnson's *Where Good Ideas Come From* (2010).

87   A playboy politician most famous as a campaigner against lesbian-
      ism: McKinstry, *Spitfire*, pp.17–18.

88   'Bloody good cup of tea, Mitchell': McKinstry, *Spitfire*, p. 20.

88   'It's either him or me!': McKinstry, *Spitfire*, p. 31.

88   'Freak machines': McKinstry, *Spitfire*, p. 29.

89   England's pride was intact: McKinstry, *Spitfire*, p. 32.

89   'The Battle of Britain was won by Chamberlain': McKinstry, *Spitfire*,
      p.194.

89   One might think that there is no problem enouraging innovation: as
      this book was going to press, Tyler Cowen's book *The Great
      Stagnation* (Dutton, 2011) appeared. Owen's book offers further evi-
      dence of an innovation slowdown in addition to that presented here.

90   Even the design of niche cars: Chris Anderson, 'In the next indus-
      trial revolution, atoms are the new bits', *Wired*, February 2010,
      http://www.wired.com/magazine/2010/01/ff_newrevolution/

90   'Failure for free': Clay Shirky, *Here Comes Everybody* (London:
      Penguin, 2008).

90   US health secretary Margaret Heckler announced: http://
      www.pbs.org/newshour/bb/health/jan-june01/aids_6-27.html

92   The whole process has become harder: Benjamin F. Jones, Brian
      Uzzi & Stefan Wuchty, 'The increasing dominance of teams in the
      production of knowledge', *Science*, May 2007, http://www.kellogg.
      northwestern.edu/faculty/jones-ben/htm/ResearchframeTeams.htm

92   Jones argues that scientific careers: Benjamin F. Jones, 'Age and
      great invention', *Review of Economics and Statistics*, forthcoming,
      http://www.kellogg.northwestern.edu/faculty/jones-ben/
      htm/AgeAndGreatInvention.pdf

92   *Elite* offered space combat: 'The making of Elite', *Edge*, 29 May
      2009,   http://www.edge-online.com/magazine/the-making-of-
      elite?page=0%2C0

93   *Duke Nukem Forever* was never finished: Clive Thompson, 'Learn to
      let go', *Wired*, January 2010, http://www.wired.com/magazine/
      2009/12/fail_duke_nukem/all/1

93   Gamers have been eagerly awaiting *Elite 4*: 'Frontier reveals Elite 4',
      http://uk.pc.ign.com/articles/092/092218p1.html

93   The plane took a quarter of a century to enter service: measuring
      time from original government specification. Sources:
      http://en.wikipedia.org/wiki/F-22_Raptor; Ben Rich & Leo Janos,
      Skunk Works (New York: Sphere, 1994), p. 350; Samuel H.
      Williamson, 'Six ways to compute the relative value of a U.S. dol-
      lar amount, 1790 to present', MeasuringWorth, 2009, http://www
      .measuringworth.com/uscompare/

93   You will discover that by the year 2000: The Hudson Institute, *The
      Year 2000: A Framework for Speculation on the Next 33 Years*, Herman
      Kahn & Anthony J. Wiener (New York: Macmillan, 1967). John Kay
      first called my attention to Kahn & Wiener's predictions.

94   The real winner of the vote was: http://www.economist.com/
      blogs/gulliver/2010/01/what_business_travellers_appreciate_most

94   The number of new drugs approved each year: Murray Aitken,
      Ernst R. Berndt & David M. Cutler, 'Prescription drug spending
      trends in the United States', *Health Affairs* Web Exclusive, 16
      December 2008.

94   The number of patents produced per researcher: Benjamin F. Jones,
      'The burden of knowledge', *Review of Economic Studies*, forthcom-
      ing, http://www.kellogg.northwestern.edu/faculty/jones-ben/htm/
      BurdenOfKnowledge.pdf

94   We should be spending fifty times *more* on research: Bjorn
      Lomborg, 'We should change tack on climate after Copenhagen',
      Financial Times, 23 December 2009, http://www.ft.com/cms/s/0/
      5369f3e8-ef69-11de-86c4-00144feab49a.html

95   'A method of swinging on a swing': Hal Varian, 'A patent that pro-
      tects a better mousetrap spurs innovation. But what about one for a
      new way to amuse a cat?', *New York Times*, 21 October 2004, Section
      C, p. 2; Jeff Hecht, 'Boy takes swing at US patents', *New Scientist*, 17
      April 2002; Adam Jaffe & Josh Lerner, *Innovation and its Discontents*
      (Princeton University Press, 2004).

96   The auction expert Paul Klemperer points out: Paul Klemperer,
      'America's patent protection has gone too far', *Financial Times*, 2
      March 2004.

96   He soon discovered that patent 6,134,548: Alex Tabarrok (2002),
      'Patent theory versus patent law', *Contributions to Economic Analysis
      & Policy*, vol. 1, issue 1, article 9, http://www.bepress.com/bejeap/
      contributions/vol1/iss1/art9

96   This was the fate of Bayer: Keith Bradsher with Edmund L.
      Andrews, 'Cipro', *New York Times*, 24 October 2001, http://
      www.nytimes.com/2001/10/24/business/24BAYE.html

97   The owner of the patent on Tamiflu: James Kanter, 'Roche offers to

negotiate on flu drug', *New York Times*, 19 October 2005, http://query.nytimes.com/gst/fullpage.html?res=9803EEDF123FF9 3AA25753C1A9639C8B63&sec=health

97   Mario Capecchi's earliest memory: Mario Capecchi's extensive and moving autobiography is available on the Nobel Prize website: http://nobelprize.org/nobel_prizes/medicine/laureates/2007/capecchi-autobio.html

101   Urges 'researchers to take risks': http://www.hhmi.org/research/investigators/

103   The Howard Hughes Medical Institute invests: the Howard Hughes Medical Institute grants are $700 million annually. Global R&D spending was $1,100,000 million in 2009. See Gautam Naik, 'R&D spending in U.S. expected to rebound', wsj.com, 21 December 2009, sec. Economy, http://online.wsj.com/article/SB10001424052748703344704574610350092009062.html

104   'Firms are reluctant to risk their money': McKinstry, *Spitfire*, pp. 34–5.

105   There is an inconvenient tale behind this: I have drawn much of this account from Dava Sobel's *Longitude* (London: Fourth Estate, 1996).

106   Compared with the typical wage of the day: Officer, 'Purchasing power of British pounds', cited above, n. 10.

107   In 1810 Nicolas Appert: http://en.wikipedia.org/wiki/Nicolas_Appert

107   Ultimately the Académie began to turn down: Maurice Crosland, 'From prizes to grants in the support of scientific research in France in the nineteenth century: The Montyon legacy', *Minerva*, 17(3) (1979), pp. 355–80, and Robin Hanson, 'Patterns of patronage: why grants won over prizes in science', University of California, Berkeley, working paper 1998, http://hanson.gmu.edu/whygrant.pdf

108   Innovation prizes were firmly supplanted: Hanson, 'Patterns of patronage'.

109   The prize was eventually awarded in September 2009: a follow-up prize was announced and then cancelled following a lawsuit over privacy. One Netflix user alleged that the data released by Netflix didn't sufficiently conceal her anonymity, and might allow others to discover that she was a lesbian by connecting her with 'anonymous' reviews. (Ryan Singel, 'Netflix spilled your Brokeback Mountain secret, lawsuit claims', *Wired*, 17 December 2009, http://www.wired.com/threatlevel/2009/12/netflix-privacy-lawsuit/)

110   'One of the goals of the prize': author interview, 13 December 2007.

110   Not everybody responds to such incentives: 'Russian maths genius Perelman urged to take $1m prize', BBC News, 24 March 2010, http://news.bbc.co.uk/1/hi/8585407.stm

111   The vaccine prize takes the form of an agreement: the advanced

market commitment idea was developed by Michael Kremer in 'Patent buyouts: a mechanism for encouraging innovation', *Quarterly Journal of Economics*, 113:4 (1998), 1137–67; but also see http://www.vaccineamc.org/ and the Center for Global Development's 'Making markets for vaccines', http://www.cgdev.org/section/initiatives/_archive/vaccinedevelopment

111 Only the very largest pharmaceutical companies spend more than: Medicines Australia, 'Global pharmaceutical industry facts at a glance', p. 3, http://www.medicinesaustralia.com.au/pages/images/Global%20-%20facts%20at%20a%20glance.pdf

111 Children in Nicaragua received: Amanda Glassman, 'Break out the champagne! The AMC delivers vaccines', Center for Global Development, Global Health Policy blog, 13 December 2010: http://blogs.cgdev.org/globalhealth/2010/12/break-out-the-champagne-the-amc-delivers-vaccines.php

111 Prize enthusiasts think that even an HIV vaccine: Tim Harford, 'Cash for answers', *FT Magazine*, 26 January 2008, http://timharford.com/2008/01/cash-for-answers/

112 'Innovation is what we do because there's nothing else to do in Mojave': Leonard David, 'Brave New World? Next steps planned for private space travel', Space.com 06 October 2004, http://www.space.com/news/beyond_spaceshipone_041006.html

112 The age of private space flight: Ian Parker, Annals of Aeronautics, 'The X Prize', *The New Yorker*, 4 October 2004; and also see the Discovery Channel footage of SpaceShipOne Flight 15P, for instance at: http://www.youtube.com/watch?v=29uQ6fjEozI

114 When first reaching the brink of space: Leonard David, 'Brave New World? Next steps planned for private space travel', Space.com 06 October 2004, http://www.space.com/news/beyond_space shipone_041006.html

4 Finding what works for the poor or: Selection

115 'An empiricist, I was willing': Muhammad Yunus & Alan Jolis, *Banker to the Poor* (London: Aurum Press, 1999), p. 65.

115 'The barrier to change': Bill Gates, Harvard University Commencement Address, 2007, http://ow.ly/JwQH

115 'They were everywhere, lying very quiet': Yunus & Jolis, *Banker to the Poor*, p. 3.

117 His facility for pragmatic problem-solving: Yunus & Jolis, *Banker to the Poor*, p. 31.

117 Nor is Grameen the world's largest microfinance lender: 'The

hidden wealth of the poor', *The Economist*, 3 November 2005, http://www.economist.com/surveys/displaystory.cfm?story_id=5079 324; and Tina Rosenberg, 'How to fight poverty: 8 programs that work', *New York Times*, 16 November 2006, http://select.nytimes.com/2006/11/16/opinion/15talkingpoints.html?page wanted=3&_r=1

118 'I thought I should rather look': Yunus & Jolis, *Banker to the Poor*, p. 5.

119 'Each time I've visited a PlayPump': Owen Scott, 'The Playpump III: the challenge of good inquiry', http://thoughtsfrommalawi. blogspot.com/2009/11/playpump-iii-challenge-of-taking-photos.html; for the hand-pump versus PlayPump trial, see http://barefoot economics.ca/2010/04/11/the-playpump-iv-playpump-vs-afridev/

119 'The message is stop immediately': Case Foundation statement is here, accessed 5 June 2010: http://www.casefoundation.org/blog/ painful-acknowledgement-coming-short, and Laura Freschi, 'Some NGOs can adjust to failure: the PlayPumps story', 19 February 2010, http://aidwatchers.com/2010/02/some-ngos-can-adjust-to-failure-the-playpumps-story/. Also see the PBS report on PlayPumps, 'Troubled Water', http://www.pbs.org/front lineworld/stories/southernafrica904/video_index.html

120 'If he vomits he's more likely': the Benjamin Spock example (and quotation) comes from *Testing Treatments: better research for better healthcare* by Imogen Evans, Hazel Thornton & Iain Chalmers, with a new foreword by Ben Goldacre, downloadable at http://www.jameslindlibrary.org/testing-treatments.html

121 It was only in 1988 that new parents: R.E. Gilbert, G. Salanti, M. Harden & S. See, 'Infant sleeping position and the sudden infant death syndrome: systematic review of observational studies and historical review of recommendations from 1940 to 2002', *International Journal of Epidemiology* (2005), 34:874–87.

121 'Let us take out of the Hospitals': Jan Baptist van Helmont, *Oriatrike, or Physick Refined: The Common Errors Therein Refuted and the Whole Art Reformed and Rectified* (London: Lodowick Loyd, 1662), p. 526, quoted in Iain Chalmers, 'Comparing like with like', *International Journal of Epidemiology* (2001), 30:1156–64. Note that van Helmont's book was published posthumously. He died in 1644.

122 Other suggestions included sea water: Evans, Thornton & Chalmers, *Testing Treatments*, p. 3.

122 Ships started to carry greater stores: G. Sutton (2004), 'James Lind aboard Salisbury'. The James Lind Library (www.jameslindlibrary. org).

123 The scales remain heavily loaded against trials: Evans, Thornton & Chalmers, *Testing Treatments*, p. 57.

125 But one young German doctor: Archie Cochrane with Max Blythe, *One Man's Medicine* (British Medical Journal, 1989), pp. 62–70.

125 It turns out that verbal reprimands: Cochrane with Blythe, *One Man's Medicine*, pp. 7, 191–2.

126 'There was dead silence': Cochrane with Blythe, *One Man's Medicine*, pp. 7, 211.

126 'I had no morphia': Cochrane with Blythe, *One Man's Medicine*, p. 82.

127 'If we don't know whether we are doing any good': Esther Duflo's talk at TED, February 2010, http://www.ted.com/talks/esther_duflo_social_experiments_to_fight_poverty.html and author interview, April 2009.

128 When Glewwe, Kremer and Moulin analysed the randomised trial: Paul Glewwe, Michael Kremer & Sylvie Moulin, 'Many children left behind? Textbooks and test scores in Kenya', NBER Working Paper 13300, August 2007.

128 The flip charts flopped: Paul Glewwe, Michael Kremer, Sylvie Moulin & Eric Zitzewitz, 'Retrospective versus prospective analyses of school inputs: the case of flip charts in Kenya', NBER Working Paper 8018, November 2000.

128 Treated for intestinal worms: Edward Miguel & Michael Kremer, 'Worms: education and health externalities in Kenya', Working Paper, May 2002.

130 'It pains me to be in a village that': Jeffrey Gettleman, 'Shower of aid brings flood of progress', *New York Times*, 8 March 2010, http://www.nytimes.com/2010/03/09/world/africa/09kenya.html

130 A randomised trial for the Millennium Villages: Michael Clemens, 'Why a careful evaluation of the Millennium Villages is not optional', *Views from the Center*, 18 March 2010, http://blogs.cgdev.org/globaldevelopment/2010/03/why-a-careful-evaluation-of-the-millennium-villages-is-not-optional.php

130 'Model villages of all kinds': Madeleine Bunting, 'The Millennium Villages project: could the development "wonk war" go nuclear?', Guardian online, Thursday, 4 November 2010, http://www.guardian.co.uk/global-development/poverty-matters/2010/nov/04/millennium-villages-sachs-clemens-demombynes?CMP=twt_gu

131 Evaluation experts such as Esther Duflo and Edward Miguel: Ian Parker, 'The poverty lab', *The New Yorker*, 17 May 2010, pp. 78–89; author interview with Edward Miguel, 16 March 2010. Also see Michael Clemens & Gabriel Demombynes, 'When does rigorous

impact evaluation make a difference? The case of the Millennium Villages', Center for Global Development Working Paper 225, http://www.cgdev.org/content/publications/detail/1424496

132 'Questions that are completely FUQed': author interview with Joshua Angrist, March 2010.

134 Olken discovered that in a typical Indonesian: Benjamin Olken, 'Measuring corruption: evidence from a field experiment in Indonesia', *Journal of Political Economy*, vol. 115, no. 2 (2007), pp. 200–49.

135 Approached Indians who were learning to drive: Marianne Bertrand, Simeon Djankov, Rema Hanna & Sendhil Mullainathan, 'Obtaining a driving license in India: an experimental approach to studying corruption', Working Paper 2006, http://www.economics.harvard.edu/faculty/mullainathan/files/driving.pdf

135 Teacher absenteeism plummeted: Esther Duflo & Rema Hanna (2005), 'Monitoring works: getting teachers to come to school', NBER Working Paper No. 11880, http://www.nber.org/papers/w11880.pdf

136 The researchers found over 400 very small businesses: Suresh de Mel, David McKenzie & Christopher Woodruff, 'Returns to capital: results from a randomized experiment', *Quarterly Journal of Economics*, vol. 123 (3) (2008), pp. 1329–72.

136 Other randomistas have teamed up with a bank: Dean S. Karlan, Margaret McConnell, Sendhil Mullainathan & Jonathan Zinman, 'Getting to the top of mind: how reminders increase saving', Working Paper, 1 April 2010, http://ssrn.com/abstract=1596281

136 And randomly selected villagers in Rajasthan: Ian Parker, 'The poverty lab'.

136 Liberians have one sixth the paltry income: World Bank, 'Liberia at a glance', September 2009, http://devdata.worldbank.org/AAG/lbr_aag.pdf

136 When former rebel-turned-president Charles Taylor stood trial: the prosecution's accusations are gathered here: http://www.charlestaylortrial.org/trial-background/who-is-charles-taylor/#four. The testimony of Joseph 'ZigZag' Marzah is reported here: http://www.charlestaylortrial.org/2008/03/13/zigzag-marzah-says-taylor-ordered-cannibalism-defense-works-to-discredit-his-testimony/

137 In Lofa County in Northern Liberia: author interview with Macartan Humphreys in New York, February 2009, and telephone interviews in May and June 2010; James D. Fearon, Macartan Humphreys & Jeremy Weinstein, 'Can development aid contribute

to social cohesion after civil war? Evidence from a field experiment in Liberia', *American Economic Review Papers and Proceedings*, 99:2 (2009), pp. 287–91; and James D. Fearon, Macartan Humphreys & Jeremy Weinstein, 'Development assistance, institution building, and social cohesion after civil war: evidence from a field experiment in Liberia', Center for Global Development Working Paper 194, December 2009.

139 'Rape capital of the world': BBC News, 'UN official calls DR Congo "rape capital of the world"', 28 April 2010, http://news.bbc.co.uk/1/hi/world/africa/8650112.stm

140 'Laughed out of court': Cochrane with Blythe, *One Man's Medicine*, p. 183.

140 'We should not try to design a better world': Owen Barder, 'What can development policy learn from evolution?', Blog Post, 27 October 2010, http://www.owen.org/blog/4018

142 Within six years, the percentage of grants: Ritva Reinikka & Jakob Svensson, 'The power of information: evidence from a newspaper campaign to reduce capture of public funds', Working Paper, http://people.su.se/~jsven/information2006a.pdf

143 Vaccination rates rose by almost a half: Martina Björkman & Jakob Svensson, 'Power to the people: evidence from a randomized field experiment of community-based monitoring in Uganda', *Quarterly Journal of Economics* (forthcoming), http://people.su.se/~jsven/PtP_QJE.pdf

144 César Hidalgo has never studied economics: César Hidalgo's research papers and maps of product space are available at: http://www.chidalgo.com/. Other sources: author interviews with César Hidalgo and Bailey Klinger, summer 2007, and with Ricardo Hausmann, September 2010.

148 Chile's salmon industry grew tenfold: 'Dying assets', *The Economist*, 30 July 2009, and 'Chilean salmon exports', PREM Notes Technology and Growth Series no. 103, World Bank, October 2005, http://www1.worldbank.org/prem/PREMNotes/premnote103.pdf

148 Taiwan is now the world's largest orchid exporter: see Dani Rodrik, *One Economics, Many Recipes* (New Jersey: Princeton University Press, 2007), p. 104; Keith Bradsher, 'Once elusive, orchids flourish on Taiwanese production line', *New York Times*, 24 August 2004, http://www.nytimes.com/2004/08/24/business/once-elusive-orchids-flourish-on-taiwanese-production-line.html?fta=y&pagewanted=all; and a press release from the Taiwan International Orchid Show 2010, http://www.tios.com.tw/tios_test/eng/5_2taiwan.php

148 Silicon Valley venture capitalists need lose little sleep: Jim Pickard,

'Venture capital fund turned £74m into £5m', *Financial Times*, 9 March 2010, http://www.ft.com/cms/s/0/76859892-2ae1-11df-886b-00144feabdc0.html; and Josh Lerner's opening statement in The Economist debate on Industrial Policy: http://www.econo mist.com/debate/overview/177/Industrial%20policy

149   The Holy Roman Emperor himself: Sebastian Mallaby, 'The politically incorrect guide to ending poverty', *The Atlantic*, July/August 2010, http://www.theatlantic.com/magazine/archive/2010/07/the-politically-incorrect-guide-to-ending-poverty/8134/1/; Wikipedia; Simon Heffer, 'Lübeck: the town that said no to Hitler', *Daily Telegraph*, 2 June 2009, http://www.telegraph.co.uk/travel/city breaks/5428909/Lubeck-The-town-that-said-no-to-Hitler.html

151   Romer has pushed the charter city concept: Paul Romer, 'For richer, for poorer', *Prospect*, issue 167, 27 January 2010.

151   Before turning down the job of Chief Economist of the World Bank: David Warsh, 'Learning by doing', *Economic Principals*, 19 July 2009, http://www.economicprincipals.com/issues/2009.07.19/571.html

151   He argues that foreign ownership: author interview with Paul Romer, 20 September 2010.

152   It's a free economic zone: Sean Campbell, 'Metropolis from scratch', *Next American City*, issue 8, April 2005, http://americancity .org/magazine/issue/i08/; and Greg Lindsay, 'Cisco's big bet on New Songdo: creating cities from scratch', *Fast Company*, 1 February 2010, http://www.fastcompany.com/magazine/142/the-new-new-urbanism.html

5 Climate change or: Changing the rules for success

154   'I think we're going to find': Prince Charles, interview with the BBC, October 2005, http://news.bbc.co.uk/1/hi/uk/4382264.stm

154   'Evolution is cleverer than you are': obituary: Professor Leslie Orgel, *The Times*, 6 December 2007, http://www.timesonline.co. uk/tol/comment/obituaries/article3006557.ece

154   A dazzling lecturer at London's Royal Institution: Gabrielle Walker & Sir David King, *The Hot Topic* (Bloomsbury, 2008), pp. 14–18; Wikipedia entry on John Tyndall, http://en.wikipedia.org/wiki/John_Tyndall; & James Rodger Fleming, *Historical Perspectives on Climate Change* (New York: Oxford University Press, 2008), pp. 68–71.

155   Earth's atmosphere contains traces of other gases: Intergovernmental Panel on Climate Change Third Assessment Report, Table 6.1,

http://www.grida.no/publications/other/ipcc_tar/?src=/climate/ipcc_tar/wg1/221.htm#tab61

156 'Comparing a single atom of oxygen': cited in Fleming, *Historical Perspectives*, pp. 70–1.

156 Richard Lindzen, a contrarian meteorologist: '350 science' at 350.org http://www.350.org/about/science; and 'Top climate scientists share their outlook', *FT Magazine*, 20 November 2009.

158 But that is what has just happened to Geoff: Geoff Mason is fictional. My wife did become an environmentalist after reading Al Gore's book, *Earth in the Balance*, in the early 1990s, so the idea of Al Gore creating born-again environmentalists is close to home.

159 Cows emit a lot of methane: Martin Cassidy, 'Tackling problem of belching cows', BBC News website, 3 June 2009, http://news.bbc.co.uk/1/hi/northern_ireland/8078033.stm

160 Add all the other inputs to the milk: 'The environmental, social and economic impacts associated with liquid milk consumption in the UK and its production', Department for Agriculture and Rural Affairs, December 2007, http://www.defra.gov.uk/foodfarm/food/industry/sectors/milk/pdf/milk-envsocecon-impacts.pdf

160 By not boiling his kettle: direct measurement of kettle's power consumption.

160 Geoff would have done better: Elizabeth Baldwin of Nuffield College, Oxford, worked this out for me. A 1000W toaster operating for 90 seconds to toast 2 slices of bread is responsible for just 7g of carbon dioxide per slice. The bread itself is 52 g of carbon dioxide per slice. Butter is 80 g of carbon dioxide per ounce according to http://www.eatlowcarbon.org/Carbon-Calculator.html and Elizabeth allows a miserly 3 grams (1/9th oz) of butter per slice of toast, for about 9 g of carbon dioxide for the butter on one slice of toast. (I spread my butter more thickly, alas, at the planet's expense.) Total 68 g of carbon dioxide per slice. Data for the milk and muesli from Prashant Vaze, *The Economical Environmentalist* (London: Earthscan, 2009) via Elizabeth Baldwin.

160 Geoff's choice of a cheeseburger: Mike Berners-Lee, *How Bad Are Bananas?* (London: Profile, 2010), p. 86.

160 Especially ones (such as herring, mackerel and whiting): Vaze, *The Economical Environmentalist*, chapter 3.

160 An entirely vegan supper: there is a school of thought that says veganism would be unnecessary, if only we farmed meat with climate change in mind. See George Monbiot, 'I was wrong about veganism', *Guardian*, 6 September 2010, http://www.guardian.

co.uk/commentisfree/2010/sep/06/meat-production-veganism-deforestation

161 Geoff's choice of British lamb over New Zealand lamb: one of several of these New Zealand studies is picked over by Michael Shuman, author of *Going Local*, at http://www.ethicurean.com/2007/08/10/shuman-on-lamb/. Shuman questions the numbers but his main point is not that they are wrong, but that they could be changed: if British farmers switched to more environmentally friendly methods and British energy came more from renewable sources, then British lamb would have a lower carbon footprint.

161 Geoff's choice of British over Spanish tomatoes: I am assuming 100g in a helping of tomatoes. Vaze, *The Economical Environmentalist*, p. 57.

161 As for avoiding Chilean wine: Berners-Lee, *How Bad Are Bananas?*, p. 78.

161 A plastic bag is responsible for only: Berners-Lee, *How Bad Are Bananas?*, p. 18.

161 A Prius in congested traffic: a Prius emits 104g/km according to http://cars.uk.msn.com/features/green-motoring/articles.aspx?cp-documentid=147863613 and 89g/km according to http://carpages.co.uk/co2/

162 Cars carry, on average, 1.6 people: Tim Harford, 'A marginal victory for the well-meaning environmentalist', *Financial Times Magazine*, 6 February 2010. Also see Justin Rowlatt's blog posts for the BBC at: http://www.bbc.co.uk/blogs/ethicalman/2009/11/why_cars_are_greener_than_buses.html and http://www.bbc.co.uk/blogs/ethicalman/2010/01/justin_piece.html

162 It's more eco-friendly to chuck them out immediately: David MacKay, *Sustainable Energy – without the Hot Air* (Cambridge: UIT, 2009), p. 58, Figure 9.3.

162 He shouldn't have scorned the dishwasher: Brendan Koerner, 'Is a dishwasher a clean machine?', Slate, 22 April 2008, http://www.slate.com/id/2189612; and Berners-Lee, *How Bad Are Bananas?*, p. 63. Berners-Lee figures 540g–8000g for washing dishes by hand, and 770 g for a 55°C machine wash. For the seriously low-carbon hand wash, use two sinks, one for soapy water and one for rinsing, and don't let your plates near running water. For pure extravagance wash by hand and *then* in the dishwasher.

162 Line instead of relying on the tumble dryer: Berners-Lee, *How Bad Are Bananas?*, p. 84.

162 One of these toy windmills: MacKay, *Sustainable Energy*, p. 268.

162 Leaving his desktop computer on standby: MacKay, *Sustainable Energy*, p. 70.

163 Magnificently puny 6 grams of carbon dioxide a day: I am assuming that mains electricity is responsible for about 600 g of carbon dioxide per 1000 watts per hour. This is about right for the UK and US, although across the European Union the figure is closer to 350 g thanks to hydroelectric and nuclear generation (MacKay, *Sustainable Energy*, p. 335).

163 75 grams of carbon dioxide for a packet of potato snacks: source: The Carbon Trust, 'Product carbon footprinting and labelling: the new business opportunity', October 2008, and author interview with Euan Murray, 4 June 2009.

164 Readers of my first book, *The Undercover Economist*, might have noticed: when I wrote the opening pages of *The Undercover Economist* I was tapping in to a modern folk tale that economists tell each other – vaguely under the impression that it might have originated with Milton Friedman. I had not realised that the folk tale had an identifiable source, but it does: Leonard Read's remarkable 1958 essay, 'I, Pencil'. You can read it online at: http://www.econlib.org/library/Essays/rdPnclCover.html

164 Starbucks alone claims to offer 87,000 different beverages: this figure was claimed in a UK Starbucks advertising campaign in 2008. A 2006 article in *The Economist* ('Face value: staying pure', 23 February 2006, http://www.economist.com/business/displaystory.cfm?story_id=E1_VVQVVJD) put it at 55,000, so the number seems to be rising quite fast.

166 37 per cent said 'nothing': opinion poll data reported in Vaze, *The Economical Environmentalist* (London: Earthscan, 2009), pp. 8–9. The polls were conducted in the UK in 2007 and each questioned over 2000 adults.

168 For power companies to build natural gas power stations: the carbon content of various fossil fuels is available here: http://bioenergy.ornl.gov/papers/misc/energy_conv.html. Wikipedia's page on carbon taxes also contains a handy table on the price implications of a carbon tax on different fuels: http://en.wikipedia.org/wiki/Carbon_tax, accessed 3 November 2010.

169 The 'Merton Rule': conversations with the energy consultant Tim Crozier-Cole alerted me to the Merton Rule and its unintended consequences. Other references include 'Councils aim to enforce microgeneration targets', ENDS Report, 28 August 2009; Bibi van der Zee, 'Renewables rule making green a reality', Guardian Unlimited, 11 December 2007; Vicki Shiel, 'Mayor's city energy

policy faces debate', *Planning*, 12 October 2007; 'Golden rule hits backlash', *Planning*, 14 September 2007; Emma Clarke, 'The truth about ... the Merton rule', Climate Change Corp, 30 Jan. 2009, http://www.climatechangecorp.com/content.asp?Content ID=5932

169 The national government then introduced the rule more widely: interview with Geoffrey Palmer, Thursday, 19 November 2009.

173 Even if the CAFE standards: on CAFE standards, see Pinelopi Koujianou Goldberg, 'The effects of the corporate average fuel efficiency standards in the US', *Journal of Industrial Economics*, vol. 46, no. 1 (Mar. 1998), pp. 1–33; Feng An & Amanda Sauer, 'Comparison of passenger vehicle fuel economy and greenhouse gas emissions standards around the world', The Pew Center on Climate Change, pp. 6–7 and Fig. 1, http://www.pewclimate.org/docUploads/Fuel%20Economy%20and%20GHG%20Standards_0 10605_110719.pdf; 'Fuel economy fraud: closing the loopholes that increase U.S. oil dependence', Union of Concerned Scientists, 2005, p. 4, http://www.ucsusa.org/assets/documents/clean_vehicles/exec utive_summary_final.pdf; and Christopher Knittel, 'Automobiles on steroids', July 2009, NBER Working Paper w15162, http://www.econ.ucdavis.edu/faculty/knittel/papers/steroids_latest.pdf

173 European Union's Renewable Energy Directive: Susanne Retka Schill, 'EU adopts 10 percent mandate', *Biodiesel Magazine*, February 2009, http://www.biodieselmagazine.com/article.jsp?article_id= 3140; and 'EU in crop biofuel goal rethink', BBC News, 11 Sept. 2008, http://news.bbc.co.uk/1/hi/world/europe/7610396.stm

173 The European rules do not yet reflect this: United Nations Environment Programme, 'Assessing biofuels', October 2009, http://www.unep.fr/scp/rpanel/pdf/Assessing_Biofuels_Full_Report.pdf, pp. 53–54; John Gapper, 'Corn kernels are no cure for oil junkies', *Financial Times*, 29 January 2007; and Gabrielle Walker, 'Biofuels: the sweet smell of power', *Daily Telegraph*, 12 August 2008.

175 Smarter than pedigree dog breeders: Nicola Rooney & David Sargan, 'Pedigree dog breeding in the UK: a major welfare concern?', a report commissioned by the RSPCA.

176 Ship them, neatly sorted and with instructions: Alan Gibbs, 'Does tariff protection cost jobs?', speech in Wellington, 25 June 1990, http://www.nzbr.org.nz/site/nzbr/files/speeches/speeches-90-91/tariff-spch.pdf

179 High energy prices spur energy-saving patents: David Popp, 'Induced innovation and energy prices', *American Economic Review*, 92(1), March 2002, pp. 160–80, http://www.jstor.org/stable/3083326

180 Almost a tenth of the total contribution to greenhouse gas emissions: George Monbiot, 'I was wrong about veganism', *Guardian*, 6 September 2010, http://www.guardian.co.uk/commentisfree/2010/sep/06/meat-production-veganism-deforestation

180 Australian scientists have realised that: 'Quest to make cattle fart like marsupials', *The Age*, 7 December 2007, http://www.theage.com.au/news/climate-watch/quest-to-make-cattle-fart-like-marsupials/2007/12/06/1196812922326.html

6 Preventing financial meltdowns or: Decoupling

181 'We have involved ourselves in a colossal muddle': John Maynard Keynes, 'The Great Slump of 1930', first published London, *The Nation & Athenæum*, issues of 20 and 27 December 1930, http://www.gutenberg.ca/ebooks/keynes-slump/keynes-slump-00-h.html

182 The rig burned for three more weeks: BBC, *On This Day*, http://news.bbc.co.uk/onthisday/hi/dates/stories/july/6/newsid_301 7000/3017294.stm; Piper Alpha Wikipedia page, http://en.wikipedia.org/wiki/Piper_Alpha; The Fire and Blast Information Group, http://www.fabig.com/Accidents/Piper+Alpha.htm

183 Parts of the spiral are still being unwound over two decades later: John Kay, 'Same old folly, new spiral of risk', *Financial Times*, 14 August 2007, http://www.johnkay.com/2007/08/14/same-old-folly-new-spiral-of-risk/ and personal communication with an insurance lawyer.

184 The connection is obvious: a number of researchers and writers have studied or commented on the link between finance and industrial accidents, including: Stephen J. Mezias, 'Financial Meltdown as Normal Accident: The Case of the American Savings and Loan Industry', *Accounting Organizations & Society*, 18: 181–92 (1994); James Reason, *Managing the Risks of Organizational Accidents* (Ashgate Publishing Limited, 1997); Charles Perrow, *Normal Accidents*, second edition (Princeton: Princeton University Press, 1999); Andrew Lo, 'The Three P's of Total Risk Management', *Financial Analysts Journal*, 55 (1999), 13–26; Richard Bookstaber, *A Dream of Our Own Design* (New Jersey: Wiley & Sons, 2007) and James Surowiecki, 'Bonds Unbound', *The New Yorker* (11 February 2008).

185 'I used to speak to bankers about risk': author interview with James Reason, February 2009.

185 Argued that in a certain kind of system: Charles Perrow, *Normal Accidents* (Princeton: Princeton University Press, 1999; first edition published by Basic Books, 1984).

186   'Exceeds the complexity of any nuclear plant': author interview with Charles Perrow, 25 February 2010.

187   The two end supports would often settle: A.M. Dowell III & D.C. Hendershot, 'No good deed goes unpunished: case studies of incidents and potential incidents caused by protective systems', *Process Safety Progress* 16, 3 (Fall 1997), pp. 132–9.

187   At the Fermi nuclear reactor near Detroit': Perrow, *Normal Accidents*, pp. 50–4.

188   It did so with the explicit permission of the regulators: Gillian Tett, *Fool's Gold* (London: Little, Brown, 2009), pp. 51–6.

188   'It's as if people used the invention of seatbelts': John Lanchester, *Whoops!* (London: Allen Lane, 2010), p. 65.

188   Innocent bystanders were among the casualties: See Steven Peterson, George Hoffer, & Edward Millner, 'Are drivers of air-bag-equipped cars more aggressive? A test of the offsetting behavior hypothesis', *Journal of Law & Economics*, University of Chicago Press, vol. 38(2) (October 1995), pp. 251–64. The evidence on the Peltzman effect is mixed, so for an alternative view see Alma Cohen & Liran Einav, 'The effects of mandatory seat belt laws on driving behavior and traffic fatalities', Discussion Paper No. 341, Harvard Law School, November 2001, http://www.law.harvard.edu/programs/olin_center/papers/pdf/341.pdf

189   And as its rating is downgraded: James Surowiecki, 'Bonds unbound', *The New Yorker*, 11 February 2008; and Aline van Duyn, 'Banks and bond insurers ponder CDS costs', *Financial Times*, 24 June 2008, http://www.ft.com/cms/s/0/f6e40e9a-4142-11dd-9661-0000779fd2ac.html#axzz1GDDrJ3OR

191   It started when engineers trying to clear: Perrow, *Normal Accidents*, chapter 1; and Trevor Kletz, *An Engineer's View of Human Error* (Rugby, Warwickshire: Institution of Chemical Engineers, 2001; first edition published 1985).

192   It was impossible even for highly trained operators: Richard Bookstaber, *A Demon of Our Own Design* (New Jersey: Wiley & Sons, 2007), pp. 149–50.

192   With better indicators of what was happening: Perrow, *Normal Accidents*, chapter 1; and John G. Kemeny, 'President's Commission: the need for change: the legacy of TMI', October 1979, Overview, http://www.threemileisland.org/resource/item_detail.php?item_id=00000138

192   'When you look at the way the accident happened': author interview with Philippe Jamet, 24 March 2010.

194 Turned back to concentrate on the Lehman Brothers problem: Andrew Ross Sorkin, *Too Big to Fail* (London: Allen Lane, 2009), pp. 235–7.

194 'Hold on, hold on': Sorkin, *Too Big to Fail*, p. 372.

195 'We're a million miles away from that at the moment': Squam Lake Working Group on Financial Regulation, 'A new information infrastructure for financial markets', February 2009, http://www.cfr.org/publication/18568/new_information_infrastructure_for_financial_markets.html; and Andrew Haldane, 'Rethinking the financial network', speech given on 28 April 2009 to the Financial Student Association in Amsterdam, http://www.bankofengland.co.uk/publications/speeches/2009/speech386.pdf, and author interview with Andrew Haldane, August 2010.

196 And that man was Tony Lomas: for the account of Lehman's bankruptcy in Europe, I have relied on the superb account by Jennifer Hughes, 'Winding up Lehman Brothers', *FT Magazine*, 8 November 2008, http://www.ft.com/cms/s/2/e4223c20-aad1-11dd-897c-000077b07658.html

198 It had one million derivatives contracts open: Andrew Haldane, 'The $100 billion question', speech given at Institute of Regulation & Risk, Hong Kong, 30 March 2010, http://www.bankofengland.co.uk/publications/speeches/2010/speech433.pdf

199 The courts refused: Jane Croft, 'Definition on Lehman client money sought', *Financial Times*, 10 November 2009; and Anousha Sakoui & Jennifer Hughes, 'Lehman creditors face long delays', *Financial Times*, 14 September 2009.

199 It is quite possible that Lehman's financial indicators: Henny Sender & Jeremy Lemer, '"epo 105" accounting in focus', *Financial Times*, 12 March 2010, http://www.ft.com/cms/s/0/1be0aca2-2d79-11df-a262-00144feabdc0.html

199 About three years after the bankruptcy process began: Sakoui & Hughes, 'Lehman creditors'.

200 Dominoes, unlike banks, are supposed to fall over: Andrew Haldane, 'The $100 billion question'.

201 The job the poor bird had started: BBC News, 'Sparrow death mars record attempt', 19 November 2005, http://news.bbc.co.uk/1/hi/world/europe/4450958.stm; and embedded video at http://news.bbc.co.uk/player/nol/newsid_4450000/newsid_4452600/4452646.stm?bw=bb&mp=wm&news=1&bbcws=1

203 The credit crunch made it clear that the banks were carrying too little: 'Reforming capital requirements for financial institutions',

Squam Lake Working Group Paper, April 2009, http://www.cfr. org/content/publications/attachments/Squam_Lake_Working_ Paper2.pdf

204   Those bonds should be held by private individuals: Lex, 'CoCo bonds', *Financial Times*, 11 November 2009, http://www.ft.com/ cms/s/3/d7ae2d12-ced1-11de-8812-00144feabdc0.html; Gillian Tett, 'A staple diet of CoCos is not the answer to bank failures', *Financial Times*, 13 November 2009, http://www.ft.com/cms/s/0/ d791f38a-cff4-11de-a36d-00144feabdc0.html; and interview with Raghuram Rajan, July 2010.

205   Worst possible decision is indecision: 'Improving resolution options for systemically relevant financial institutions', Squam Lake Working Group Paper, October 2009, http://www.cfr.org/content/ publications/attachments/Squam_Lake_Working_Paper7.pdf

206   Bridge bank continues to support the smooth running: Willem Buiter, 'Zombie solutions: good bank vs. bad bank approaches', VoxEU, 14 March 2009, http://www.voxeu.org/index.php?q= node/3264; Robert Hall & Susan Woodward, 'The right way to create a good bank and a bad bank', VoxEU, 24 February 2009; Tim Harford, 'A capital idea to get the banks to start lending again', *FT Magazine*, 4 April 2009, http://timharford.com/2009/04/a-capital- idea-to-get-the-banks-to-start-lending-again/

207   John Kay points out that in some ways it is less meddlesome: John Kay, 'The reform of banking regulation', 15 September 2009, http://www.johnkay.com/2009/09/15/narrow-banking/; and author interview, September 2010.

208   'We cannot contemplate keeping aircraft': John Kay, 'Why too big to fail is too much for us to take', *Financial Times*, 27 May 2009, http://www.johnkay.com/2009/05/27/why-%E2%80%98too-big- to-fail%E2%80%99-is-too-much-for-us-to-take/

208   This one cost £200 million: Leo Lewis, 'Exchange chief resigns over "fat finger" error', *The Times*, 21 December 2005, http://business .timesonline.co.uk/tol/business/markets/japan/article775136.ece

210   Includes all the famous scandals such as WorldCom: Alexander Dyck, Adair Morse & Luigi Zingales, 'Who blows the whistle on corporate fraud?', European Corporate Governance Institute Finance Working Paper No. 156/2007, January 2007, http://faculty.chicago booth.edu/finance/papers/Who%20Blows%20The%20Whistle.pdf

211   He says that he was thanked by the Chairman: HBOS Whistleblower Statement: http://news.bbc.co.uk/1/hi/uk_politics/ 7882581.stm; and Paul Moore's interview on the Radio 4 documen- tary *The Choice*, Tuesday, 9 November 2009.

211 Moore walked out on to the street: Paul Moore took HBOS to an employment tribunal and the bank settled with him. The terms of the settlement included a gagging order, which Moore later ignored after he heard God telling him to 'bear witness'.

211 Crosby's account is different: Crosby's full statement can be seen here: http://news.bbc.co.uk/1/hi/business/7883425.stm

212 Dirks fought his case for ten years: Brian Trumbore, 'Ray Dirks v. the SEC', http://www.buyandhold.com/bh/en/education/history/2004/ray_dirks.html; and Ronald Soble & Robert Dallos, *The Impossible Dream* (New York: G.P. Putnam's Sons, 1975).

213 Unwise to dismiss whistleblowers too casually: John Gapper, 'King Lear proves the point: listen to that whistleblower', *Financial Times*, 14 February 2009, http://www.ft.com/cms/s/0/09a0a19c-fa07-11dd-9daa-000077b07658.html

213 'Don't you make a fucking enemy of me': Paul Moore's interview in *The Choice*, 9 November 2009.

214 The sums of money at stake are much larger now: David Kocieniewski, 'Whistle-blowers become investment option for hedge funds', *New York Times*, 19 May 2010, http://www.nytimes.com/2010/05/20/business/20whistleblower.html?pagewanted=all

214 The deputy chairman of the FSA at the time?: BBC News, 'Timeline: The Bank of Scotland', http://news.bbc.co.uk/1/hi/scotland/7620761.stm; Robert Peston, 'Lloyds to buy HBOS', 17 September 2008, http://www.bbc.co.uk/blogs/thereporters/robertpeston/2008/09/lloyds_to_buy_hbos.html; and BBC News, 'UK Banks receive £37bn bail-out', http://news.bbc.co.uk/1/hi/business/7666570.stm

216 Celebrate seven years without a notable accident: Ben Casselman, 'Gulf rig owner had rising tally of accidents', *Wall Street Journal*, 10 May 2010. http://online.wsj.com/article/SB10001424052748704307804575234471807539054.html

217 Just as his own computer monitor exploded: 'Blowout: the Deepwater Horizon disaster', *CBS 60 Minutes*, 16 May 2010, http://www.cbsnews.com/stories/2010/05/16/60minutes/main6490197.shtml

218 Last been inspected five years before the accident: David Hammer, 'Rig's blowout preventer last inspected in 2005', *Times-Picayune*, 26 May 2010, http://www.nola.com/news/gulf-oil-spill/index.ssf/2010/05/hearings_rigs_blowout_prevente.html

218 For months BP engineers had been expressing concern: Ian Urbina, 'Documents show early worries about safety of rig', *New York Times*, 29 May 2010, http://www.nytimes.com/2010/05/30/us/30rig.html?_r=1

218　The Macondo well's manager reported problems: Julie Cart & Rong-Gong Lin II, 'BP testimony: officials knew of key safety problem on rig', *Los Angeles Times*, 21 July 2010, http://articles.latimes .com/2010/jul/21/nation/la-na-oil-spill-hearings-20100721

219　The company was showing signs of stress after a merger: Casselman, 'Gulf rig owner had rising tally of accidents'.

219　Oil companies, like banks, need to find ways: Elena Bloxham, 'What BP was missing on Deepwater Horizon: a whistleblower', *CNN Money*, http://money.cnn.com/2010/06/22/news/companies/bp_ horizon_macondo_whistleblower.fortune/index.htm. Transocean defended its safety record.

7 The adaptive organisation

221　'One doesn't have to be a Marxist': Gary Hamel with Bill Breen, *The Future of Management* (Harvard Business Press, 2007), p. 130.

221　'Your first try will be wrong': Cory Doctorow, 'How to prototype and iterate for fun and profit', 9 November 2010, http://www.boing boing.net/2010/11/09/howto-prototype-and.html

222　Endler decided to test his hypothesis: Richard Dawkins, *The Greatest Show on Earth* (London: Bantam Press, 2009), pp. 135–9, and http://highered.mcgraw-hill.com/sites/dl/free/0072437316/ 120060/evolution_in_action20.pdf

225　Sales were $8 billion in 2009: Whole Foods Presentation at Jeffries 2010 Global Consumer Conference, 22 June 2010, http:// www.wholefoodsmarket.com/pdfs/jefferieswebcast.pdf

226　The description of many of the management practices: Hamel with Breen, *Future of Management*, chapter 4.

226　Timpson has several hundred: Timpson website accessed July 2010, http://www.timpson.co.uk/

227　And he drops in frequently: details about Timpson's management methods, and interview with John Timpson, from *In Business: Hell for Leather*, broadcast Thursday, 7 August 2009, 8.30 pm, BBC Radio 4, http://www.bbc.co.uk/programmes/b00lvlv3

228　Nor do we want to allow a situation: John Kay, 'Too big to fail? Wall Street, we have a problem', *Financial Times*, 22 July 2009, http://www.johnkay.com/2009/07/22/too-big-to-fail-wall-street- we-have-a-problem/

229　'It made us pay more attention': Glynn Davis, 'Interview with James Timpson', *HR Magazine*, 4 January 2010, http://www.hrmagazine .co.uk/news/974936/View-Top-Interview-James-Timpson- managing-director-Timpsons/

230 Views his role at Google as: Hamel with Breen, *Future of Management*, p. 119.

230 Schmidt took the second desk without protest: Ken Auletta, *Googled* (London: Virgin Books, 2010), p. 71.

230 'If you tell anybody what to do here': Hamel with Breen, *Future of Management*, pp. 88–92.

231 The instant correction of a problem: author visit to Hinkley Point, Somerset, 22 July 2010.

231 A machine he'd built himself: Auletta, *Googled*, p. 95.

232 The book went from paper to pixels in forty minutes: Hamel with Breen, *Future of Management*, p. 115.

232 *Every* engineer at Google had the same deal: Auletta, *Googled*, p. 18; and Google website, 'What's it like to work in Engineering, Operations, & IT?'

232 An astonishing portfolio of failures: Auletta, *Googled*, p. 286.

232 The aim is not to stifle more projects: 'Creative tension', *The Economist*, 19 September 2009, pp. 80–1.

233 No room for people who don't play their part: Hamel with Breen, *Future of Management*, p. 108.

233 Much longer than the World Wide Web: Hamel with Breen, *Future of Management*, chapter 5.

233 Gore had no experience in the music industry: Hamel with Breen, *Future of Management*, pp. 90–1.

234 Because people will remember the ones that stick: Hamel with Breen, *Future of Management*, p. 104.

234 Two of the five worst technology products: Jason Hiner, 'The five worst tech products of 2009', *TechRepublic*, 14 December 2009, http://blogs.techrepublic.com.com/hiner/?p=3430

234 The few big successes seem to justify: Kevin Maney, 'What scares Google', *The Atlantic*, September 2009, p. 28.

235 Use of randomised experiments on the website: Ian Ayres, *Supercrunchers* (London: John Murray, 2007), p. 54.

236 Thomas Edison may have been known: Stefan H. Thomke, *Experimentation Matters* (Harvard Business School Press, 2003), chapter 3.

236 'If I find 10,000 ways': Thomke, *Experimentation Matters*, p. 24.

236 'The real measure of success': A. Millard, *Edison and the Business of Innovation* (Baltimore: Johns Hopkins University Press, 1990), p. 40, cited in Thomke, *Experimentation Matters*.

236 Thousands of different chemical compounds: Thomke, *Experimentation Matters*, pp. 40–1

237 When a problem reaches a certain level of complexity: Thomke, *Experimentation Matters*, pp. 36–88; and Malcolm Gladwell, 'The treatment', *The New Yorker*, 17 May 2010.

237   Ariely could use the collaboration: Dan Ariely, 'Why businesses don't experiment', *Harvard Business Review*, April 2010, http://hbr.org/2010/04/column-why-businesses-dont-experiment/ar/1

239   The 'technology mudslide': Clayton M. Christensen, *The Innovator's Dilemma* (Harvard Business School Press, 1997).

242   Lockheed's basic corporate culture: Ben Rich & Leo Janos, *Skunk Works* (Little, Brown, 1994).

243   Schwab itself would likely have been marginalised: Clayton M. Christensen, *The Innovator's Solution* (Harvard Business School Press, 2003), p. 198.

243   Whole structure of Virgin Group has always been: Richard Branson, *Business Stripped Bare* (Virgin Books, 2008), pp. 169–214.

244   'I'll be damned if I permit': anonymous officer quoted in John Nagl, *Learning to Eat Soup with a Knife* (University of Chicago Press, 2005), p. 172.

8 Adapting and you

247   'He was not a very careful person': Shimura is quoted in 'Andrew Wiles and Fermat's Last Theorem', MarginalRevolution.com, 29 August 2010, http://www.marginalrevolution.com/marginal revolution/2010/08/andrew-wiles-and-fermats-last-theorem.html

247   'Let us try for once not to be right': Tristan Tzara, *The Dada Manifesto*, 1918.

247   'Stupefyingly clichéd and almost embarrassingly naïve': Hedy Weiss, 'Good music, flashy moves can't fill emotional void', *Chicago Sun-Times*, 21 July 2002.

247   'Crazily uneven': Michael Phillips, '"Movin' Out"? Maybe not; Broadway-bound Tharp-Joel show has to get acts together', *Chicago Tribune*, 22 July 2002.

248   'If you stand in Twyla's way': Cathleen McGuigan, 'Movin' to Broadway: Twyla Tharp heads uptown with Billy Joel', *Newsweek*, 28 October 2002.

248   *Oklahoma!* started as the flop: Linda Winer, 'Top secret? Get out of town!', *Newsday*, 11 August 2002.

249   'I was completely lost': Robin Pogrebin, 'How Twyla Tharp turned a problem in Chicago into a hit on Broadway', *New York Times*, 12 December 2002.

249   'Shimmering portrait of an American generation': Pogrebin, 'How Twyla Tharp ...'

249 'To understand why two separate': Anna Kisselgoff, 'The story is in the steps', *New York Times*, 25 October 2002.

249 'How did this happen?': Michael Phillips, 'Manhattan transfers successful and not so', *Los Angeles Times*, 20 December 2002.

249 'The best failures are the private ones': Twyla Tharp and Mark Reiter, *The Creative Habit: Learn it and Use it for Life* (New York: Simon & Schuster, 2003), p. 213.

250 'Like a jazz musician jamming': Tharp & Reiter, *The Creative Habit*, p. 99.

251 'It requires you to challenge': Tharp & Reiter, *The Creative Habit*, p. 218.

251 This odd phenomenon was first pinned down: Leon Festinger & James M. Carlsmith, 'Cognitive consequences of forced compliance', *Journal of Abnormal and Social Psychology*, 58 (1959), 203–10.

252 'It means that the sperm found': Carol Tavris & Elliot Aronson, *Mistakes Were Made (But Not by Me)* (London: Pinter & Martin, 2008), p. 150.

252 Bromgard had spent fifteen years in prison: Kathryn Schulz, *Being Wrong: Adventures in the Margin of Error* (London: Portobello, 2010), pp. 233–8.

253 'One of the worst professional errors': Tavris & Aronson, *Mistakes Were Made*, p.130.

253 'I didn't promote myself as a star': Twyla Tharp, *Push Comes to Shove* (New York: Bantam, 1992), p. 82.

253 'That experience remains intensely painful': Tharp, *Push Comes to Shove*, p. 84.

253 'Bob and I had lost a baby': Tharp, *Push Comes to Shove*, p. 98.

255 Naturally the subject usually chose: M. D. Lieberman, K. N. Ochsner, D. T. Gilbert, & D. L. Schacter, 'Do amnesics exhibit cognitive dissonance reduction? The role of explicit memory and attention in attitude change', *Psychological Science*, 12 (2001), 135–40.

255 'Happiness being synthesised': Dan Gilbert at TED, February 2004, http://www.ted.com/talks/dan_gilbert_asks_why_are_we_happy. html

256 Taught Petraeus that everyone is fallible: David Cloud & Greg Jaffe, *The Fourth Star* (New York: Crown, 2009), p. 43.

257 'She didn't try to console me': Tharp & Reiter, *The Creative Habit*, p. 221.

257 The reviews are harsh but fair: Reviews by Hedy Weiss, Michael Phillips & Sid Smith, references above.

257 'All you need are people': Tharp & Reiter, *The Creative Habit*, p. 229.

258   People with regular jobs tend to receive feedback: Andrew Oswald, 'What is a happiness equation?', May 2006, http://www2.warwick. ac.uk/fac/soc/economics/staff/academic/oswald/happinessformula 06.pdf

260   Vaulted from one vantage point to another: Tim Harford, 'What really counts', *FT Magazine*, 28 January 2006, http://timharford.com/2006/01/what-really-counts/; Malcolm Gladwell, 'Late bloomers', *The New Yorker*, 20 October 2008, http://www.gladwell.com/2008/2008_10_20_a_latebloomers.html; David Galenson, *Old Masters and Young Geniuses: The Two Life Cycles of Artistic Creativity* (Princeton University Press, 2005).

262   State of profound uncertainty that comes with: Kathryn Schulz, *Being Wrong*.

Acknowledgements

263   'Ever tried. Ever failed': Samuel Beckett, *Worstward Ho* (1983) published in *Nohow On* (The Limited Editions Club, 1989).

Index

A Note About the Author

Tim Harford is an economist, columnist and broadcaster. He writes a weekly column in the *Financial Times* called 'The Undercover Economist'. He also writes the only economics-based problem page in the world, 'Dear Economist', in which readers' personal problems are answered, tongue-in-cheek, with the latest economic theory. Tim presents Radio 4's guide to numbers in the news and in life, *More or Less*, and was the presenter of a TV series for BBC2 called *Trust Me, I'm an Economist*. Tim has worked at the World Bank, Shell and on the editorial board of the *Financial Times*. He is a visiting fellow at Cass Business School, London, and at Nuffield College, Oxford. He was the winner of the Bastiat prize for economic journalism in 2006 and runner-up in 2010, and with the team from *More or Less* he won the Royal Statistical Society's prize for excellence in journalism in 2010. Tim's other books include *The Undercover Economist*, *The Logic of Life* and *Dear Undercover Economist*. He lives in London with his wife and two daughters.